inner
torment

Living Between
Conflict and Fragmentation

SALMAN AKHTAR, M.D.

JASON ARONSON INC.
Northvale, New Jersey
London

Production Editor: Judith D. Cohen

This book was set in 11 pt. Baskerville by Alpha Graphics of Pittsfield NH and printed and bound by Book-mart Press, Inc. of North Bergen, NJ.

Library of Congress Cataloging-in-Publication Data

Akhtar, Salman, 1946 July 31–
    Inner torment : living between conflict and fragmentation / Salman Akhtar.
        p. cm.
    Includes bibliographical references and index.
    ISBN 0-7657-0159-6
    1. Psychoanalysis.   2. Object relations (Psychoanalysis)
3. Emotions.   4. Conflict (Psychology)   I. Title.
RC506.A38   1998
616.89'17—dc21   97-50487

Printed in the United States of America on acid-free paper. Jason Aronson offers books and cassettes. For information and catalog write to Jason Aronson Inc., 230 Livingston Street, Northvale, New Jersey 07647-1726. Or visit our website: http://www.aronson.com

TO THE MEMORY OF MY PARENTS

Safia and Jan-Nisar Akhtar

CONTENTS

Preface ix

Acknowledgments xv

PART I: FOUNDATIONS

1. Object Constancy 3

The Initial Achievement of Object Constancy • Subsequent
Reverberations • Syndromes Associated with Disturbed
Object Constancy • Technical Implications • Summary

2. Aggression 29

Etymology, Meaning, and Psychoanalytic Terminology
• Freud's Views on Aggression • Melanie Klein and Heinz
Hartmann, and Their Respective Followers • British Object
Relations Theory and Self Psychology • Contemporary
Reformulations • Synthesis and Reflections

PART II: FEELINGS

3. Love   **65**

Freud's Views on Love • Views of Contemporary Psycho-
analysts • Inability to Fall in Love • Inability to Remain in
Love • Falling in Love with the "Wrong" Kinds of People
• Inability to Fall out of Love • Inability to Feel Loved •
Concluding Remarks

4. Hatred   **95**

Hatred and Its Manifestations • The Relationship of Hatred
with Rage, Envy, and Arrogance • Origins of Hatred • Sociocultural Vicissitudes • Hatred in Transference and Countertransference • Technical Implications • Concluding Remarks

PART III: FRICTIONS

5. Kohut Versus Kernberg   **129**

Relationship to General Psychiatry • Regard for the Theo-
retical Contributions of Predecessors and Contemporaries
• Relationship to Mainstream Psychoanalysis • Views on the
Narcissistic Personality • Summary and Conclusions

6. Needs Versus Wishes   **165**

Freud's Views on the Need-Wish Distinction • Subsequent
Contributions • Synthesis, Caveats, and Beyond • Technical Implications • A Theoretical Postscript

PART IV: FANTASIES

7. "Someday . . ." and "If Only . . ." Fantasies   **205**

Some Caveats • The "Someday" Fantasy • The "If Only"
Fantasy • Sociocultural Vicissitudes • Technical Implications
• Summary

8. Tethers, Orbits, and Invisible Fences **235**

Definitions • Developmental Perspective • Psychopathology
of Optimal Distance • The Tether Fantasy and Its Variants
• Sociocultural Vicissitudes • Technical Implications •
Summary

References 271

Credits 309

Index 311

PREFACE

This book has grown out of my clinical experience, my integrative strivings, and serendipity. Working with patients whose difficulties arose from an area between psychotic and neurotic organizations, and yet who were not explicitly borderline, posed many theoretical and technical challenges for me. To meet these challenges, I read, assimilated concepts from different psychoanalytic traditions, tried aspects of their technical approaches, and then began to integrate the conceptual diversity into a composite whole of my own. Serendipity, in the form of invitations to speak and to contribute chapters on topics that had already begun to interest me, became my ally. My task was now clear.

The result is this book. It is divided into four sections labeled, with logic and playful alliteration, Foundations, Feelings, Frictions, and Fantasies. Each section embodies a dialectical tension between two opposing concepts. The book thus moves forward in an undulating fashion. Like a river.

Part I of the book is labeled Foundations and is composed of chapters on object constancy and aggression. The former sustains the self, the latter attempts to break it apart. The patients I was dealing with fluctuated between coherence and splintering of self experience. They showed abrupt shifts in their transferences and in their self-estimations. It was therefore important for me to grapple with issues of object constancy. I was fortunate in having been supervised by Selma Kramer, who had been a close associate and friend of Margaret Mahler, the theorist, to champion this concept. I was also fortunate to be invited to prepare a paper on this topic for the 2nd International Mahler Symposium held in Cologne, Germany, in July 1993. The result, in a further developed form, is Chapter 1. In this chapter, I summarize Margaret Mahler's views on the initial acquisition of object constancy in early childhood and then trace its vicissitudes through oedipal phase, latency, adolescence, and various phases of adult development. Translating these developmental observations into clinical matters, I delineate six psychopathological syndromes of adult life associated with impaired object constancy. I then move on to the technical implications of these concepts and, in a step-by-step fashion, describe the various important tasks in analytic work with such patients.

In the next chapter, I deal with aggression. An invitation by Burness Moore to contribute an essay on this topic to the American Psychoanalytic Association's *Psychoanalysis: The Major Concepts* (Moore and Fine 1995) became the impetus for this chapter. I begin it with Freud's changing views on aggression and then discuss the two major post-Freudian trends in detail. These refer to the theoretical paths taken by Melanie Klein, Heinz Hartmann, and their respective followers. Following this, I review other significant contributions to the understanding of aggression including those of British object relations theory and self psychology. Then I address two major contemporary reformulations of aggression, namely those provided by Otto Kernberg and Henri Parens. Though the chapter is heavily weighted with theory, it does attempt to link up with phenomenology in an area of controversy and ambiguity. I am referring to the notion of death instinct, which, toward the end of this chapter, I attempt to reformulate in experience-near, object-related, and fantasy-based terms.

The tension between object constancy and aggression, characterizing Part I of the book, gives way to the tension between love

and hate. Part II, entitled Feelings, is devoted to these two great
human emotions. I begin the chapter on love with Freud's views
on the topic and follow up by delineating the views of important
contemporary theorists including Martin Bergmann, Otto Kernberg, and Janine Chasseguet-Smirgel. Returning to clinical concerns, I describe the psychopathological syndromes of love life. To
the relatively well-known maladies of inability to fall in love, inability
to remain in love, and the tendency to fall in love with "wrong"
kinds of people, I add the syndromes of inability to fall out of love
and inability to feel loved. The individuals in the former category
are given to "love addictions" of various sorts and, in the treatment
setting, malignant erotic transference. The individuals in the latter category are seen frequently in clinical practice but not diag-
nosed as such. It is important to recognize their darkly poignant
dynamics. To extend a currently popular psychoanalytic metaphor,
they do not lack mirrors, they lack vision! Among the factors that
impede their assimilating the love that others offer them are dread
of dependence, profound self-loathing, and hatred of others.

Such hatred is the topic of the next chapter, which grew out of
my discussion of Otto Kernberg's presentation on hatred at the
Twenty-Fifth Mahler Symposium held in Philadelphia in May 1994.
Viewing hatred as a complex, characterologically anchored affective state, I describe its various manifestations and distinguish them
from the related affects of rage, envy, and arrogance, relying on
the writings of Melanie Klein, Wilfred Bion, Ping-Ne Pao, Harold
Blum, and Otto Kernberg. After a brief digression into the sociocultural vicissitudes of hatred, which allows me to include Vamık
Volkan's important psychopolitical observations, I discuss three
transference configurations (schizoid, psychopathic, and paranoid) associated with hatred. I also discuss countertransference
hatred and then move on to the technical implications of these
ideas. Attempting to synthesize the profoundly significant contributions of Otto Kernberg with the somewhat opposite conceptualizations of Donald Winnicott, I outline an integrated, affirmative-
interpretive approach to intensely hateful patients.

It is to the implicit tension between these classic and romantic
visions of psychoanalysis, to use Carlo Strenger's phrase, that I

devote the next part of the book. This part is called Frictions and is composed of chapters on the Kohut–Kernberg controversy of the late 1970s and the need-wish distinction that characterizes the romantic and the classic paradigm at their motivational base. Each of these chapters highlights a tension that, in one form or other, has existed in psychoanalysis since the early Freud–Ferenczi debates on technique. There is, however, a tension between the two chapters as well. The first, written much earlier in my career, has the intensity of voice that results from underscoring differences. The second, being more recent, has greater conceptual suppleness. They seem to lean in different directions, a theoretical architecture representing an accommodation to new ideas, not a departure from prior convictions. More important than this, however, is the fact that these chapters address what is at the core of the psychopathology under consideration. In the first chapter I highlight the manifestations of pathological narcissism, and the varying dynamic explanations of the transferences narcissistic patients develop in the course of their treatment. In the second chapter, I synthesize the scattered contributions of early metapsychologists, child development observers, analysts of the independent tradition in England, and self psychologists in order to elucidate the concept of a psychological need and distinguish it from the concept of a wish. Grounded in clinical concern, I proceed to delineate six basic psychological needs and their technical implications. In a theoretical postscript, I then link these experience-near concepts with the early Freudian notion of ego instincts.

Such criss-cross between old and new, between developmental observation and ego psychology, and between instinct theory and object-relations perspective characterizes the next part of the book as well. It is called Fantasies and contains two chapters. The first chapter was written when Judith Feher Gurewich, acting upon the recommendation of Otto Kernberg, invited me to participate in a French-American dialogue on borderline states, held in Paris in November 1994. In this chapter, I describe the "someday" and "if only" fantasies. The "someday" fantasy idealizes the future and fosters optimism, and the "if only" fantasy idealizes the past and lays the groundwork for nostalgia. The two fantasies originate in the narcissistic disequilibrium consequent upon early separation experiences, though the oedipal conflict also contributes to them. Both can be used as defenses against defective self and object constancy and the existence of too much unneutralized aggression within oneself. After highlighting their developmental and metapsychological correlates, and taking intellectual cues from Amy Angel, Jacqueline Amati-Mehler, Anna Potamianou, and Arnold Cooper, I outline the technical guidelines in situations where such fantasies acquire a tenacious quality and unconsciously sadomasochistic aims.

In the next and final chapter of the book, I discuss the "tether" fantasy and its variants: psychosocial orbits in which people live and invisible fences that surround and, at times, imprison them. I review the pertinent work of Maurice Bouvet, Michael Balint, and Margaret Mahler in this context and elucidate the dilemmas of negotiating optimal distance that underlie such fantasies. I define optimal distance as that gap between a self and object representation that permits individuation without total psychic disjunction from early objects of identification and that allows refueling from the good internal objects without the dread of fusion. I describe various impairments of the capacity to maintain optimal distance. I also delineate the important role of this concept in understanding the psychology of games, travel, vacation, and, more importantly, immigration. Predictably, I return to psychoanalytic technique and demonstrate that from the beginning of the treatment through interruptions, extra-analytic encounters, transference-based oscillations of intimacy, termination-phase advances and regressions, and even afterward, the issue of optimal distance affects technique.

Not insignificantly it is by way of mentioning termination that I arrive at the end of this survey of my book's contents. Let me conclude by saying that completing a book is like the end of a long journey. At the same time, the end of every journey is the beginning of another one. The temporary relief for one's work ego is soon replaced by the need to consider matters not addressed in the current voyage.

ACKNOWLEDGMENTS

Drs. Arnold Cooper, Otto Kernberg, Selma Kramer, Sydney Pulver, and Vamık Volkan have facilitated my professional growth in an enduring manner. They took note of my effort, encouraged me, sent creative opportunities in my direction, and sponsored me in ways that were both explicit and subtle. My admiration for their stature is surpassed only by my gratitude for their kindness.

I have received valuable encouragement from many other distinguished senior colleagues including Drs. Harold Blum, the late Alvin Frank, John Kafka, George Klumpner, Marvin Margolis, Donald Meyers, Helen Meyers, Robert Michels, Burness Moore, Bernard Pacella, Warren Poland, Arnold Richards, Theodore Shapiro, Charles Socarides, and Allen Wheelis. I am deeply thankful for their help and support.

My friends and contemporaries on the national scene have also benefited me. The unerring old-world generosity of Dr. Axel Hoffer, the confident encouragement of Dr. Dorothy Holmes (who prompted me to write on immigration), the urbane intellect of Dr. Nicholas Kouretas, the easygoing camaraderie of Dr. Lawrence Lifson, the admiring protectiveness of Dr. Nadia Ramzy, the brotherly eloquence of Dr. Owen Renik, the intriguing observations of Dr. Elizabeth Lloyd Mayer, the sparkling authenticity of Dr. Dominic Mazza, the playful warmth of Dr. Harvey Rich, the ever-welcoming hospitality of Dr. John Munder Ross, and the matter-of-fact tenderness of Dr. Stuart Twemlow, have sustained me through easy and tough times. To all of them, my heartfelt thanks.

Colleagues at the Philadelphia Psychoanalytic Institute have been indispensable to the development of my ideas. Drs. Alexis Burland, Philip Escoll, Henri Parens, and Thomas Wolman have read rough drafts of portions of this book, and have offered valuable comments. Drs. Ira Brenner, Leroy Byerly, Newell Fischer, Daniel Freeman, Edward Hicks, William O'Brien, Joseph Rudolph, and Barbara Young have enriched my thinking in more informal ways. My participation in an ongoing psychoanalytic study group has allowed me the opportunity to benefit from the clinical and theoretical insights of Drs. Ted Cohen, Hossein Etezady, Ruth Fischer, Joan Gross, Eric Lager, Louis Leaff, and Leo Madow. I wish to express my gratitude to all these individuals.

I also wish to thank Dr. Troy Thompson, the chairman of the Department of Psychiatry at Jefferson Medical College for most of the time I was involved in writing this book, and Dr. Stephen Schwartz, the department's current acting chairman, for providing the intellectual environment conducive to such endeavors. Dr. Gregg Gorton offered helpful suggestions in informal discussions while Drs. Edward Silberman and Mitchell Cohen, the directors of residency training and medical student education, respectively, provided me opportunities to share my ideas with younger people. To all of them, my sincere thanks.

The trust and admiration I have received from those professionally junior to me has also strengthened my work ego. Among those whom I must mention by name are Drs. Aisha Abbasi, Roberta Ball, Sean Blitzstein, Jennifer Bonovitz, Jodi Brown, Karl Doghramji, Jacqueline Haimes, Carmen Harlan, Hanan Hassenein, Wendy Jacobson, Erich Kosowitz, Veena Luthra, Julie Jaffee Nagel, Syed Shujaat Naqvi, Steve McNamara, Meena Narayan, David Nichols, Barbara Novak, Satish Reddy, Shaharzad Siassi, Barbara Stern, Richard West, and Sharon Zalusky, as well as Ms. Bobbi Grant, Marilyn Minrath, and Julie Speacemaker. Drs. Michelle Berlinerblau, Barbara Shapiro, Andrew Smolar, David Steinman, and Ms. Susan Levine, whose psychoanalytic work I have directly supervised, have also enriched my thinking. To individuals in both these groups, I offer not only my thanks but best wishes also for their own respective futures.

Dr. Purnima Mehta provided much-needed support during the writing of one of the chapters and I am deeply thankful to her. Many other friends including Drs. Steven Samuel, J. Anderson Thompson, Jr. (with both of whom I have written many papers), Subhash Bhatia, Dusica Lecic-Tosevski, Harish Malhotra, Dwarkanath Rao, Rokeni Safavi, and Julian Stern have always been available in professional and personal ways. The continuing support of my residency classmates from the University of Virginia, Drs. Bruce Greyson, Ron Heller, William Rheuban, and Paul Wilkins, has meant a lot to me. Ms. Panna Naik of the Van Pelt Library at the University of Pennsylvania found many hard to locate references for me. I wish to express my sincere appreciation for the generosity of all these individuals.

It is hard to describe my appreciation for the outstanding skill and industriousness that Maryann Nevin, my secretary, has shown in preparing the manuscript of this book. That all this was offered me with patience and grace makes my gratitude even more enduring.

My personal analysts, my family members, and my patients have enhanced my strength and given me sight and direction. To them, my debt is indeed profound.

Part I

FOUNDATIONS

1

OBJECT CONSTANCY

The term *object constancy* was introduced in the psychoanalytic literature by Hartmann (1952a) to denote a stage when the growing child's tie to its love object becomes a stable and enduring inner relation independent of need satisfaction. Hartmann viewed this achievement as depending on the development of "object permanence" (Piaget 1937), that is, the cognitive persistence of an object's mental representation in its physical absence, and "a certain degree of neutralization" (Hartmann 1952a, p. 15) of the aggressive and libidinal drives. Anna Freud (1965) too, in tracing the development from dependency to self-reliance, spoke of "the stage of object constancy which enables a positive inner image of the object to be maintained, irrespective of either satisfactions or dissatisfactions" (p. 65). The palpable notion that "object" in this context referred mainly to the mother became explicit in Spitz's (1946a, 1965) concept of the "libidinal object," that is, the child's developing an exclusive and stable tie to its mother. It was, however, in the work of Margaret Mahler that the gradual acquisition of object constancy within the context of mother–child relationship found its most thorough exposition.

In this chapter, I highlight Mahler's contributions to the concept of object constancy and its attainment during early childhood.

I also discuss the challenges to object constancy posed by the subsequent developmental phases including the Oedipus complex,
latency, adolescence, young adulthood, and middle age. I then
describe various adult psychopathological syndromes associated
with failure to achieve object constancy. Finally, I comment on the
implications of these concepts to the psychoanalytic process and
technique.

THE INITIAL ACHIEVEMENT
OF OBJECT CONSTANCY

> Things that always love us, i.e., that constantly satisfy
> all our needs, we do not notice as such, we simply
> reckon them as part of our subjective ego; things
> which are and always have been hostile to us, we sim-
> ply deny; but to those things which do not yield un-
> conditionally to our desires, which we love because
> they bring us satisfaction, and hate because they
> do not submit to us in everything, we attach special
> mental marks, (and) memory-traces with the qual-
> ity of objectivity. [Ferenczi, 1926 p. 371]

> Object constancy can be said to have been reached
> when one particular defense—the splitting of object
> image—is no longer readily available to the ego.
> [Mahler 1968, p. 224]

> The predominance of love is the glue of the unified
> self-representation. [Settlage 1992, p. 352]

Based on extensive observational studies done alone or in collaboration with her colleagues, (Mahler 1958a, Mahler and Furer
1968, Mahler and McDevitt 1980, Mahler et al. 1975) Mahler distinguished the psychological birth of the human infant, that is, the beginning in the child of a coherent sense of personhood, from the
biological birth. She emphasized that two conditions must be met
for organization of the ego and neutralization of drives to arrive at
a sense of such personhood: (1) the enteroceptive-proprioceptive
stimuli must not be so continual or intense as to prevent structure

formation, and (2) the mother must be able to buffer and organize inner and outer stimuli for the infant. She also postulated the sequence of symbiosis and separation-individuation through which the child must pass in order to achieve a fairly stable sense of self and others.

While the "basic core" (Weil 1970) of the infant awakens in a state of enmeshment with the mother's self in the *symbiotic phase*, it is only during the *differentiation subphase* (from about 4–5 to 8–9 months), which is the first subphase of separation-individuation,[1] that the child, inwardly propelled by autonomy strivings, starts to discern his psychic separateness through rudimentary exploration of the self, the mother, and their environment. This is a period of much manual, tactile, and visual exploration of the mother's face and body. There may be engagement in peek-a-boo games in which the child still plays a passive role (Kleeman 1967). Alongside the seeking of distance from mother is also a greater awareness of her as a special person.

The differentiation subphase is followed by the *practicing subphase* (from 9 to 16–18 months) in which the crawling child, and later, the walking toddler, elatedly asserts his newfound psychic autonomy and motoric freedom. Buoyed by pervasive secondary narcissism and relatively impervious to external challenges, the child seems involved in a "conquest of the world." The elation is, perhaps, also an affective celebration of the escape from engulfment by the mother. Although the child often looks back at the mother for "emotional refueling" (Furer, quoted in Mahler et al. 1975, p. 69), his main preoccupation is to exercise his ego apparatuses and widen the orbit of his explorations.

Next is the *rapprochement subphase* (from about 16 to about 24 months), in which the child senses that his autonomy and psychomotor freedom have their limits and that the external world is more complex than he at first imagined. Narcissistically wounded, the child regresses in the hope of refinding the symbiotic oneness with

---

[1]Not included in this brief description are the subtle differences in the separation-individuation process of boys and girls (Mahler 1966, 1971, Mahler et al. 1975, McDevitt 1991, Parens 1991).

the mother. The return, however, is an ambivalent one since the drive of individuation is at work with great force and the child has become familiar with the ego pleasures of autonomous functioning. This ambivalence has its behavioral counterpart—"ambitendency" (Mahler 1974, p. 161)—insofar as the child poutingly clings to mother for reassurance, safety, even fusion at one moment, and valiantly distances himself from her for asserting autonomy, control, and separateness the next moment. If his vacillations are resiliently responded to by the mother and if loving feelings between them predominate over hostile ones, new regulatory structures begin to emerge (McDevitt 1975). The rapprochement subphase, while turbulent, is also the most significant since its successful negotiation results in profound intrapsychic alterations including:

> (1) mastery of the cognitively intensified separation anxiety; (2) affirmation of the sense of basic trust; (3) gradual deflation and relinquishment of the sense of omnipotence experienced in the symbiotic dual unity with the mother; (4) gradual compensation for the deflated sense of omnipotence through development of the child's burgeoning ego capacities and sense of autonomy; (5) a firming up of the core sense of self; (6) establishment of a sense of capacity for ego control and modulation of strong libidinal and aggressive urges and affects (e.g., infantile rage); (7) healing the developmentally normal tendency to maintain the relation with the love object by splitting it into a "good" and a "bad" object, thus also healing the corresponding intrapsychic split; and (8) supplanting the splitting defense with repression as the latter defensive means of curbing unacceptable affects and impulses toward the love object. [Settlage 1977, p. 817]

The last subphase of separation-individuation is termed *on the way to object constancy* (from about 24 to about 36 months) and associated self constancy. This subphase is characterized by the emergence of a more realistic and less shifting view of the self. It is also characterized by the consolidation of a deeper, somewhat ambivalent but more sustained internalized maternal object representation, the libidinal attachment to which does not get seriously compromised by temporary frustrations.[2] The attainment of object constancy assures the mother's lasting presence in the child's mental structure. The attainment of self constancy establishes a coherent, single self representation with minimal fluctuations under drive pressures. Together these achievements result in (and in a dialectical fashion, are themselves contributed to by) the disposal of aggression toward self and object by repression rather than splitting. Capacity for tolerating ambivalence now emerges on the psychic horizon. The child becomes capable of more complex object relations (Kramer and Akhtar 1988). Inner presence of a "good-enough mother" (Winnicott 1962) diminishes the need for her external presence. Clinging and darting away from her give way to the capacity to maintain "optimal distance" (Bouvet 1958, Mahler 1974), that is, "a psychic position that permits intimacy without loss of autonomy and separateness without painful aloneness" (Akhtar 1992a, p. 30).

The achievement of self and object constancy, however, is not a once-and-for-all step but an ongoing process. Mahler (1968, 1971, 1974) emphasized that while her descriptions focused upon the separation-individuation *phase*, the separation-individuation *process* continues to evolve and stabilize through subsequent development, even during adult life.

SUBSEQUENT REVERBERATIONS

Both achievements—consolidation of individuality and emotional object constancy—are easily challenged by the struggle around toilet training, and by the awareness of the anatomical sexual difference, a blow to the narcissism of the little girl and a danger to the little boy's body integrity. [Mahler 1975, p. 199]

---

[2]Parallel is the development of "reality constancy" (Frosch 1966). which enables the autonomous ego functions "to tolerate alterations and changes in the environment without psychic disruption or adaptational dysfunctions" (p. 350). Kafka (1989) has further elaborated these concepts, interweaving cognition, spatiality, and temporal perspective in this regard.

> Not until the termination of adolescence do self
> and object representations acquire stability and firm
> boundaries, i.e., they become resistant to cathectic
> shifts. [Blos 1967, p. 163]

Since the subphase *on the way to object constancy* overlaps with
the beginning of the phallic-oedipal phase of psychosexual
development (Mahler et al. 1975, Parens 1980, 1991), the issues
characteristic of it also play a role in the latter. These issues are
the replacement of splitting with repression, the emergence
of capacity for ambivalence, and the establishment of optimal
distance. The oedipal experience requires a unified self with a
capacity for intentionality, and objects that are experienced as
distinct from oneself and toward whom ambivalence can be tole-
rated. However, these requirements put the newly acquired self
and object constancy to the test. Indeed, there exists a reciprocal developmental influence (Parens 1980) between difficulties
in separation-individuation and the oedipal phase conflicts. The
recently mended split between "good" and "bad" (libidinally and
aggressively derived) maternal representations is especially vulnerable to reactivation as the child confronts the contradictory
maternal imagos ("Madonna" and "whore") of the oedipal phase.
Earlier fears of losing the good mother too might resurface in
the face of intense castration anxiety. The structuring of object
constancy can also be damaged if experiences with the two parents are quite different,[3] as is likely, to some extent at least, during the oedipal phase. The temptations and restrictions of this
period also test the capacity for optimal distance. After all "the
task of mastering the oedipal complex is not simply to renounce
primary oedipal objects, but to do so in a way that simultaneously
permits individual autonomy together with valued traditional
continuity" (Poland 1977, p. 410). Moreover, the establishment
of an incest barrier need not eliminate aim-inhibited subtle
affirmations of attractiveness between parents and children. In-

---

[3]Freud's (1923) comment regarding the "conflicts between various identifications into which the ego comes apart" (p. 31) is pertinent here.

deed, there might exist an "oedipally optimal" distance (Akhtar 1992a, p. 35) that is neither incestuously intrusive nor oblivious of cross-generational eroticism and neither slavishly submissive to early parental injunctions nor totally unmindful of family legacies.

Latency is ushered in by the internalization of parental prohibitions in the form of superego, and characterized by greater cognitive and motor skills. Object constancy is more or less certain. Concerns regarding separation do exist, albeit with a manageable intensity and in amalgamation with subterranean oedipal drives. Many games played by latency age children betray such condensation in displaced, ego syntonic forms (Glenn 1991).

It is, during adolescence, however, that the issues of self and object constancy are once again brought to the surface with full force. This developmental phase, with its characteristic drive upsurge, fosters regression. Adolescents of both sexes tend to retreat from oedipal conflicts, seeking refuge in struggles over issues of control, autonomy, and distance. Regressive tendencies intensify primary self and object relations. Progressive trends, both defensive and autonomous, herald new self-configurations and loosening of infantile object ties. On the one hand, renunciation of earlier forms of object relations paves the way for more age-adequate relationships; on the other hand, regression allows a return to abandoned ego states including those involving intense idealizations and devaluations. There is insistent disengagement from the earlier parental mores internalized in the form of the superego; there is an equally strong reliance on the values of one's peers. Trial identifications and role experimentations within the latter context gradually broaden the ego autonomy and help consolidate a resilient, mature self representation. The same is true in the realm of object representation. In the process of disengagement from primary love and hate objects, there is a temporary, often intense regression to split object relations (Blos 1967, Kramer 1980a). The decathexis of parental object representation is accompanied by heightened narcissism before libidinal investments in phase-specific, nonincestuous objects become possible. Once the progressive trends begin to dominate, how-

ever, the capacity for object relations deepens in a most meaningful way. "Indeed, it remains the ultimate task of adolescence
to strengthen post-ambivalent object relations" (Blos 1967,
p. 179).

Subsequent life tasks (e.g., separation from parents and home;
engagement and marriage; career choice, often requiring the overcoming of ambivalent ties to one's mentors) also revive the vicissitudes of the rapprochement subphase (Escoll 1991). Thus young
adulthood, too, tests self and object constancy, though to a lesser
degree than adolescence. Object constancy can also be strained
later by the challenges of raising children. Being the recipient of
a child's rapprochement subphase turbulence, the mother especially has to modulate her own reciprocal drives and contradictory
object representations of the child. Here the maternal object constancy comes to serve the "container" (Bion 1967) function for the
child's contradictory affects, scattered self representations, and
vacillating object ties. Subsequently, the capacity to tolerate the
child's sexual intrusions, competitiveness, and hostility during the
oedipal phase tests the parental capacity to retain optimal distance.
The child's diminished need of parents during latency and the
intense, often maddening, oscillations in attitudes, affect, and distance during adolescence similarly require parental object constancy if all is to go well. Still later, middle age mobilizes a final
mourning of the mute and unexpressed self representations. This
is accompanied by broadening of the core self representation,
and a compensatory deepening of what one indeed has become.
Object constancy is also reworked as aggression, envy toward the
youth, including one's offspring, can no longer be denied, and
identifications with one's parents, with all their implicit oedipal
ambivalence, are finally buttressed (Kernberg 1980). Finally, during old age, as one approaches death, a deep and postambivalent
view of the world that one has lived in and is about to leave needs
to be developed in order for this final transition to be smooth.

Having defined object constancy, delineated its initial achievement, and traced its vicissitudes through subsequent development,
we are prepared to discuss the adult psychopathology associated
with its disturbances.

SYNDROMES ASSOCIATED WITH
DISTURBED OBJECT CONSTANCY

The literature abounds in papers and symposia dealing with the sequelae of the failure of internalization,
increased separation anxiety, and other clinical signs
that indicate, for example, the following: that the
blending and synthesis of "good" and "bad" self
and object images have not been achieved; that
ego-filtered affects have become inundated by sur-
plus unneutralized aggression; that delusions of
omnipotence alternate with utter dependency and
self-denigration; that the body image has become
or remains suffused with unneutralized id-related
erogeneity and aggressive, pent-up body feelings,
and so on. [Mahler 1971, p. 181]

The lack of internalization of the comforting constant
mother is associated with a lack of ego integration.
Poor frustration tolerance and impulse control, fragile self-esteem, and unneutralized aggression leave the
patient predisposed to severe sadomasochistic dispositions and rage reactions. [Blum 1981, p. 801]

Disturbances of Optimal Distance

The failure to achieve object constancy leads to a continued propensity to rely excessively on external objects for self regulation.
Aggression toward them mobilizes fears of having internally destroyed them, and this, in turn, fuels the need to closely monitor
them in reality. Libidinal attachment and anaclitic longings, in contrast, stir up fears of enslavement by external objects, necessitating
withdrawal from them. All this results in a profound difficulty in
maintaining optimal distance (for more details, see Chapter 8).
Severe personality disorders constitute a cardinal example of such
psychopathology. Included here are narcissistic, borderline, schizoid, paranoid, hypomanic (Akhtar 1988a), infantile, "as-if" (Deutsch
1942), and antisocial personalities. For them, involvement with
others stirs up a characteristic "need-fear dilemma" (Burnham
et al. 1969): to be intimate is to risk engulfment and to be apart is to
court aloneness. This leads to a variety of compromises. The border-

line continues to go back and forth (Akhtar 1990a, Gunderson 1985, Melges and Swartz 1989). The narcissist can sustain allegiances longer, and less frequently shows such oscillations (Adler 1981, Akhtar 1989a, Kernberg 1970b). The paranoid bristles at any change in distance initiated by others (Akhtar 1990b), preferring the "reliability" of his fear of being betrayed (Blum 1981). The schizoid opts for withdrawal on the surface while maintaining an intense imaginary tie to his objects (Akhtar 1987, Fairbairn 1952a, Guntrip 1969). Antisocial and hypomanic individuals, though internally uncommitted, rapidly develop superficial intimacy with others. This tendency to be highly attuned to others, even magically identifying with them, is most evident in the "as-if" personalities (Deutsch 1942) and underlies the fraudulent tendency in all individuals with severe character pathology (Gediman 1985).

Splitting, Emotional Flooding, and Violence

Another result of failed object constancy is the persistence of split self and object representations. Splitting gives rise to repeated, intense, and convincing oscillations of self-esteem (Akhtar and Byrne 1983, Kernberg 1967, Mahler 1971), which contribute to an uncertain sense of identity. Such "identity diffusion" (Akhtar 1984a, Akhtar and Samuel 1996, Erikson 1950, Kernberg 1967) results not only in markedly contradictory character traits but also in temporal discontinuity in the self experience; it is a "life lived in pieces" (Pfeiffer 1974). The inner world remains populated with caricatured part objects. There is an incapacity to understand others in their totality, intolerance of ambivalence, and a tendency to react to realistic setbacks with negative mood swings (Mahler 1966, 1971, Mahler and Kaplan 1977). In patients with action-prone egos, such flooding with unneutralized aggression might result in destructive and violent acts.

Case 1

Mr. G., a severely borderline young man with an exquisite sensitivity to rejection, was seen in thrice-weekly, face-to-face, psychoanalytic psychotherapy. Once, early in his treatment, I informed him of an upcoming interruption in schedule. He responded by pained silence, gaze avoidance, and a noticeable drop in his voice. My empathic affirmation of this and encouragement for him to put his feelings into words met with little success. Later that evening (he told me amid sobs during the next session), Mr. G. saw in his front yard a little frog that appeared sad and lonely to him. He picked up the frog, took it inside, and made a home for it in a little box. He tried to cheer up the frog by talking to it and giving it bread crumbs. The frog, however, jumped out of the box and soon was nowhere to be found. Mr. G. looked for it all over his place. He repeatedly called for it and with the absence of any response began to feel rejected and angry. This grew into rage. Then suddenly he saw the frog. Cursing loudly, he chased it around the room damaging many of his belongings in the process. In a fury, he caught the frog and repeatedly smashed it against the wall with all his might. Later, a dawning awareness that he was "committing murder" stopped him. He let the now badly injured frog out of a window.

The good frog–bad frog split, the shift from caretaker to murderer self, the incapacity for ambivalence, and the flooding of the ego with raw aggression are as explicit in this enactment as are the transference themes of feeling abandoned by me (the bad frog), and the consequent loneliness and rage.[4] Blum (1981) notes that in such cases, because of the blurring of the self-object boundaries, the object's wish for independence is experienced as an agonizing, hence unforgivable, betrayal.

Paranoia and the "Inconstant Object"

Less dramatic outcomes are perhaps more common. The distortions of self and object representations seen in paranoid personality constitute one such instance. The paranoid individual has a close and deep tie with his "inconstant object" (Blum 1981), an ambivalently loved object who appears both needed and persecutory. The inconstant object cannot be allowed to have an indepen-

---

[4]This case has also been mentioned elsewhere (Volkan and Akhtar 1979).

dent existence. The issue is not that of closeness with the external object, but intrapsychic separation and the attainment of object constancy. The hatred and the associated constant hostile persecution (see also Chapter 4) is the reciprocal of libidinal object constancy and "a desperate effort to preserve an illusory constant object while constantly fearing betrayal and loss" (Blum 1981, p. 807).

Inordinate Optimism and the "Someday" Fantasy

In other individuals, what appears more prominent is the continued inner clinging to the coenesthetically remembered good-mother representation of the symbiotic phase. This may prompt a search for an "all good" object in external reality. Often this is coupled with a fantasy of "someday" (Akhtar 1991a; see Chapter 7 for more details) there being complete absence of pain and conflict in life. A complex set of psychodynamic mechanisms helps maintain the structural integrity of "someday." These include (1) a tenacious denial and negation of sectors of reality that challenge it; (2) splitting-off of those self and object representations that mobilize conflict and aggression; (3) a defensively motivated feeling of inauthenticity (Gediman 1985) in those areas of personality where a healthier, more realistic, compromise formation level of mentality and functioning has indeed been achieved; and (4) a temporal displacement from past to future of a preoedipal, preverbal state of blissful unity with the "all good" mother of the symbiotic phase (Mahler 1974, Mahler et al. 1975). The speculation that this fantasy alludes to a profound longing for a luxurious (and retrospectively idealized) symbiotic phase gains strength from these patients' descriptions of relative inactivity, timelessness, wordlessness, thoughtlessness, unexcited bliss, and the absence of needs in "someday." However, other factors, including early parent or sibling loss, intense castration anxiety, and problematic oedipal scenarios, also play a role in the genesis of the "someday" fantasy.

On an overt level, patients differ in how they strive to reach this "someday." Those with a narcissistic personality (Akhtar 1989b) actively seek to bring "someday" to life by hard work and social success. Those with an antisocial bent seek similar magic through swindling, gambling, and get-rich-quick schemes. Paranoid individuals (Akhtar 1990b) focus on the obstacles in their path to "someday." Borderline individuals frantically look for "someday" through infatuations, perverse sexuality, and drugs. Schizoid individuals (Akhtar 1987) adopt a passive stance of waiting for a magical happening, a windfall or a chance encounter with a charismatic guru. All individuals with a severe personality disorder seem to be seeking a restitution of an inner homeostasis that was disturbed years ago. All are in chronic pursuit.

Malignant Erotic Transference

This pursuit at times gets condensed with positive oedipal strivings. Condensation of the "good-mother" representation with that of the desired oedipal partner[5] gives rise to intense longings experienced as unquestionable "needs" (Akhtar 1992b, 1994a). During analytic treatment, such powerful erotic transference often turns out to be an upward defense against faulty self and object constancy. Four aspects of "malignant erotic transference" are especially to be noted: (1) predominance of hostility over love in the seemingly erotic overtures, (2) intense coercion of the analyst to indulge in actual actions, (3) inconsolability in face of the analyst's depriving stance,[6] and (4) the absence of erotic counterresonance in the analyst who experiences such "erotic" demands as intrusive, desperately controlling, and hostile. The choice of the modifier *malignant* to describe such erotic transference is to highlight these features and to extend the context in which this modifier has been earlier used in psychoanalysis, for example, "malignant regression" (Balint 1968) and "malignant narcissism" (Kernberg 1989). In such

---

[5]The parallel amalgamation of the "bad-mother" representation with the oedipal rival creates vengeful hostility which is often split-off, denied, or enacted in a contradictory but unassimilated manner toward the analyst.

[6]Referring to their inconsolability, Freud (1915a) termed such patients as "children of nature who refuse to accept the psychical in place of the material" (p. 166).

cases, intense narcissism, oral insatiability, and the underlying sadomasochism soon become apparent. "These patients cannot reciprocate love and are devouring and consuming with fears of depletion and engulfment. Seeking comfort and contact, they struggle with problems of infantile narcissism, separation, and symbiosis" (Blum 1973, p. 69).

Inability to Mourn, Nostalgia, and the "If Only" Fantasy

The pressure to recapture the preseparation, symbiotic bond impairs the capacity to mourn and underlies the "if only" fantasy (Akhtar 1991a). Individuals with this fantasy lack all interest in the future. They constantly wring their hands over something that happened in the past. Focusing their attention on this event, they insist that "if only" it had not occurred, everything would have turned out all right. Life before that event is retrospectively idealized with a consequent vulnerability to intense nostalgia.[7] The metapsychological structure of the "if only" fantasy is similar to that of the "someday" fantasy. It too involves splitting, denial, and primitive idealization. It too serves defensive purposes and reflects incomplete mourning over both preoedipal and oedipal traumas. Most frequently, though, the "if only" fantasy is a product of incomplete mourning over the loss of the all-good mother of symbiosis. It expresses a position whereby the idealized primary object is neither given up through the work of grieving nor is assimilated into the ego through identification.

Case 2

Ms. H., a socially withdrawn, white divorced accountant in her mid-forties, was persuaded by her sister to seek help for a rather severe depression of about a year's duration. This was precipitated by her being abruptly left by her married lover of quite some time. Since

---

[7]Here my views parallel those of Sterba (1940), who saw a longing for mother's breast at the kernel of homesickness, and of Chasseguet-Smirgel (1984), who speaks of the "pervert's nostalgia for primary narcissism" (p. 29).

then, Ms. H. had been in constant agony, pining for him, crying, and contemplating suicide. After some initial stabilizing measures, twice weekly psychotherapy was begun.

For a long time, our work remained focused on this relationship. Session after anguished session Ms. H. spoke of this man. They used to meet for a fixed number of intoxicating hours each week. They laughed, played, talked, and made deeply satisfying love. Theirs had been an "ideal relationship" and now she was hopelessly unable to let go of it. Indeed, she had held on to everything associated with him: the pillow case on which he last rested his head, his used napkin, the tissue papers with which he had cleaned himself whenever they made love, his comb, a newspaper he had left in her apartment, and so on. Her place—indeed her heart—was a shrine and he a god. He was all to her: "mommy, daddy, teddy bear, friend, lover, everything."

As these details unfolded amid heart-wrenching crying, all I could do was to affirm her experience and empathize with her loss. Whenever a discordant note appeared in her descriptions of this man (e.g., his inconsistencies, lying, racial slurs against black people), I underscored it, hoping it would help her de-idealize him and facilitate mourning. Ms. H., however, responded to such interventions with anxiety, hurt, and denial of the significance of his "other side." Soon, I saw the premature nature of my interventions and began keeping material regarding his "bad" side to myself.

Over the subsequent months, Ms. H. brought to my office the "linking objects" (Volkan 1981) that connected her with him, often with much emotional flooding. This gradually diminished her preoccupation with him. Still, she was unable to get rid of the things that linked them. Clearly, he had been profoundly important to her. But why? With this, a floodgate opened to themes involving a highly deformed self-image consequent upon childhood neglect and abuse.

Ms. H. had been raised by a cold, rule-bound mother and an uninvolved father whose only role was to dole out the violent punishments ordered by his wife. Though affluent, the family bought few things for the children, who often lacked sufficient clothing.

Ms. H. had always been called "a monster" and "a disaster" by her mother, who predicted nothing but failure for her life. She had few memories of warmth between them, none of physical closeness. She had grown up afraid that she was bad, even evil. After a forlorn latency and parentally unguided adolescence, Ms. H. entered an out-of-town college. Soon after her graduation, she married a man who turned out to be "a crook and a swindler." Divorced shortly afterward, she underwent a brief period of promiscuity and then settled into a solitary, cynical life. Ten years passed and then she met the older, married man who became her lover.

Significantly, as this information unfolded, Ms. H. talked only of her being bad, ugly, mean, and so on. It had never occurred to her that she had been abused and neglected. Only much later in treatment did she begin to question how her parents had raised her: being sent to a summer camp at age 4, going to get a haircut by herself at age 6, total absence of physical affection (except from a black maid), and repeated beatings by her father. Ms. H. now felt that her "badness" was a taking on of the blame for how things were and letting her parents off the hook. This realization led, on the one hand, to the emergence of violent rage and murderous fantasies toward her parents, and, on the other hand, to an intensified idealization of her departed lover (now also seen by us as a reincarnation of the kind black maid of her childhood).

Significantly, Ms. H. tenaciously avoided the transference allusions of either extreme object representation. She kept me in a neutral though benevolently positive position, sort of like the black maid. Only gradually did it become clear that, having practically no one else in her life, she deeply feared violence from putting me in the "bad" (mother) role and abject dependency from placing me into the "good" (lover) role. We decided to continue working in the extratransference realm. Gradually, after some angry confrontations with her parents, Ms. H. began to be more tolerant, though understandably never too kind, toward them. Her relationship with her sister and brother-in-law now began to deepen and they slowly came to serve as surrogate parents for her. In this relationship, Ms. H. became more tolerant of ambivalence. She gradually got rid of the useless items belonging to her lover. She also began to jokingly (therefore still partly denying) talk of his weaknesses and her disappointment in him. As these changes occurred, she developed a fascination for zebras and, at times, laughingly referred to herself as "neither black nor white but striped like a zebra." A restructuring of self and object constancy was evident.

In sum, lack of object constancy impairs the capacities to mourn, tolerate ambivalence, and maintain optimal distance. Lacking inner cohesion, such individuals tend to develop compensatory structures leading to paranoia, erotomania, and inconsolable nostalgia. These dynamic and structural configurations have considerable bearing on their treatment.

TECHNICAL IMPLICATIONS

Rather than recalling, talking about, and reflecting upon the theme, the patient lives out the problem of object constancy with the therapist in the present. For psychotic and borderline patients, object constancy is externally represented by their content in whatever form of ideation, whether of love, politics, films, trash or weather, that serves to maintain the contact with the therapist. Contact between patient and therapist constitutes the agent of both inner and outer negotiation and interaction, out of which emerges the psychological construct of object constancy. [Ekstein and Friedman 1967, p. 362]

Certain configurations persist in transference or acting out patterns which seem to be the outcome of unresolved conflicts in the separation-individuation process. [Mahler 1971, p. 181]

The analytic relationship embodies both therapeutic process and developmental process, and . . . these processes function in a complementary way in the restructuring of object and self constancy. [Settlage 1993, p. 474]

Starting with Loewald (1960) and extending through the later contributions of many analysts (Blum 1971, 1977, Burland 1986, Fleming 1972, Greenacre 1975, Lax 1986, Robbins, in Escoll 1977, Schlessinger and Robbins 1983, Settlage 1977, 1991, 1993, Zetzel 1965), there has evolved a view that the psychoanalytic process has overlaps with the developmental process. A corollary of this position is to see similarities between the analyst–analysand relationship and the mother–child dyad. The technical significance of such conceptualization depends not only on the analyst's theoretical predilection but also on the analysand's character organization. For the reasonably individuated, neurotic analysand, the analyst's consistent and empathic stance is significant insofar as it permits and safeguards their interpretive undertaking. For the analysand with deficient object constancy, the situation is quite different. The availability of someone empathic, reliable, and constant is a new experience. It stirs up a wide gamut of intense, often contradictory, emotions: disbelief and excitement, anaclitic yearning and anxious withdrawal, hate transferred from early frustrating objects and hope that such hate will not destroy this relationship, and so on.[8] Analysis in such cases remains focused, for a long time, on the anxiety regarding intimacy and separateness, issues of ambivalence, defensive warding-off of aggression, and fears of psychic growth and individuation. Based on my analytic experience with such patients (although, for complex professional reasons, only psychotherapy cases have been reported in this chapter), I have delineated six technical aspects of significance in working with them. I must emphasize, though, that I am not recommending specific strategies, only a background[9] for the "evenly suspended attention" (Freud 1912c, p. 111) mandatory for our work.

---

[8]Manifestations of such affective stirrings are hidden underneath a veneer of oedipal transferences. However, such material is frequently distorted and suspiciously intense. Indeed, "it is often the distortions of the oedipal features that serve as the first clues to unresolved preoedipal issues" (Burland 1986, p. 301).

[9]"A background," said the eminent British photographer Lord Snowdon, "has to be just this side of being something, and just the other side of being nothing" (Lacayo 1984, p. 54).

First and foremost, the analyst has to have a greater than usual regard for his "holding" (Winnicott 1960a) and "containing" (Bion 1967) functions. Underscoring the role of such noninterpretive ingredients of the analytic technique, Stone (1981) stated, "The 'love' implicit in empathy, listening, and trying to understand, in nonseductive devotion to the task, the sense of full acceptance, respect, and sometimes the homely phenomenon of sheer dependable patience, may take their place as equal or nearly equal in importance to sheer interpretive skill" (p. 114). This is nowhere more true than in the course of treating individuals with disturbed object constancy.

Second, the analyst has to keep in mind that individuals who lack object constancy frequently employ splitting and related defense mechanisms of denial, projective identification, idealization, and devaluation (Kernberg 1967). Their transferences abruptly shift and so do their self-estimations. The analyst therefore must retain these contradictory self and object representations in mind since the patient has a tendency to affectively "forget" one or the other extreme of his experience. The analyst's interpretations, for a long time, might be usefully tempered by his display that he, at least, has not "forgotten" the opposite transference configuration (e.g., "This hate that, despite your parallel love, you feel for me at this time is . . ."). The analyst's allegiance to the "principle of multiple function" (Waelder 1936) also helps reduce his own vulnerability to either/or conceptualizations regarding love and hate, drive and defense, deficit and conflict, oedipal and preoedipal, and so on.

Third, the analyst has to be extraordinarily attentive to matters of "optimal distance" (Akhtar 1992a, Bouvet 1958, Escoll 1992, Mahler et al. 1975). Starting from the time the patient begins to use the couch—or fails to use it (Frank 1992)—through interruptions, vacations, accidental extra-analytic encounters, transference-based oscillations of intimacy, termination-phase advances and regressions, and even afterward, the issue of optimal distance affects analytic technique (Akhtar 1992a), and more so with individuals who lack object constancy. The analyst has to be constantly mindful of their need for closeness and autonomy and the two corresponding anxieties of fusion and abandonment. He must avoid "interpretative intrusions" (Settlage 1994, p. 46) and often knowingly restrict the expanse of his comments. The first stirrings of longing in a previously detached schizoid patient or a violent enactment in an otherwise agreeable borderline patient, for instance, are better interpreted in the extratransference realm without too quickly unmasking their transference allusions. The optimal distance concept also enriches the understanding of "negative therapeutic reactions" (Freud 1923), as these might also arise from separation-based concerns and fears of losing the analyst by getting better (Asch 1977, Grunert 1979, Modell 1965).

Fourth, the analyst has to be sharply attuned to nonverbal communications of the patient. Individuals who lack object constancy often behave rather than remember. Their regressive struggle to recapture the symbiotic bond with their mothers defies customary discourse. Fantasy elaboration is meager and "the raw data pointing to interruptions early in ego development tend to be affectual rather than verbal or intellectual" (Burland 1975, p. 317). The "unrememberable and the unforgettable" (Frank 1969) residues of the preverbal trauma, however, lie unabated under the adult persona and are often discernible only through the patient's posture and movements on the couch, mannerisms, tone of voice, and style of entering and leaving the office. Paying attention to one's countertransference, where such "behavioral dance and somatic music" (McLaughlin 1992, p. 151) reverberates at its loudest, opens new vistas for reconstruction and insight.

Fifth, the analyst must keep in mind the dialectical relationship between the interpretive resolution of psychopathology and the resumption of arrested development (Settlage 1992). With each undoing of some aspect of pathology, there is the opportunity for resumed development in that area, and with each such developmental advance there is an increase in the patient's tolerance for the exposure of repressed, anxiety-provoking wishes and fantasies. Abrams's (1978) concept of "developmental interpretation" might be a specific tool in this regard. When a hitherto unexpressed healthy tendency emerges as a result of interpretive work, the ana-

lyst might underscore the inherent progressive trend and "facilitate the emergence of experiential building-blocks" (p. 397).
Settlage's (1993b) recommendation that the analyst acknowledge
and encourage the patient's developmental initiatives and achievements belongs in the same realm.

Finally, the analyst has to recognize that mourning-like elements,
integral to all analyses, carry greater significance in the treatment
of these patients. This is in part because they have often suffered
severe, actual trauma in their childhoods. More importantly, they
have not gone through the incremental steps of loss (of external
support, of omnipotence) and gain (of internal structure, of reality principle) typical of separation-individuation process. They
lack this prototype of mourning; in Klein's (1940) terms they have
not experienced the "depressive position." Separations from the
analyst, guilty recognitions of their aggression toward him, dawning gratitude, and the renewed anguish of loss during termination—all awaken and consolidate the process of mourning. The
same applies to the loss of their infantile omnipotence and their
not infrequent tendency to live in a world of illusions (Burland
1986).

In sum, there are six tasks that seem especially important for the
analytic work with such patients: (1) safeguarding the analyst's
"holding" functions; (2) interpreting splitting mechanisms, especially as they pertain to negative transference; (3) maintaining
optimal distance; (4) discerning nonverbal communications,
especially through countertransference; (5) encouraging developmental initiatives; and (6) facilitating mourning, not only of past
losses but also of those inherent in the analytic situation. To balance things out, I will conclude by quoting Blum's (1981) caution-
ary note about preoedipal reconstructions:

> The transference patterns in cases of very severe developmental
> arrest and distortions and in cases of severe ego regression do
> not revive actual infantile relationship in their original forms. . . .
> Analytic reconstruction in these cases is a very complicated effort.
> Because of projection, denial, splitting, and other infantile
> defenses, and because of the general invasion of the cognitive pro-
> cess with the primary process, self-object representations are dis-

torted, not only by the patient's specific psychological disturbance, but by the general characteristic of unconscious transformations. [p. 803]

An analytic approach tempered by Blum's wise counsel and yet attending to the six tasks outlined above seems the one best suited for treating individuals with disturbed self and object constancy.

SUMMARY

The capacity to maintain and to utilize a stable mental representation of the libidinal object is the product of an interdependent, reciprocal relationship among the maturation, modulation, and fusion of the libidinal and aggressive drives; the development of the ego, including the perceptual and the memory apparatuses and the defensive and adaptive functions; and the real experiences of gratification and frustration in the child's life, particularly the degree of the emotional availability of the mother and the quality of the mother–child interaction. [McDevitt 1975, p. 715]

In this chapter, I have summarized Mahler's views on the initial acquisition of object constancy in early childhood. I have delineated its vicissitudes during oedipal phase, latency, adolescence, and various phases of adult development. I have described, with the help of brief clinical vignettes, six psychopathological syndromes of adult life associated with disturbed object constancy: (1) impaired optimal distance; (2) persistent splitting of self and object representations, with the concomitant intensification of affects; (3) paranoia; (4) inordinate optimism and the "someday" fantasy; (5) malignant erotic transference; and (6) impaired capacity to mourn, intense nostalgia, and the "if only" fantasy. Finally, I have outlined the technical implications of these concepts and attempted to show that six tasks seem especially important for analytic work with such patients: (1) safeguarding the analyst's "holding" functions; (2) interpreting splitting mechanisms, especially as these pertain to negative transference; (3) maintaining optimal distance; (4) discerning nonverbal communications, especially through countertransference; (5) encouraging developmental initiatives; and (6) facilitating mourning, not only of past losses but also of those inherent in the analytic situation. Through all this, I have attempted to highlight, elucidate, and modestly extend the work of Margaret Mahler.

2

AGGRESSION

Aggression is a broad and inherently interdisciplinary topic. Many fields, besides psychology, psychiatry, and psychoanalysis, have contributed to our understanding of it, including neurology and neurophysiology, genetics and evolutionary sciences, ethology, political science, sociology, anthropology, and other branches of the humanities. Clearly, it is not possible to review this vast literature here. Even to provide a comprehensive summary of just the psychoanalytic writings on the topic is difficult. The classical literature needs to be synthesized with the contemporary views. The differing viewpoints of drive theory, structural model, object relations approach, Kleinian formulation, developmental perspective, and self psychology need to be taken into account. Data gathered from varying sources, for example, logical and deductive theory building, reconstructions in psychoanalytic treatment of adults, analytically sophisticated observation of infants and children, analytic treatment of children, and the "applied" arena of psychopolitical studies, need to be pooled and brought together in some kind of conceptual harmony.

The task is indeed daunting, perhaps not even possible within the confines of a single chapter. My focus here is quite restricted.

I do not address the admittedly important areas of (1) neurophysi-
ological, biochemical, hereditary, and phylogenetic substrates of
aggression; (2) the neurotic, perverse, and characterological syndromes associated with sadomasochism, self-destructiveness, and
violence; (3) the impact of intense, unneutralized, overt aggression on the feasibility and technique of adult and child psychoanalysis; and (4) the application of the psychoanalytic understanding
of aggression to parent education for preventing the development
of excessive hostility in children, and to the study of law and justice, and ethnic, racial, and international conflicts. Instead, I devote this chapter to the various views of the nature and origins of
human aggression as these have evolved through the history of
psychoanalysis. I begin with Freud's changing views on aggression.
Then I highlight the two major divergent post-Freudian trends (i.e.,
the theoretical paths taken by Melanie Klein and Heinz Hartmann)
in the study of aggression. Following this, I summarize other
significant contributions including those of the British object relations theory, and self psychology. I then address some contemporary reformulations, and conclude by summarizing, synthesizing,
and noting the newer vistas of theoretical concern and application.
It seems best to begin by defining our terms.

ETYMOLOGY, MEANING,
AND PSYCHOANALYTIC TERMINOLOGY

> I view the phenomenon of aggression, and its psy-
> chological functions and representations, as the
> aggregate of diverse acts, having diverse origins, and
> bound together, sometimes loosely, by the nature of
> their impact on objects rather than by a demonstra-
> bly common and unitary drive. . . . This does not
> mean that certain elements of aggression do not
> have an instinctual origin or affiliation. [Stone 1971,
> p. 195]

It is difficult to provide a straightforward psychoanalytic definition of the word *aggression* for many reasons. First, too many words
(*aggression, aggressivity, aggressiveness, aggressive behavior, aggressive*

drive, aggressive instinct etc.) are used interchangeably in this realm. Second, the word *aggression* has come to stand for an enormous variety of phenomena and manifestations (Stone 1971). It is an "unfortunate fact that we use the term 'aggression' when we also mean many other things" (Sandler, quoted in Lussier 1972, p. 13) and that aggression has become "an umbrella concept . . . [denoting] forms of energy, various types of drives, and a wide range of motivation and behavior" (Marcovitz 1973, pp. 226–227). Third, confusion about what the word denotes also results from a tautological leap in psychoanalytic theorizing. To explain aggressive behavior, an underlying aggressive drive was postulated. As a result, a "descriptive concept was elevated into an explanatory one, and it was then assumed that aggressive drive (i.e., the impetus to be aggressive) did not always result in aggressive behavior" (Sandler, quoted in Lussier 1972, p. 14). No wonder that the denotative focus of aggression was lost. Finally, the rarity of linear correlations among drive, affect, fantasy, wish, defense, and behavior also makes it puzzling as to which conceptual or phenomenological level is most suitable for the word *aggression*. Is it better, for instance, to reserve it only for the hypothesized instinctual drive and not use it in a behavioral context or in the context of fantasy or affects?

In search of clarity, one turns to the literal meaning of *aggression*. Both the *Oxford English Dictionary* (1961, p. 182) and *Webster's New Universal Unabridged Dictionary* (1983, p. 36) emphasize the hostile, menacing meaning of the word. Yet, in citing its derivation from Latin and in discussing its verb form *aggress*, both note two roots (*aggredi*: to attack, and *ad+ gradi*: to step, to move toward). This expands the meaning of aggression to include not only hostile gestures but also active and assertive ones. Indeed, five out of the six meanings given in the *Oxford Latin Dictionary* (1982, p. 84) for the root word *aggredior* refer to nonhostile, nondestructive actions.

The tension between an active-assertive and an attacking-destructive view of aggression is also evident in the psychoanalytic glossaries (Eidelberg 1968, English and English 1976, Moore and Fine 1968, 1990, Rycroft 1968). Some of these seem to have taken opposite sides in this dilemma. In a somewhat puzzling manner, Eidelberg (1968) states that aggression "also referred to as an aggressive instinct-fusion, is a mixture of Eros and Thanatos, with Thanatos dominating" (p. 21). He does, however, make an interesting distinction between aggressive and sexual drives: aggressive pleasure is felt when the subject overcomes the resistance of the object, whereas sexual pleasure is felt by both the subject and the object, and is achieved by the actions of both. Although tangential and idiosyncratic, Eidelberg's definition is a resolutely intrapsychic one. The American Psychoanalytic Association's first glossary (Moore and Fine 1968), on the other hand, declares bluntly that aggression means "attack or hostile action . . . (that) may take the form of physical assault as one extreme, or gentle, implicit verbal criticism as the other" (p. 18). This definition, making no mention of nondestructive aggression, equates aggression with hostility. While it goes on to mention an underlying aggressive instinctual drive, its emphasis is upon overt behavior.

In contrast, Rycroft (1968) defines aggression as a

> hypothetical force, INSTINCT, or principle imagined to actuate a range of acts and feelings. It is frequently regarded as antithetical to SEX or LIBIDO, in which case it is being used to refer to destructive drives. Even when being used as a synonym for destructiveness, controversy exists as to whether it is a primary drive, i.e., whether there is an aggressive, destructive instinct, or whether it is a reaction to FRUSTRATION. [p. 4]

Rycroft maintains an intrapsychic focus, hints at controversies, and in regarding the traditional meaning of aggression to be "dynamism, self-assertiveness, expansiveness, [and] drive" (p. 5), firmly disengages aggression from inherent destructiveness. English and English (1976) adapt an intermediate stance between Moore and Fine (1968) and Rycroft (1968). However, by portraying aggression as including hostile acts, behaviors consequent upon frustration, and manifestations of the will to power and of the hypothesized death instinct, these authors tend to become theoretically and phenomenologically overinclusive.

A more succinctly stated compromise position is that of the new glossary of the American Psychoanalytic Association (Moore and Fine 1990). Here *aggression* is seen as referring to the "manifest strivings, either physical or verbal, to subjugate or prevail upon others" (p. 10). Various expressions of aggression are noted as well as the fact that the word *aggression* is "sometimes broadened to include acts that seem to originate from initiative, ambition, or the just demand for rights. Such acts are sometimes designated *assertion* in order to indicate that they do not seem to arise from hostile motives" (p. 10, author's italics). The definition goes on to discuss the aggressive drive underlying these manifestations. It notes the continuing debate as to whether the aggressive drive is innately destructive or might become so as a result of frustration and conflict. It mentions that Freud's notion of death instinct is not widely accepted by psychoanalysts while acknowledging its assimilation into Kleinian theory. Further, the definition notes that it is unclear whether aggression and libido are separate drive energies at birth or only gradually differentiate into separate strands. Finally, it touches upon the developmental vicissitudes of aggressive drive including its influence upon the structuralization of the superego.

This overview of the various definitions of aggression highlights "certain dichotomies" (Rangell 1972, p. 5) that surface repeatedly in discussing aggression: constructive versus destructive aggression, drive to mastery versus drive to destroy, and innate versus reactive origin of destructiveness. These dichotomies have complex conceptual sources and historical origins.

FREUD'S VIEWS ON AGGRESSION

I cannot bring myself to assume the existence of a special aggressive instinct alongside the familiar instincts of self-preservation and sex, and on an equal footing with them. [Freud 1909a, p. 140]

Starting from speculations on the beginning of life and from biological parallels, I drew the conclusion that, besides the instinct to preserve living substance

> and to join it into even larger units, there must exist
> another, contrary instinct seeking to dissolve those
> units and to bring them back to their primaeval, in-
> organic state. That is to say, as well as Eros there was
> an instinct of death. [Freud 1930, pp. 118–119]

The above statements portray the two nodal points in the evolution of Freud's thinking on aggression. The turning point in this
long journey came in 1920 with the publication of *Beyond the Pleasure Principle*, somewhat late in the course of Freud's theory building. He himself acknowledged this by asking, "Why have we ourselves needed such a long time before we decided to recognize an
aggressive instinct?" (Freud 1933, p. 102). However, the time lag
involved only metapsychological theorizing and not clinical observation (Laplanche and Pontalis 1973). Freud had been keenly
aware of aggression for a long time before assimilating it into his
theory. He had discerned the workings of aggression within himself, including his early death wishes against his younger brother,
his hostile oedipal feelings toward his father, and his need for an
enemy in his life (Freud 1900, Gay 1988, Masson 1985). Besides,
he had noted the significance of aggression in clinical work. As early
as 1896, he talked about the "sexual aggression" (p. 165) passively
suffered by hysterics and the "acts of aggression carried out with
pleasure" (p. 168) by obsessional neurotics during their childhoods. The following year, in a letter to Fliess (Masson 1985), he
showed his awareness of aggressiveness as a resistance to treatment.
Then in *The Interpretation of Dreams*, his earliest exposition of the
Oedipus complex contained a combination of libidinal and hostile trends and appeared under the heading of "Dreams of the
Death of Persons of Whom the Dreamer is Fond" (1900, p. 248).
Five years later, in his analysis of jokes, Freud noted how often these
served "the purpose of aggressiveness" (1905a, p. 97). The same
year, in the Dora case, he underscored the ubiquity of the emergence of aggressiveness in psychoanalytic treatment (1905b).

The publication of *Three Essays on the Theory of Sexuality* (1905c)
was, however, an event of greater import to the study of aggression. It is here that Freud began to develop his first instinct theory,
though it was a few years later that he first explicitly referred to

the "instincts of self-preservation and of sex" (1909a, p. 140). It was in the *Three Essays,* however, that he first focused attention on sadism and masochism, terms he acknowledged having borrowed from Krafft-Ebing. In tracing the roots of sadism, Freud observed:

> [The] sexuality of most male human beings contains an element of aggressiveness—a desire to subjugate; the biological significance of it seems to lie in the need for overcoming the resistance of the sexual object by means other than the process of wooing. Thus sadism would correspond to an aggressive component of the sexual instinct which has become independent and exaggerated and, by displacement, has usurped the leading position. [1905c, pp. 157– 158]

Sadism was a component of the sexual instinct and masochism was sadism turned around upon the subject's own self. Freud noted the "intimate connection between cruelty and the sexual instinct" (p. 159) and wondered if

> this aggressive element of the sexual instinct is in reality a relic of cannibalistic desires—that is, it is a contribution derived from the apparatus for obtaining mastery, which is concerned with satisfaction of the other and, ontogenetically, the older of the great instinctual needs. [1905c, p. 159]

The statement added a preoedipal substrate to sadism, and hinted at connections between sadism and the striving for mastery. Both these themes gain strength by Freud's later stating that it "may be assumed that the impulse of cruelty arises from the instinct of mastery and appears at a period of sexual life at which the genitals have not yet taken over their later role" (sentence added in 1915b to 1905c, p. 193). Finally, not only did Freud correlate sadism, activity, instinct for mastery, and "the agency of the somatic musculature" (p. 198), he also spoke of masochism as a passive "instinct of cruelty" (p. 193). Thus, in 1905 Freud took three positions on aggression: (1) it is a component of sexual instinct, (2) it arises from an instinct of mastery (with the latter concept still waiting to be elevated to a full instinct status), and (3) there might be an instinct of cruelty.

Four years later, however, he could not bring himself "to assume the existence of a special aggressive instinct" (1909a, p. 140). To do so, he felt, would be to attribute to a single facet of the sexual instinct characteristics that were essential to instincts in general— namely a source, aim, and object, and a pressing quality and capacity to initiate action.

The criteria for an instinctual drive were made more specific and explicit in *Instincts and Their Vicissitudes* (1915b). Freud held on to the dichotomy between sexual and ego instincts, once again assigning sadism to the sexual instinct. However, as Parens (1979) has cogently argued, a tension similar to that in the *Three Essays* between viewing aggression as a component of sexual instinct versus as a component of ego instinct, exists here as well. This is most evident in Freud's views (1915b) on hate. First he saw hate as resulting from transformed love, but then concluded that "the true prototypes of the relation of hate are derived not from the sexual life, but from the ego's struggle to preserve and maintain itself" (p. 138). This dilemma of placing aggression under sexual instincts or ego instincts was automatically laid to rest with Freud's postulation of his second instinctual theory in *Beyond the Pleasure Principle* (1920a). Freud now relegated ego instincts to the sexual instinct and elevated aggression to an independent instinctual drive. In a "startling" (Jones 1957) theoretical move, he declared this aggressive drive to be the derivative of a death instinct that together with sexual instinct formed the two main forces in the struggle of life.

Based upon observations regarding children's turning passive traumatic experiences into play, certain analysands' returning over and over again to painful past experiences, the behavior of those who must go repeatedly through similar calamities, and the painful preoccupations of war veterans, Freud suggested that there might be a wicked, self-destructive, "daemonic force" (1920a, p. 35) at work in them. This force seemed to work in opposition to the pleasure principle. It is as though these individuals never comprehend the futility of their repetitions. Freud argued that this force was aligned with a fundamental attribute of mind that involved a search for reduction of all excitation to quiescence. At its deepest, this search for quiescence—the "Nirvana principle"[10] (Freud 1920a, p. 56)—was aimed at returning the living organism to its previous, inorganic state. He concluded that "*the aim of all life is death*" (1920a, p. 38, author's italics) and thus gave voice to his celebrated concept of the death instinct.

The death instinct, at birth, is a threat to the self. Therefore, it is deflected outward by the influence of libido and ego using the agency of somatic musculature. Freud termed this outwardly deflected part of the death instinct the "aggressive instinct" (*Aggressionstrieb*).[11] Such conceptualization altered his earlier views of sadism and masochism. Freud now proposed that a portion of the death instinct

> is placed directly in the service of the sexual function, where it has an important part to play. This is sadism proper. Another portion does not share in this transposition outwards; it remains inside the organism and, with the help of accompanying sexual excitation . . . becomes libidinally bound there. It is in this portion that we have to recognize the original, erotogenic masochism. [1924a, pp. 163–164]

The earlier formulation of sadism being primary and masochism secondary appears reversed here. The death instinct, after all, is at first self-directed, and only later outer directed. However, such thinking misses the point that neither the primary self-direction nor the primary outward direction of the death instinct

---

[10]Freud acknowledged borrowing this expression from Barbara Low, a Sanskrit expert. The notion of "death instinct" thus, from the beginning, had an Eastern touch. Fechner, the renowned physicist whose "constancy principle" led Freud to the "Nirvana principle" was himself involved in Buddhism (Jones 1957). And, Romain Rolland, from whom Freud (1930) obtained the semi-related concept of "oceanic feeling," was an avid reader and biographer of the nineteenth-century Indian mystics Ramakrishna and Vivekananda. It thus seems that the Indian mystic tradition was a background conceptual source for Freud's death instinct. This may have been part of why the concept appeared alien to Western minds.

[11]The term, with differing emphasis, was introduced by Adler in 1908 (see Jones 1957).

are libidinally charged, a requirement for aggression to be either masochistic or sadistic. Indeed, Freud continued to imply (e.g., 1930) that there were both an inward and outward discharge of aggression free of erotism.[12] Moreover, he retained the earlier formulation of masochism being self-directed sadism, only renaming it "secondary masochism" (1924a, p. 164).

Over the subsequent years, Freud became increasingly committed to his second dual-instinct theory. In *The Ego and the Id* (1923), he repeated this theory, adding that the death instinct operates silently. In *Civilization and Its Discontents*, he emphasized that "aggression is an original, self-subsisting instinctual disposition in the man . . . [and] . . . aggressive instinct is the derivative and the main representative of the death instinct" (1930, p. 122). In polar opposition to his 1905 view that destructive aggression ("cruelty") may result from thwarted instinct of mastery, Freud now suggested that the instinct of destruction, moderated and tamed, and, as it were, inhibited in its aim, must, when it is directed towards objects, provide the ego with the satisfaction of its vital needs and with control over nature" (1930, p. 121).

Thus we see Freud attempting to reconcile aggression with the instinct for mastery. In this connection, Parens's (1979) observation that Freud often spoke of "an instinct of aggressiveness *and* destructiveness" (Freud 1930, p. 119, italics added) or of "nonerotic aggressivity *and* destructiveness" (p. 120, italics added) is significant. Parens wonders if Freud was intending to distinguish destructive and nondestructive aggression. Perhaps. However, even if this were true, the source of this latter form of aggression appears far from settled in Freud's writings. In 1905, the striving for mastery arose in its own right; in 1930, it resulted from the aim-inhibition of innate destructiveness.

In *Analysis Terminable and Interminable* (1937b), Freud again referred to the death instinct and related masochism, negative thera-

---

[12]Gaddini (1972) later noted that such outward discharge occurs through striated muscles, while the "discharge on the inside takes place through the smooth muscles of the vessels and mucous membranes" (p. 191). The significance of the latter for psychosomatic illness merits further exploration.

peutic reaction, and unconscious guilt to its derivative, the aggressive drive. Again, in passing, he seemed to distinguish "the instinct of aggression *or* of destruction according to its aims" (p. 243, italics added). And, finally, in the *Outline,* he reiterated his formulation of "two basic instincts" (1940, p. 148). The aim of one was to establish unities and that of the other to undermine connections and destroy things. Freud noted the lack of a term analogous to libido for the energy of the death instinct.[13] He also reiterated that this instinct silently operates internally and only comes to our notice when it is diverted outward as an instinct of destruction. Freud emphasized that the two basic instincts, besides being opposed, frequently combine with each other. Indeed, this "concurrent and mutually opposing action of the two basic instincts gives rise to the whole variegation of the phenomena of life" (1940, p. 149).

MELANIE KLEIN AND HEINZ HARTMANN, AND THEIR RESPECTIVE FOLLOWERS

> As far as a theory of drives is concerned, the analytic world has remained, since 1920, divided into two factions, with convictions ranging from complete or even extreme commitment to Freud's dualistic theory of drives to an equally complete rejection of the assumption of a death instinct with aggression as its representative. [Anna Freud 1972, p. 170]

The conceptual chasm between Freud's pre- and post-1920 views on aggression ultimately resulted in a bifurcation of the Freudian theory of aggression. One group of analysts followed the death instinct route. The other chose to concentrate on the distinct nature of the aggressive drive, its modulation by the ego, and its role in psychic structure formation. Melanie Klein and Heinz

---

[13]The terms *destrudo* and *mortudo* were suggested by Stekel and Weiss but never gained Freud's favor. The same is true of the term *Thanatos,* coined by Stekel in 1909 and later used by Federn to denote the death instinct (see Jones 1957).

Hartmann are representatives par excellence of these two lines of theoretical advance.

Klein became the most "uncompromising" (Gay 1988, p. 402) exponent of death instinct, the Freudian postulate that had been accepted by only a few early analysts (Ferenczi 1929, Menninger 1938; Weiss 1935; also Eitingon, Federn, and Nunberg, according to Jones 1957). In a series of striking, though controversial, contributions (Klein, 1932, 1933, 1935, 1946, 1948, 1952), she elaborated a theory of the neonatal instinctual life and its role in object relations of that period. While Klein's wide-ranging views on instincts, internal objects, primitive ego defenses, and psychic structuralization—and their subsequent extension by others (Bion 1956, 1959, Grotstein 1981, Heimann 1952, Rosenfeld 1965, Segal 1964)—need not be summarized here, her particular emphasis upon inborn aggression is worth noting. Klein felt that the infant is threatened by destruction from within immediately following birth. Giving concreteness and specificity to Freud's (1920a, 1930) notion of the death instinct being deflected outward, Klein proposed that such deflection results in the creation of an "all bad" external object. This, in turn, leads to persecutory anxieties. The primitive ego, which Klein saw as operant from birth, defends by splitting itself, introjecting the bad object, and also by projecting a portion of the life instinct outward to create "all good" objects. Thus both life and death instincts are intimately linked with early object relations.

The tendency to view objects as "all good" or "all bad" with the concomitant affects of greed and envy, and defensive splitting of the ego, is characteristic of the earliest phase of life (the "paranoid position"). With increasing ego maturation, however, the inner origins of aggression are acknowledged and projective mechanisms recede. The conviction of a lack of inner aggression and guilt over it can no longer be maintained. Synthesis of good and bad part objects becomes possible with the resultant deepening of object relations (the "depressive position"). Now the predominant ego anxiety is in the nature of ambivalence, guilt, and sadness, the defenses against which center around either hypomanic denial or gratitude and reparation.

Klein extended this scheme further and presented an altered view of the Oedipus complex and superego structuralization. However, her views pose problems by (1) pushing the developmental timetable to earlier and earlier infancy, (2) attributing unrealistically elaborate fantasy life to early ego (for a rebuttal of this particular criticism see Hayman 1989), (3) positing a priori images of objects by viewing the first objects of the drives as extensions of the drives themselves, and (4) ignoring the importance of the actual behavior of early caregivers in laying the foundations of the psychic structure. Yet, some of her concepts, for example, the splitting defense, the gradual emergence of the capacity for ambivalence, mourning, and sadness, and the powerful role of constitutional givens (especially intense aggression) in severe psychopathology, have received increasingly serious consideration.[14]

Heinz Hartmann, in contrast, has had a much more widespread influence on psychoanalytic theorizing, especially in the United States. While firmly adhering to a "primary aggressive propensity in man," Hartmann discarded Freud's notion of death instinct as a nonverifiable and clinically inapplicable "biological speculation" (Hartmann 1939, p. 11). Highlighting the human–animal differences, he proposed the term *instinctual drive* (drive, for short) to be preferable over *instinct* in the human context. Contrasting the aggressive drive with its libidinal counterpart, he noted that the two were alike in regard to *impetus* but differed in source, aim, and object. The source of libido, especially in its sequential relation to the erogenous zones, was clear. The proposed relationship between aggression and musculature (Freud 1915b), however, explained discharge, not genesis. Moreover, both libidinal and aggressive tensions could be discharged by motor activity. The *source* of aggression, therefore, remained unclear. The sexual aims varied greatly but the *aim* of aggression appeared "less diversified" (Hartmann et al. 1949, p. 18). Active aggression involved the "wish to harm, to master, or to destroy an object; passivity refers to the

---

[14]For recent assessments of Klein's contributions see Kernberg (1975a, 1980) and Greenberg and Mitchell (1983).

wish to be mastered, harmed, or destroyed" (p. 17). However, aggressive aims varied with the means of expression and the degree of instinctual discharge. With respect to the *object*, too, libido and aggression differed insofar as a full discharge of aggression endangered the object, whereas a full discharge of libido did not.

Hartmann delineated other important characteristics of aggression: (1) aggressive discharge is less structured than libidinal discharge, which follows specific time curves; (2) aggressive and libidinal impulses might be more efficiently dealt with by different defenses; (3) aggressive and libidinal aims can both be inhibited by ego and superego dictates, but aim-inhibition of aggression also results from the object's investment with libido; (4) aggression, in a sublimated form, is more integrated into the ego and superego structure than libido, which, being capable of full discharge, is tied more closely to the object; (5) the discharge of aggressive tension, more than that of libidinal tension, depends on muscular activity; and (6) aggressive drive, when neutralized, contributes to the self-preservatory function. Hartmann also noted that four types of conflict lead to aim-inhibition of aggression: instinctual conflict, conflict with reality, structural conflict involving the ego, and structural conflict involving the superego. In addition, there existed four processes to modify the impact of aggression: displacement, aim-inhibition, fusion with libido, and sublimation. The last mentioned involved an energy change. The resultant neutralized aggressive energy fueled ego's motor activity and ego and superego's countercathectic measures. Hartmann thus added a third form to the two types of inward discharge of aggression (one silent and nonerotic, the other libidinized and hence masochistic) already outlined by Freud. He emphasized that the capacity to neutralize aggression is a criterion of ego's strength and lack of such neutralization betrays a weak ego.

Regarding the origins of aggression, Hartmann (1939) began with the assumption of an undifferentiated phase of psychic structure during which both libido and aggression are centered in the self. Gradual localization of unpleasure outside the body invites the cathexis of its source with aggression. This protects the self and is pleasurable too since it discharges aggressive tension. Such association of aggression and pleasure forms the basis of sadism, which, however, requires the additional element of libidinal pleasure at inflicting pain and humiliating. It therefore can only be viewed in the context of a well-developed object relation. Not all aggressive tendencies directed against objects are sadistic. Hartmann noted that while aggression was fueled by an inner driving force akin to libido, it could also be mobilized by deprivations and frustrations. However, what is found frustrating by the growing child and ways of expressing aggression over it vary according to developmental phases (Abraham, 1924a, Freud 1905c). Characteristic manifestations include biting during the oral phase, spite and obstinacy during the anal phase, and hostile competitiveness with (and by projection, fear of) the rival parent during the oedipal phase. During the second and third year of life, much transformation of aggression occurs to equip the ego with neutralized energy. In the oedipal phase, the aggression vested in the parents is internalized with relatively less neutralization into the superego, which consequently retains an instinctual quality. The subsequent latency is characterized by further neutralization of aggression and a widening of ego functions in the conflict-free sphere (Hartmann 1939).

Hartmann's exposition of the genetic, dynamic, economic, and structural aspects of aggression became a touchstone for all the later theoretical contributions to this topic. Waelder (1956), while accepting the proposition of an essential or primary destructiveness, drew attention to the adaptive aspects of aggression and to the relation between ego mastery and aggression. Jacobson (1964) too showed Hartmann's influence in her view of a primary undifferentiated phase, gradual drive differentiation, role of aggression in demarcating real from wishful self presentations, and the importance of an assimilation of aggression to the deepening of object relations and to the structuralization of superego.

In 1971, a panel discussion focused on the role of aggression in adaptation. Hamburg (1973), representing an evolutionary approach, highlighted the "anlage of aggressive tendencies, transmitted genetically yet requiring environmental stimulation for full development" (p. 194). Marcovitz (1973) described the spectrum of aggression from curiosity, exploration, and self-assertion to dominance, exploitation, hostility, and hate. While he acknowledged its destructive aspects, he emphasized that without aggression there would be "no survival, no active drive towards learning, nor to the mastery of our own inner drives, and of the challenges of the world around us" (p. 231). However, he viewed aggression and libidinal gratification to be inseparable in processes of adaptation. Joseph (1973), reinvoking Hendrick's (1942) "instinct of mastery," suggested that preoccupation with clinical problems precluded attention to the nonhostile aspects of aggression. He advocated a broadening of the definition of aggression to include all forceful behavior that involves approaching an object, and saw the rooting reflex of the nursing infant as the prototype of aggression in the service of adaptation. Arlow (1973) noted that the innate aggressive propensity is modified by experience, especially by the earliest interactions of the individual with his environment. The macrocosm of society is established within the microcosm of the individual, and social structure, cultural history, and group values all play a significant role in the modulation of aggression, and, in turn, adaptation. Psychoanalysis, however, permits the reconstruction of the omitted, that is, unconscious, motivations indispensable to the process of adaptation.

Papers presented at the 27th International Psycho-Analytical Congress in Vienna echoed the Klein–Hartmann divergence (see, for instance, the contradictory positions of Gillespie 1971, and Rosenfeld 1971a). However, Hartmann's powerful influence was amply evident (Heimann and Valenstein 1972). Anna Freud (1972), for instance, concurred with him in rejecting death instinct and in regard to the ambiguity of source and changing aims of aggression. In contrast to Hartmann, however, she felt that libidinal aims were more specific to the drive, while aggressive aims associated themselves with varying purposes. The two drives also differed in regard to object. Libidinal development proceeded from a need-satisfying object to object constancy but aggression did not take this step toward sustained commitment. A good lover is faithful, a good hater promiscuous; even the "fixed hate" (p. 165) of the paranoic is a vicissitude of the libido rather than of aggression.[15] At the same meeting, Sandler (quoted by Lussier 1972) attempted to clarify the dichotomy between the innate versus reactive origins of aggression. He proposed a "capacity to be aggressive" that exists alongside an instinctual drive and is mobilized by the ego to avoid unpleasure. Brenner (1971) emphasized that aggression and libido bear similar relationship to the pleasure principle: their discharge causes pleasure, the lack of discharge unpleasure. He noted that aggression had variable aims and that aggression and libido play comparable roles in psychic conflict. It remained unclear whether aggression and sexuality differentiate gradually from a common matrix or are separate from birth on. Eleven years later, Brenner reiterated this stance and emphasized that once separated, both "libido and aggression are within the pleasure principle, not beyond it" (1982, p. 39). At this time, he sought to resolve the dilemma about the source of aggression by declaring that the drives have "no special, extracerebral source. Like all other psychic phenomena, they are an aspect of cerebral functioning" (p. 39).

After reviewing the post-Hartmann contributions from within the ego psychology tradition, we can go back full circle and now add that while Melanie Klein and Heinz Hartmann did represent the two major theoretical trends following Freud, there was a third viewpoint as well.

BRITISH OBJECT RELATIONS THEORY AND SELF PSYCHOLOGY

Four theoretical shifts from classical psychoanalytic theory . . . were variously made by object relations theorists: the movement from a one-body to a multi-

---

[15]Blum's (1981) concept of the "inconstant object" is a contemporary elaboration of this "fixed hate" theme. It refers to an ambivalently loved object that is felt as both persecutory and needed. It cannot be allowed to have a separate existence. The threat of betrayal by it must be tenaciously maintained. In a sense, such constant fear of persecution is the reciprocal of libidinal object constancy and a desperate effort to preserve an illusory constant object.

> body psychology; the relegation of instinctual moti-
> vation from the center towards the periphery; the
> recognition of significant linkages other than the in-
> stinctual between the self and the object; and, the
> emphasis on the importance of self-development.
> [Bacal and Newman 1990, p. 11]

> Self-psychology has freed itself from the distorted
> view of psychological man espoused by traditional
> analysis [which] . . . had to carry the burden imposed
> on it by its need to make a bow to biology—via the
> quasi-biological conception of primary drives which
> are seen as being processed by a mental apparatus.
> [Kohut 1982, p. 402]

While the Anna Freud–Melanie Klein controversy occupied the center stage in British psychoanalysis, another scenario, involving the development of the object relations theory, silently unfolded in the wings. Evolved by Suttie, Balint, Fairbairn, Winnicott, and Guntrip, this perspective either downplayed (Balint, Winnicott) or totally rejected (Suttie, Fairbairn, Guntrip) the instinctual under-pinnings of aggression.[16] In this group of theorists, none is "more remarkable nor more unsung than Ian Suttie" (Bacal and Newman 1990, p. 5). As early as 1924, he rejected instincts and declared human behavior to be basically motivated by a need for safety and companionship. Some years later (Suttie 1935), he proposed that after an early phase of "infantile solipsism" (p. 29), the child under-goes a process of "psychic parturition" (p. 27) before being capable of independent existence. During this process, the need for mother's love is intense, hence the vulnerability of separation anxi-ety. Anger or hate is

> a development or intensification of separation-anxiety which in turn
> is roused by a threat against love. It is the maximal ultimate appeal
> in the child's power. . . . Its purpose is not death-seeking or death

---

[16]Rejecting the concept of innate destructiveness results in an idealized view of human nature reminiscent of its portrayal by Rousseau and Goethe. Such "romantic vision" has enormous implications for psychoanalytic theory and tech-nique (Strenger 1989).

dealing, but the preservation of the self from the isolation which is death, and the restoration of a love relationship. [Suttie 1935, p. 31]

Balint (1935) arrived at a similar conclusion regarding aggression. He, too, minimized the instinctual underpinnings of hate and aggression and located their origin in the absence of a gratifying relationship. However, it was Fairbairn (1943, 1944) who, in this entire group, presented the most clearly spelled out theory of psychic development and endopsychic structures. In sharp disagreement with Klein, who had paid only lip service to the environment, Fairbairn emphasized the actual role of early caregivers in the child's personality formation. He proposed that an ego is present from birth on, and that libido is not pleasure seeking but object seeking. It could attach itself to good as well as bad objects, and the latter investment explained aggression.

What Freud describes under the category of "death instincts" would thus appear to represent for the most part masochistic relationships with internalized bad objects. A sadistic relationship with a bad object which is internalized would also represent the appearance of a death instinct. As a matter of fact, such relationships are usually of a sadomasochistic nature with a bias on the masochistic side of the scale; but in any case they are essentially libidinal manifestations. [Fairbairn 1943, p. 79]

Winnicott too rejected the death instinct while retaining the notion of innate aggression in the infant.[17] He seemed, however, to feel that such "aggressiveness is almost synonymous with activity" (1950, p. 204). Or, even more emphatically,

"Aggression is seen more as evidence of life. Under favorable conditions, fusion occurs between the erotic and the motility impulses, and then the term oral sadism becomes applicable, followed by all the developments of this theme. This is matched by the mother's

---

[17]Winnicott was the only one among these five theorists to have had extensive clinical experience with infants and children. This may partly explain his inability to reject innate aggression and its usefulness for development.

wish to be imaginatively eaten. Failure of fusion, or loss of fusion that
has been achieved, produces a potential element of pure destructiveness (i.e., without guilt-sense) in the individual. [1959, p. 127]

Winnicott saw even such destructiveness as developmentally
necessary since its expression enables the child to discover that
his mother can survive it. This facilitates his awareness (and later,
acceptance) of their separateness, making deeper relations between them possible. Consequently, Winnicott (1956) held that
aggressive and outrageous behavior frequently implied the hope
of someone's rectifying the deficiencies of care felt in childhood.
Guntrip (1969) even more strongly viewed conflicts over aggression (and sex) as upward defenses against a ruptured and tormented self. He asserted that the "frustration-aggression theory is
the only one supported by clinical observation" (1971, p. 131). The
notion that a powerful cauldron of instincts governs human behavior is itself a defensive postulate that protects us from viewing
ourselves as fundamentally weak and vulnerable. Guntrip attributed self-destructiveness to a deep hatred of one's own vulnerability, which, in turn, had resulted from anaclitic betrayals by
others during infancy.

This bare-bones summary of the rich ideas of these innovative
analysts does not do justice to them. Yet, the inclusion of this
significant post-Freudian trend helps underscore the conceptual
ancestry of the contemporary self-psychology view of aggression.
The resemblance between Fairbairn's and Kohut's (1972, 1977)
ideas, for instance, is striking (Akhtar 1989b, Bacal and Newman
1990, Robbins 1980). Both regard a pristine, whole self to exist from
the beginning and both view its growth to depend more on satisfactory object relations than on libidinal gratification. Both view
regression as a separate pathway, not a reversal of developmental
steps previously taken. Both discard the pleasure principle and
instinctual drives, especially inborn aggression. While Kohut does
recognize an "elemental aggression" (1977, p. 120) that helps in
the establishment and maintenance of the self, he does not view it
as a drive-related phenomenon. Moreover, he believes that such
"non-destructive aggressiveness . . . has a developmental line of its

own—it does not develop out of primitive destructiveness" (p. 121). Destructive aggression, on the other hand, is a reaction to chronic and traumatic frustration of the phase-appropriate need for omnipotent control over the self-objects of infancy and childhood.

While the resemblance between Fairbairn's and Kohut's views is clear, Fairbairn's influence on Kernberg's (1976, 1982a, 1991b) theory of aggression is less recognized. Indeed, he seems to have influenced both Kohut and Kernberg, albeit in different ways (Akhtar 1989b). Kohut seems to have elaborated on Fairbairn's "external" or environmental emphasis, and Kernberg on Fairbairn's "internal" or structural focus. Such influence of the British object relation theorists, however, extends beyond Kohut and Kernberg. Certain aspects of Parens's (1979, 1989a,b) formulation of aggression, for instance, echo Winnicott's near equation of activity and aggression. This brings up the important contributions of Parens and Kernberg for consideration.

CONTEMPORARY REFORMULATIONS

The psychoanalytical study of child development would fill an urgent need, might usefully function as center of integration of various approaches and promises the only way to answer the questions with which we all are occupied, questions in which the problem of prevention is omnipresent. [Kris 1950, p. 37]

With birth . . . pleasurable and unpleasurable sensations begin to be perceived and become attached to, though still confused with, beginning outside perceptions. Energic differentiation occurs; libidinal and aggressive cathectic gathering poles are formed around nuclei of as yet unorganized and disconnected memory traces. [Jacobson 1964, p. 52]

Responding to the appeals by Hartmann (1950, 1958) and Kris (1950), and following their own intuition, a number of child analysts began observing infants and young children in order to complement the reconstructive data of clinical psychoanalysis. Among the outstanding concepts derived from their work are structuring of the libidinal object (Spitz 1946b, 1950, 1965), developmental lines (A. Freud 1963), and separation-individuation theory (Mahler 1965, Mahler and Furer 1968, Mahler and McDevitt 1968, Mahler et al. 1975). In the specific context of aggression, too, many of these investigators (Downey 1984, McDevitt 1983, Parens 1973, 1979, 1980, 1984, 1989a,b, 1991, Solnit 1966, 1972) have made enormously significant contributions. The work of Parens especially offers a systematic reformulation of the concept of aggression.

In his long-term, weekly observation of infants and young children, Parens noted that there is, practically from birth onwards, "an inner-drivenness, a pressured internal thrust, to assert the infantile self upon the environment via sensori-motor functioning" (1989a, p. 112). Such activity puts into question the classical assumption of aggression being inherently destructive, since it was in no way destructive. Instead, it served the purpose of "apprehending, assimilating and bringing the environment under control" (1979, p. 66). Parens wondered how to explain this activity. If it were an aspect of the primary ego autonomy, then what was its energy source? This could not be "deinstinctualized" ego energy since that results from drive neutralization, and an ego with capacity to neutralize drives does not emerge until about 6 months of age (Hartmann 1952b, McDevitt 1983, Parens 1979, 1989a, Schur 1966, Spitz 1965, Weil 1976). Yet, the activity was evident before that age. A second explanation was that the early ego possessed "noninstinctual energy" (Hartmann 1939) of its own. But how is the noninstinctual energy different from the "deinstinctualized" one? Do they mix, or change into each other? Are they used for similar or different purposes? More significantly, how could such activity derive from noninstinctual energy when it had unmistakable instinctual qualities, for example, inner drivenness and pressure?

Noting such discordance between observable data and the classical theory of aggression, Parens undertook further longitudinal study of children's manifestations of aggression. He detected four categories of aggressive behaviors (1) unpleasure-related destructive behaviors (e.g., rage reaction of infancy); (2) nonaffective destructive behaviors (akin to "prey aggression" in animals and represented by feeding activity);[18] (3) nondestructive aggressive behaviors (e.g., exploration, assertion, etc.); and (4) pleasure-related destructive behaviors (e.g., teasing—convincingly discernible only from the beginning of the second year of life). Based upon this data, Parens proposed three fundamental trends of aggressive drive: (1) nondestructive aggression, (2) nonaffective destructiveness, and (3) hostile destructiveness. Each held a powerful heuristic value of its own. The first trend cast doubt on the death instinct theory of aggression and the continued assertion (e.g., Brenner 1982) that, even without the death instinct, the primary aim of aggression is destruction. This trend showed that aggression "is not inherently only destructive" (Parens 1989a, p. 115). The second trend disengaged destructiveness from hostility by demonstrating destructiveness for alimentation and, therefore, self-preservation. The third trend had the most significant repercussions. While infantile rage reaction was its built-in prototype, hostile destructiveness emerged only gradually and in the context of greater ego maturity. Moreover, it required excessive unpleasure for its activation. Therefore, hostile destructiveness should be avoidable by reducing excessive unpleasure, a deduction of enormous preventive potential (Parens et al. 1987).

Parens notes that many others (Gunther 1980, Kohut 1977, McDevitt 1983, Rochlin 1982, Storr 1968) had also concluded that an innate motivational force of nondestructive aggression does exist, and that rage and hostility are not inborn but experientially provoked. He also emphasizes that aggression is influenced by experience and maturation. Following the landmarks derived from Mahler's separation-individuation theory, Parens traced the epigenetic unfolding of aggression. The development of aggression

---

[18]Drawing a parallel with animal "prey aggression" and "rival aggression," Lantos (1958), too, distinguished between nonaffective and affect-laden aggression in humans. While she viewed both as basically instinctual, she saw them as having different genetic origins and she recommended that the former be simply labeled "activity."

is, however, not as schematic as that of libido. Briefly, all trends of aggression are evident at birth. At about 8 months of age "a biologically determined upsurge" (Parens 1991, p. 12) of aggression occurs. The structuring of the libidinal object (Spitz 1965) around this time also affects the vicissitudes of aggression.

> During the last two months or so of the first year of life, this structuring of the libidinal object is crucial to the *beginnings* of internalization and of superego precursor formations. These are especially the product of the powerful thrust to autonomy that is fueled by nondestructive aggression. This thrust to autonomy and normal narcissism combine to create battle of wills with the libidinal object from near the end of the first year on which leads to ambivalence, intrapsychic conflict, and internalization of superego precursors and will later, at about 18 months, influence the character of the anal conflict. . . . During the second year of life, . . . the vicissitudes of both nondestructive aggression and hostile destructiveness are significantly influenced by the character and quality of the child's rapprochement crisis (Mahler et al. 1975). During the 2½- to 6-year period, differences in aggression in boys and girls now first become manifest, especially under the influence of phallic aggression. [Parens 1991, p. 12]

Parens further elucidates the vicissitudes of hostile destructiveness during the oedipal phase and their role in the structuralization of the superego.[19] Throughout his epigenetic model, Parens emphasizes the reciprocal influence of the three trends of aggressive drive—nondestructive aggression, nonaffective destructiveness, and hostile destructiveness—upon each other.

---

[19]With varying degrees of emphasis upon its instinctual dimension, many other investigators have addressed the vicissitudes of aggression either throughout the life span (Erikson 1950) or through the specific periods of infancy and early childhood (Downey 1984, A. Freud 1972, Freud 1924b, Jacobson 1964, Mahler et al. 1975) adolescence (Blos 1967), young adulthood (Escoll 1991), middle age (Kernberg, 1980), and senescence (Erikson 1982). For the period of early childhood, Downey's (1984) comments regarding the relationships between aggression and differentiation, aggression and transitional object formation, and aggression and visual modality are highly pertinent.

In contrast, Kernberg (1976)—who has made profound contributions to the clinical aspects of severe character pathology associated with pronounced aggression (1984), sadomasochism (1991a), and pathological hatred (1991b)—assigned the nondestructive and nonaffectively destructive aspects of aggression to the primary autonomous functions. His view of their energic source, though incompletely spelled out, appears to follow Hartmann's (1939, 1950) locating it in noninstinctual ego resources and in the energy resulting from drive neutralization. Kernberg (1982a, 1991c) regards only hostile destructiveness as relevant to the origin of aggression as a drive. Emphasizing the distinction between Freud's terms *Trieb* and *Instinkt*, and echoing Hartmann and colleagues (1949), Kernberg (1982a) reiterates that while instincts are discontinuous, rigid, innate predispositions, drives are relatively continuous motivational systems at the psychophysical interface. He therefore preferred the expression *drive* in connection with (libido and) aggression. At this point, Kernberg parts company with Freud and Hartmann, and proposes a considerably different formulation of drives (including of course the aggressive drive) resulting in a "modification of the dual instinct theory" (1982a, p. 915).

Kernberg collects the building blocks of his theory from the modern instinct theory in biology (Lorenz 1963, Tinbergen 1951, Wilson 1975), Jacobson's (1971) psychoanalytic theory of affects, Mahler's (1968, 1975, Mahler and Furer 1968, Mahler et al. 1975) research on separation-individuation, and the empirical findings of Arnold (1970), Izard (1978), Knapp (1979), and Emde (1987). He suggests that affects are the earliest motivational system and are intimately involved in the fixation by memory of an internalized object relationship. Affects, emanating from "wired-in" instinctive components, are simply pleasurable or unpleasurable in the beginning. They link primitive object relations in two corresponding parallel series of gratifying and frustrating or aversive experiences. With ego growth and increasing sophistication of internalization processes, these pleasurable and unpleasurable affects are organized as love and hate.

Love and hate thus become stable intrapsychic structures, in genetic continuity through various developmental stages, and, by that very continuity, consolidate into libido and aggression. Libido and aggression, in turn, become hierarchically supraordinate motivational systems. . . . Affects, in short, are the building blocks or constituents of drives. [Kernberg 1982a, p. 908]

In Kernberg's view, aggression "as a drive results from the integration of negative, or aversive affects" (1991c, p. 111). Like Hartmann, Kernberg holds a tighter view of instinctual aggression. Unlike Hartmann, he declares that drives are not external givens but evolve from affects. Like Klein, Kernberg emphasizes the role of instinctual aggression in the earliest internalizations. Unlike Klein, he discards death instinct. Like Fairbairn, Kernberg retains the importance of early object relations in the genesis of aggression. Unlike Fairbairn, he regards the underpinnings of aggression to be fundamentally instinctual in origin. Kernberg's theory, in essence, is a reconciliation of the Klein-Fairbairn schism under the influence of Hartmann's ego psychology. It therefore brings the three major psychoanalytic trends in the study of aggression together.

SYNTHESIS AND REFLECTIONS

Those who reject the death drive are not aware that, when they do so without introducing another set of explanations for the phenomenon of death, they are simply scotomatizing the most relevant part of psychology, and then going on as if their theories still had some chance of being correct. [Eissler 1971, p. 27]

A fire becomes, not less, but more truly a fire as it burns faster. It's the being consumed that pushes back the darkness, illumines whatever there is of good in our days and nights. If it weren't brief it wouldn't be precious. Let me say it flatly: We are lucky we die, and anyone who pushes away the awareness of death lives but half a life. [Wheelis 1971, p. 68]

This survey of psychoanalytic theories about the nature and origins of aggression highlights the difficult questions in this area: Is there an instinctual aggressive drive? Does it derive from the so-called death instinct? Or does it emanate from the integration of unpleasurable affects of early infantile life? Are libido and aggression of comparable metapsychological status? Does aggression serve adaptation? What is the relationship between self-preservation and aggression? Does the self-preservative capacity result from neutralized aggression? Or does a threat to self-preservation lead to the emergence of destructive aggression? Is aggression fundamentally destructive or are there nondestructive forms of aggression? Is aggression rendered constructive only by its fusion with libido? Or do the wholesome forms of aggression originate as such? Are cruelty, destructiveness, and sadomasochism inherent in human nature? Or are these consequences of frustrated libidinal aims, thwarted vigor, injured narcissism?

Attempts to answer these questions must, at the outset, tackle a more basic issue. This pertains to the very definition of *aggression*. The foregoing overview of the literature demonstrates that this fundamental question is far from settled. Clinical observations of aggressive behavioral equivalents are ubiquitous, and there seems to be a consensus that aggression manifests in myriad forms (direct, indirect; verbal, physical; active, passive; subtle, crude; full, aim-inhibited, etc.). However, there is dispute about what can be legitimately included under the rubric of aggression. It is here that the term seems to be employed in two different ways that might not be compatible. Some theorists restrict the definition of aggression to hostile destructiveness while others extend it to include assertion and activity. Indeed, the word *aggression* has increasingly been used as if it accommodated both possibilities. The practice, however, does not justify the conclusion that such an accommodation has truly been achieved or is even possible. In fact, a careful scrutiny reveals that the psychoanalytic discourse on aggression is riddled with tautological leaps, semantic overflow, and confusion between matters of fact and matters of definition. Circular reasoning also abounds. This is evident, for instance, in observing assertive, nondestructive behavior, calling it "aggressive" and then advancing it as proof that not all aggression is destructive in aim. The unfortunate use of the same language for empirical data and speculative theories adds to confusion in this area. My own discussion of aggression might, as a result, provide a greater clarification of the problems involved in the concept rather than a clarification of the concept itself.

Yet in a recapitulation aimed at raising further questions, I wish to note that five theoretical positions exist in this realm. One extreme holds steadfastly to the death instinct theory (Freud, Ferenczi, Klein, Federn, Menninger, Eissler, and Rosenfeld), positing aggression to be a fundamentally destructive outward deflection of such an instinctual substrate. The other extreme is represented by those theorists who have dissociated themselves from the instinctual basis of human motivation altogether (Suttie, Fairbairn, Guntrip, and Kohut). While their view does allow for innate[20] assertiveness, which under the influence of frustration might turn into destructiveness, it definitely rules out innate destructiveness.

Between these extremes, lie three other views that discard death instinct while firmly adhering to the instinct theory and viewing aggression as one of the two basic instinctual drives. The first of these three views regards the aim of aggression to be variable though mainly involving destruction. It sees the infant's assertion, motility, and activity as emanating from a noninstinctual energy source to which neutralization of aggression might also add (Anna Freud, Hartmann, Kris and Loewenstein, Waelder, and Brenner). The second position extends the scope of the instinctual aggression to include infantile activity, assertion, and attempts at mastery. It considers both nondestructive and destructive aggression to be fueled from the same energy source. Moreover, it emphasizes that hostile destructiveness is only elicited by unpleasure (Winnicott and Parens). The third position excludes nondestructive activity from aggression and presents a concept of drive that is considerably

---

[20]The distinction between "innate" and "instinctual" is significant here since these theorists do not totally negate the former. In a different, broader context, this distinction is also exemplified in the various fundamental human motivational systems outlined by Lichtenberg (1989).

different from the traditional view. It proposes that early pleasurable and unpleasurable affects (and their associated neonatal object relations) gradually consolidate into the libidinal and aggressive drives that subsequently become supraordinate motivational systems (Kernberg). The roots of all five positions can, in one way or another, be traced to Freud, a fact that attests to both the richness of Freud's ideas and the latitude of its interpreters. Such latitude of interpretation is, however, a minor problem compared to the definitional confusion that affects these theories. Moreover, the degree to which testable hypotheses can be derived from these viewpoints remains unclear. Finally, the fact that these theories have been derived from varying sources of data puts their comparability into question. Before closing, however, I would like to make some further remarks about two issues, one pertaining to death instinct and the other to the relationship between assertion and aggression.

First, the issue of the death instinct. Klein's (1933, 1935, 1952) fierce allegiance to this concept, Eissler's (1971) loyal protest in favor of its retention, and Wheelis's (1971) poignant reminder of its experiential rumblings notwithstanding, most analysts have laid the postulate of death instinct to rest. Yet, a close examination of psychoanalytic literature shows a recurring notion that there is, in humans, a vague drive-like internal pull toward the loss of the boundaries, if not the existence, of the psychic self. Such concepts include (1) the merger fantasies, often associated with feeding and with sleep (Lewin 1950); (2) the deep seated wish for loss of human identity by "metamorphosis" (Lichtenstein 1961); (3) the everlasting wish for "the lost, original union with the mother" (Jacobson 1964, p. 39); (4) in the context of neonatal life, "the drive to return to an earlier state where all was gratified automatically" (Stone 1971, p. 236); (5) man's eternal yearning to recapture the "coenesthetically remembered harmony of dual-unity stage" (Mahler 1971, p. 186); (6) the "search for oneness" (Kaplan 1977); (7) the neonates' "inborn and immediate wish to return to the intrauterine state" (Chasseguet-Smirgel, quoted in Akhtar 1991b, p. 751) and man's "nostalgia for primary narcissism" (Chasseguet-Smirgel 1984, p. 29); (8) the "someday" and "if only" fantasies

(Akhtar 1991a); and, (9) an attempted reconciliation of "every-thing" and "nothing" fantasies, which occurs "transiently in dream-less sleep and in the ecstasy of orgasm—but the promise of per-manence can be realized only after our individual lives are over" (Shengold 1991, p. 7).

To be sure, these concepts have diverse theoretical foundations, involve fantasy content not attributable to instinctual primitivity, and contain an unmistakable libidinal admixture with aggression. Yet collectively these notions do demand a contemporary recon-ceptualization of the death instinct concept. Such examination might confirm the ubiquitous existence in humans of a deep-seated wish for the loss of self-boundaries, perhaps an echo of an early desire for (and memory of) fusion with the mother. It might be that this preverbal pull subsequently accrues fantasies from vari-ous levels of psychosexual development. Death too may enter this scenario, though much after infancy and childhood, perhaps truly not even until middle age. From then onward, the deep-seated desire for fusion with mother might become intermingled with a longing for peace via death; a "death instinct" has thus been set into motion. On the other hand, individuals who are traumatized by early losses through death or themselves have faced early life-threatening crises might incorporate the notion of death into this substrate of fusion/oblivion seeking much earlier. They might give evidence of possessing a "death instinct" even before middle age. Such a formulation of death instinct is clearly different from the one originally described under this designation. In the context of this reconceptualization, both *death* and *instinct* might be words that seem misplaced. Clearly, greater thinking and more precise ter-minology are needed here.

Newer ways of thinking also seem needed in reference to the second issues mentioned above, namely healthy, nonconflictual activity and vigor and its relationship to aggression. Should it be called "nondestructive aggression" (Parens 1979) or is it better to simply designate it "activity" (Lantos 1958) and put it beyond the scope of studies of aggression? One reasonable way out of this theo-retical impasse has recently been suggested by Stechler (Stechler 1987, Stechler and Halton 1987) and Lichtenberg (1989). Stechler suggests that assertion derives from a universal exploratory tendency and aggression from a universal self-protective system. This system reacts strongly and with dysphoric affects to threats from outside. If the child's assertions meet a punitive response from parents, the child reacts with dysphoria, which results in a contamination between assertion and aggression. When this is extensive, to all appearances an aggressive instinctual process has been set in motion. Lichtenberg voices a similar sentiment. He too regards assertion and aggression as being derived from separate and distinct biopsychological origins. He concurs with Stechler that "the assertion system activates spontaneously in response to exploratory opportunities in the environment, whereas the aggression system is reactive to stimuli perceived as threatening or distress inducing" (p. 172). However, Lichtenberg prefers *aversion* rather than *aggression* as being the optimal designation for this latter system since the innate response pattern composing it is not only antagonism but withdrawal as well. The important thing to note, however, is that both Stechler and Lichtenberg are seeking to retain the innate, "hard-wired" nature of assertion *and* aggression while conceptualizing their potentially dialectical ebb-and-flow within the modern systems theory context.

While further thought is needed to resolve this and other related questions, for example, the role of aggression in adaptation, efforts are already being directed at rendering the theoretical insights on aggression useful for day-to-day clinical work with difficult, sadomasochistic, perverse, suicidal, and borderline patients (Kernberg 1975b, 1976, 1984, Kernberg et al. 1989, Rosenfeld 1965, Stone 1980, Volkan 1976, 1987a). More significantly, the psychoanalytic understanding of aggression is beginning to yield guidelines for the prevention of excessive hostility and destructiveness. In this realm, the parent education strategies devised by Parens and colleagues (1987) are most promising. A related development is the psychoanalytically informed processes of negotiating for peace with antagonistic nations (Volkan 1986, 1987b, 1988). While conceptual difficulties continue to exist and unresolved questions still beckon from afar, the psychoanalytic study of aggression has clearly come a long way.

Part II

FEELINGS

3

LOVE

Romantic love brings friendship and erotic desire together in a sustained, mutually gratifying, nonincestuous relationship between two adults (Freud 1912a, Kernberg 1974a). In discussing its nature and its maladies, I begin with a brief summary of Freud's views on love. Then I highlight the contemporary psychoanalytic contributions to this area. Following this, I delineate five types of psychopathology involving love. The first three of these are relatively well recognized and include: (1) the inability to fall in love, (2) the inability to remain in love, and (3) the tendency to fall in love with the "wrong" kinds of people. The other two are less recognized and center upon (4) the inability to fall out of love, and (5) the inability to feel loved. After commenting on each malady, I offer some caveats to the proposed classification and thus render it clinically more realistic.

FREUD'S VIEWS ON LOVE

The affectionate fixations of the child persist throughout childhood, and continually carry along with them eroticism, which is consequently diverted from its

> sexual aims. Then at the age of puberty they are
> joined by the powerful "sensual" current which no
> longer mistakes its aims. [Freud 1912a, p. 181]

> The careless way in which language uses the word
> "love" has its genetic justification. People give the
> name "love" to the relation between a man and a
> woman whose genital needs have led them to found
> a family; but they also give the name "love" to the
> positive feelings between parents and children,
> and between the brothers and sisters of a family,
> although *we* are obliged to describe this as "aim-
> inhibited love" or "affection." Love with an inhib-
> ited aim was in fact originally fully sensual love, and
> it is so still in man's unconscious." [Freud 1930,
> pp. 102–103]

    In laying an intricate groundwork for understanding the nature
of human sexuality, Freud (1905c) pointed out that the process of
the choice of love object in human beings is essentially diphasic.
The first move toward the object begins between the ages of 2 and
5 and is characterized by infantile sexual aims. This is brought to
a halt by latency. Puberty then sets in the second and more explicitly sexual movement toward the object. Meanwhile, the repression
of the infantile sexual aims renders the earlier longings as merely
an "affectionate current" thus causing a gap between it and the later
appearing "sensual current. Should these two currents fail to con-
verge, the result is often that one of the ideals of sexual life, the
focusing of all desires upon a single object, will be unattainable"
(p. 200).
    What was implicit in this statement was developed seven years
later by Freud (1912a) in a seminal statement that still forms a cornerstone of the psychoanalytic understanding of love. He noted
"two currents whose union is necessary to ensure a completely
normal attitude in love. . . . These two may be distinguished as the
affectionate and the *sensual* current" (p. 180, italics in the original).
The affectionate current was ontogenetically the earlier one. It
arose in connection with the early body and psychic care provided
by the primary objects, especially the mother. The second, more

specifically sexual, current arrived on the scene with puberty. It had to be synthesized with the affectionate current. Romantic love could then be expressed towards nonfamilial objects with whom a sexual union was permissible and possible. At times, however, the two currents could not be brought together and this resulted in a psychopathological state. The sphere of love in such people remained bifurcated into tenderness and sexual passion. "Where they love they do not desire and where they desire they cannot love" (Freud 1912a, p. 183).

Freud went on to make distinctions in the erotic life of men and women. In men, there was a ubiquitous tendency for "overvaluation of the sexual object" (p. 181). Women, in contrast, continued to correlate sexuality with its earlier, childhood prohibition. To heighten sexual pleasure, therefore, men needed to debase their love objects (e.g., choose a woman who was socioculturally inferior to them) and women needed to mentally evoke (or actually create) the condition of prohibition.

Bemoaning the diminution of erotic pleasure in marriage,[21] Freud (1912a) declared that "the psychical value of erotic needs is reduced as soon as their satisfaction becomes easy" (p. 187). However, he added that there perhaps was something inherent in the nature of sexual desire that rendered its complete satisfaction elusive. The diphasic onset of sexual desire in human development led to adult object choices being mere substitutes for the original ones. This, coupled with the inoptimal expressibility in adult sexuality of sadistic and coprophilic component instincts, made complete gratification difficult.

Two years after this contribution, Freud (1914) addressed the topic of love from a different perspective. He now distinguished between narcissistic (arising from the ego's self-affirming needs) and anaclitic (arising from the ego's desire for the object's help-giving qualities) forms of love. He emphasized that the

---

[21]While showing a greater optimism toward second marriages, Freud (1917b, 1931a) held on to the idea that marriage reduces the intensity of erotic pleasure. Ross (1996) has elucidated the dynamics of this development in men in greater detail.

highest phase of development of which object libido is capable is
seen in the state of being in love, when the subject seems to give up
his own personality in favour of an object cathexis. . . . A person who
loves has, so to speak, forfeited a part of his narcissism, and it can
only be replaced by his being loved. . . . Loving in itself, insofar as
it involves longing and deprivation, lowers self regard; whereas being
loved, having one's love returned, and possessing the love object
raises it once more. [pp. 76, 98, 99]

Noting the interdependence of the two lovers, Freud hinted at
the potential of mental pain inherent in romantic passion. He also
noted the transcendent longing in love since each lover comes closer
to his or her own ego ideal through unification with the beloved.

In a subsequent paper, Freud (1915e) noted that a synthesis of
libidinal and aggressive aims was necessary for true, deep love.
"Nature, by making use of this pair of opposites, continues to keep
love ever vigilant and fresh, so as to guard against the hate which
lurks behind it" (p. 299). He emphasized that transference love
differs from normal love only in degree and "being in love in ordinary life, outside analysis, is also more similar to abnormal than to
normal mental phenomena" (p. 168). This echoed his statement
of a year earlier that love has "the power to remove repression and
reinstate perversions" (1914, p. 100).

Still later, Freud (1921) elaborated upon the sexual overvaluation of the love object and traced such idealization to the love
object's

being treated in the same way as our own ego, so that when we are
in love a considerable amount of narcissistic libido overflows onto
the object. . . . We love it on account of the perfections which we
have striven to reach for our own ego, and which we should now
like to procure in this roundabout way as a means of satisfying our
narcissism. . . . *The object has been placed in the place of the ego ideal.*
[pp. 112, 113; italics in the original]

Then, in 1930 Freud again addressed the "unusual state" of being
in love, stating that at the peak of such experience "the boundary
between ego and object threatens to melt away" (p. 66). While ac-

knowledging the exaltation that accompanies love, Freud once again emphasized the potential of pain in it: "We are never so defenseless as when we love" (p. 82). He went on to note that many individuals protect themselves against the pain emanating from the loss of the love object by directing their love not to one person but to mankind in general and its cultural institutions. Such "aim-inhibited affection" (p. 102) constitutes the basis of friendship and familial ties as well.

In sum, Freud's view of love incorporates (1) its origin in the earliest mother–infant experience, (2) its narcissistic foundations, (3) the necessity for a fusion of affectionate and erotic aims, (4) the necessity for a synthesis of libidinal (affectionate and erotic) and aggressive aims, (5) a significant amount of renunciation of oedipal strivings, (6) the affirmation of ego ideal through the narcissistic strength drawn from the partner, and (7) an ego structure that can sustain a potential threat to its boundaries and the periodic emergence of the erotic scenarios dictated by various component instincts.

VIEWS OF CONTEMPORARY PSYCHOANALYSTS

> From the perspective of varieties of awareness, we may note that the act of love demands an extraordinary interplay, synthesis, and flexibility of both subjective and objective self-awareness. [Bach 1985, p. 55]

> Normal love, like transference love, has its infantile prototypes; it, too, is repetitive, idealizing, and replete with conflictual transferences; it, too, is a complex mix and not simply a new and pure experience. [Schafer 1993, p. 77]

Later psychoanalytic contributors to the understanding of love followed divergent paths that, ironically, were along the two "currents" Freud had outlined as being intrinsic to romantic love. Some authors (e.g., Balint 1948, Guntrip 1969, Winnicott 1963) focused their attention on tenderness, concern, and affection.

Balint (1948), for instance, noted that a special form of identification is needed for love, an identification through which the "interest, wishes, feelings, sensitivity, shortcomings of the partner attain—or are supposed to attain—about the same importance as our own" (p. 115). Other investigators explored the erotic dimension of love, focusing their attention on inhibited (e.g., Bychowski 1963, Moore 1964), homosexual (e.g., Ovesey 1969, Socarides 1978), and perverse (e.g., Gillespie 1952, 1956, Ostow 1974, Stoller 1975) forms of sexuality. Transcending this bifurcation, some later psychoanalysts indeed made significant contributions to the study of romantic love. Prominent among these are Altman (1977), Benedek (1977), Bergmann (1971, 1980, 1982), Kernberg (1974a,b, 1991a,d, 1993, 1995a), Chasseguet-Smirgel (1985), and Person (1988).

Bergmann (1971) suggested that the bliss associated with falling in love involved a refinding of a lost ego state, namely that experienced during early mother–child symbiosis. Later (1980), he outlined five functions of the ego that are associated with this experience. First and foremost, the ego has to realistically assess the qualities of the love object and evaluate the future of a relationship with it. Too much reliance on reality can, however, spoil love. Second, the ego must integrate aspects of many childhood love objects into the love object of adult life. This task might be difficult if the early love objects were either at conflict themselves or simply too numerous. Bisexual identifications also need to be integrated and a mixture of the two components, corresponding and complementary to that in oneself, found in the partner. Third, the ego has to counteract the superego so that the love object does not become incestuous in the mind even though some similarity with the primary objects will be inevitable, and even desirable. Fourth, the ego must counteract the inner pressure on "refinding the impossible, the replica of the longed-for symbiosis" (p. 69). Finally,

> when one is under the pressure of the repetition compulsion and the new object has the same pain-evoking qualities that character-ized the old, every effort will be made to transform the new ob-

ject to conform to the original object before disappointment took
place. It becomes the fifth task of the ego to find other solutions.
[p. 69]

Bergmann emphasized that enduring love depends, to a large
extent, upon "the transmutation of the idealization into gratitude
for the refinding and for the healing of the earlier wounds" (1980,
p. 74). He also declared that love's potential to give to the adult
what he had never received as a child imparts to love a great
restitutional quality. Ultimately it is the harmonious coexistence
of three elements that characterizes happy love relationships: (1)
refinding of the early love object on many levels of development,
(2) improvement on the old objects by receiving what one had not
received during childhood, and (3) mirroring affirmation of the
self.

The capacity to fall and remain in love also received attention
from Kernberg (1974a,b, 1995a). In his view, two developmental
achievements are necessary for this capacity:

a first stage, when the early capacity for sensuous stimulation of
erogenous zones (particularly oral and skin erotism) is integrated
with the later capacity for establishing a total object relation; and a
second stage, when full genital enjoyment incorporates earlier body-
surface erotism into the context of a total object relation, including a complementary sexual identification. [1974a, p. 185]

The first stage is related to the integration of contradictory self
and object representations, attainment of object constancy (Mahler
et al. 1975), and the capacity for in-depth relations with others. The
second stage corresponds to a successful resolution of the oedipal
conflicts. In a highly original statement, Kernberg (1995a) pointed
out a hitherto unrecognized aspect of being in love, stating that it

also represents a mourning process related to growing up and becoming independent, the experience of leaving behind the real
objects of childhood. In this process of separation, there is also re-
confirmation of the good relations with internalized objects of the
past as the individual becomes confident of the capacity to give and

receive love and sexual gratification simultaneously—with a growth-promoting mutual reinforcement of both—in contrast to the conflict between love and sex in childhood. [1995a, pp. 58, 59]

Kernberg also emphasized that it is important that higher forms of idealization persist within the loving couple. Such idealization

represents the idealized identification, not with the body or even the person of the love object but with the values for which this person stands. Intellectual, aesthetic, cultural, and ethical values are included here; and I think this represents, in part, integration of the superego on a higher level, one linked to the new capacity for integrating tender and sexual feelings and to the definite overcoming of the oedipal conflict. At the same time, in this establishment of identifications with the love object involving value systems, a movement from the interrelation of the couple to a relationship with their culture and background is achieved, and past, present, and future are thereby linked in a new way. [1974a, p. 210]

Elaborating upon love relations in middle age, Kernberg (1974b) highlighted the vicissitudes of the reactivation of oedipal conflicts, at this time, in relationship to one's children. He also noted that the continuity between falling in love, remaining in love, and establishing a stable relationship does not guarantee a couple's staying together forever. The increasing capacity for empathy with another person and the heightening awareness of one's own self that accompanies such a relationship paradoxically might lead to one's finding others who could serve as better partners. A deep commitment to one person and to the values and experiences of a sexual and intellectual life lived together prevents the couple's breakdown. Under such circumstances, renunciation of newer possibilities might even add depth to the couple's emotional and erotic life.

In a series of contributions spanning over two decades and culminating in a recent book, Kernberg (1995a) addressed the barriers to falling and remaining in love (1974a), the nature of mature love (1974b), aggression and love in the relationship of a couple (1991d), the nature of erotic desire (1991a), and the role of superego functions in the life of a couple (1993). Kernberg also discussed the impact of gender on the experience of mature sexual love. Citing Braunschweig and Fain's (1971) theories, he noted that, for both the boy and girl, the early bodily care by the mother kindles the potential for sexual excitement. However, the mother's implicitly "teasing" erotic relationship to her boy remains a constant in male sexuality, whereas her subtle rejection of sexual excitement regarding her daughter inhibits the girl's awareness of her vaginal sexuality. As a result, men have greater difficulty in dealing with ambivalence toward women and need to synthesize the affectionate and the sexual imagos of women, whereas women are slower to integrate sexuality in the context of love. The way men and women handle discontinuities regarding love relations also differs.

> Women usually discontinue sexual relations with a man they no longer love and establish a radical discontinuity between an old love relationship and a new one. Men are usually able to maintain a sexual relationship with a woman even if their emotional commitment has been invested elsewhere, that is, they have a greater capacity for tolerating discontinuity between emotional and erotic investments and for a continuity of erotic investment in a woman, in reality and in fantasy, over many years, even in the absence of a real ongoing relationship with her. [Kernberg 1995a, p. 84]

In keeping with the impressive breadth and depth of his contributions to the psychoanalytic study of love, it should not be surprising that it is Kernberg who has recently offered the most comprehensive contemporary definition of love. However, before quoting that definition, I will mention the contributions of Altman (1977), Benedek (1977), Chasseguet-Smirgel (1985), and Person (1988).

Altman (1977) highlighted the role of assimilated aggression and a benevolent superego in the experience of love. More important, he traced a "developmental line" (A. Freud 1963) of love. At the dawn of psychic life, a discernible self hardly exists and love is synonymous with primary narcissism. Gradually, through separation-individuation, libidinal investment of others, especially the mother, becomes possible. She becomes the primary love object. The phallic stage of development leaves a powerful imprint on love and when this imprint survives unalloyed in later life,

> much of what masquerades under the guise of love is simply a compulsive effort to prove that one is the possessor of the penis, that one was never deprived of it, that one will some day obtain it, or that there is no danger attached to its employment. Satyriasis fulfills the need for reassurance of potency; nymphomania is the expression of a collector's avidity for the penis, albeit attached to a man. [p. 41]

The Oedipus complex, of course, introduces further specificity in the choice of love object, laying the groundwork for subsequent options in this regard. In latency and adolescence, altruistic and self-seeking components in love battle with each other. The characteristic drive upsurge in adolescence mobilizes both regressive conflicts of ambivalence and progressive trends toward inner disjunction from primary objects. Young adulthood permits the actualization of a sustained romantic tie to a nonincestuous object. Then marriage assigns new interpersonal tasks to love, the successful negotiation of which leads to a deepening commitment and gratitude in the couple. Middle and old age bring their own turbulence while offering new avenues for the expression of love.

> One recompense for the inevitable feeling of chagrin . . . that comes with advancing age resides in the relation grandparents have with their children. This love, like its predecessors, contains a narcissistic core. A grandchild embodies the grandparents' self-ideals and is loved as the grandparents would love themselves. [p. 40]

Altman also noted that women have a greater sense of commitment in love relations than do men. He traced this relative contentment to an earlier event in the girl's development, namely the shifting of her love from mother to father.

> This renunciation prepares her for renunciation in the future in a way the boy is unable to match. The steadfastness of commitment

is, in this view, the renunciation of alternative possibilities, and the future woman has already made it in childhood. The boy has not, can not, and will not. [p. 48]

Benedek (1977) emphasized that the fundamental dynamic processes of love replicate those involved in a mother–child dyad. Through the repetition of mutually gratifying acts, each lover is internalized by his or her partner. Each becomes a part of the self system of the other. The demarcation between narcissistic and anaclitic love also diminishes within a couple over time. Marriage is sustained by continuation of sexual love and presence of mutual respect. Its permanence depends on the ego organization of the two partners and on their libidinal investment in the institution of marriage itself. Parenthood establishes a "biological link" (p. 75) between husband and wife and consolidates the psychological bond between them.

Chasseguet-Smirgel (1985) elucidated the picture of the ego ideal as it emerges within the context of mature love. She noted that four elements characterize this situation: (1) the nostalgic search for oneness with the primary object is not given up, but the ways of achieving it become different; (2) the sexual satisfaction within the couple and their autonomous (and mutually supported) sublimations enhance secondary narcissism of the ego and diminish the ego-ego ideal gap; (3) those aspects of internal and external reality that facilitate these sexual and narcissistic gratifications get positively cathected and the ego ideal is, to some extent, projected on the very means of access to such realities; and (4) the pain over remnant longings for oneness with primary objects and incestuous gratifications is compensated for by the attachment to the love object and its sustained availability.

In a book replete with illustrations from history, literature, and movies, Person (1988) elaborated upon various aspects of falling and remaining in love. She noted that there are physical counterparts of the elation and the fear that accompany falling in love. She described falling in love as a complex affective state that included "agitation, a mixture of hope, anxiety, and excitement" (p. 38). Echoing Freud (1914, 1930), Person noted the potentiality of pain and torment in love. However, love also eradicates all uncertainties, dissolves sexual inhibitions, leads to a recovery of lost parts of the self, and gives purpose to living. She emphasized that brevity is an essential feature of passionate love. However, the capacity of the two partners for mature object relations helps them convert the flame of intense emotions into the steady glow of affectionate companionship.[22]

The relationship of the lovers to each other and, as a couple, to the larger group have also received Kernberg's (1991a,d, 1995a) attention. However, rather than summarizing his views in this regard, I will conclude this section by quoting his latest definition of mature love since it meaningfully synthesizes practically all the literature I have reviewed here. According to Kernberg (1995a), love is

> a complex emotional disposition that integrates (1) sexual excite-ment transformed into erotic desire for another person; (2) ten-derness that derives from the integration of libidinally and aggres-sively invested self and object representations, with a predominance of love over aggression and tolerance of the normal ambivalence that characterizes all human relations; (3) an identification with the other that includes both a reciprocal genital identification and deep empathy with the other's gender identity; (4) a mature form of idealization along with deep commitment to the other and to the relationship; and (5) the passionate character of the love relation in all three aspects: the sexual relationship, the object relationship, and the superego investment of the couple. [p. 32]

It is against the backdrop of such mature romantic love that the following five psychopathological syndromes of love life should be considered.

---

[22]However, romantic love can only "survive and thrive if the partners are *cognizant* of difficulties as they arise, *communicate* their feelings to each other, and resolve their differences. There must be a real *commitment* to the relationship, which in turn, will encourage the *compromises* that are needed" (Madow 1982, p. 135, italics in the original).

INABILITY TO FALL IN LOVE

> Children who are received in a harsh and unloving
> way die easily and willingly. Either they use one of
> the many proffered organic possibilities for quick
> exit, or if they escape this fate, they retain a streak
> of pessimism and aversion to life. [Ferenczi 1929,
> p. 105]

> Patients who are promiscuous and have intense feel-
> ings of frustration and impatience when desired
> sexual objects do not become immediately available
> to them may obscure the fact that they have never
> been in love. [Kernberg 1974a, p. 186]

Inability to fall in love is perhaps the most severe form of psychopathology involving love life (Kernberg 1974b). Individuals
suffering from this malady have pronounced deficits in their capacities for concern, empathy, and basic trust. They cannot develop
closeness with others. They lack spontaneity and manage their
interpersonal lives on a factual basis. They also lack the capacity
for "sexual overvaluation" (Freud 1921) and idealization (Bergman
1980, Kernberg 1974a), which is a mandatory initial ingredient
of falling in love. They are too "realistic" in their estimation of
others and cannot allow themselves the perceptual compromise
needed for idealization of another individual.[23] An inward obliteration of gender markers, at times covered over by a patina of conventional gestures, also characterizes such individuals (Akhtar
1992b). Often they are celibate and given to masturbation with
repetitive and banal fantasies. Even when they have somehow
managed to enter into a marriage, they lack erotic desire and only
go through the motions in their sexual life. Kernberg (1974b) also
notes that, in certain narcissistic men, the inability to fall in love is
"hidden beneath an externally stable relationship with a woman"
(p. 196).

---

[23]Some capacity for idealization might be retained but is channeled away from
human relationships into philosophical systems, politico-religious ideologies, or
work-related realms.

Diagnostically, such psychopathology is associated with schizoid, paranoid, and severe sadomasochistic characters, as well as with the malignantly narcissistic (Kernberg 1984) and disaffiliated antisocial personalities. Dynamically, the inability of such individuals to fall in love emanates from a "lack of activation of early eroticism" (Kernberg, quoted in Akhtar 1991b, p. 751) coupled with impaired basic trust and poor capacity for a sustained idealization of others. Attachment to others stirs up affects that are too intense for their deficit-riddled ego to manage. Loving is given up in order to avoid the dual terror of abandonment and engulfment (Burnham et al. 1969, Guntrip 1969, Lewin and Schulz 1992). Yet another difficulty arises from the unconscious envy that gets stirred up toward the potential love object because, if loved, it appears to be receiving the libidinal supplies that the subject desires himself. Not being able to fall in love under such circumstances acts as a defense against envy. The inability to fall in love, therefore, has both deficit- and conflict-related origins.

The developmental background of such individuals almost invariably reveals a history of severe, unmitigated childhood trauma. Physical and sexual abuse, parental desertion through divorce or death, and pronounced neglect of anaclitic and mirroring "ego needs" (Casement 1991) from the earliest years of life often form the background of this psychopathology.

Such individuals usually do not seek psychotherapeutic help at all. Instead, their ill-developed and frozen erotic life forces those around them into self-doubt, rage, depression, and, at times, a desperate search for libidinal supplies. These significant others might appear at the professional's door, carrying a message of their partner's mute agony. Or, the erotically dry individuals themselves might seek help though not so much for their deficient sensuality but for vague persecutory anxieties and psychosomatic ills. In the treatment setting, a long, drawn-out withdrawal that, in its most forgiving interpretation, can be seen as a "cocoon transference" (Modell 1976), tends to ensue. The patient avoids all curiosity regarding the analyst, seems totally unaffected by the latter's comings and goings, and appears insistent on doing analysis in an externalized, rational manner. In other words, the patient's characterological inability to fall in love becomes a major resistance against "transference love" (Freud 1915a) in the course of treatment. Such development is usually indicative of an "ominous prognosis" (Kernberg 1974a, p. 191) for psychoanalytic treatment.

INABILITY TO REMAIN IN LOVE

> Just as the setting (people they were involved with in work) or the person (with whom they were excitedly involved) began to be actively emotional and hopeful about them, the patients would experience a sort of panicky anxiety and dread. In conscious behavior and self-perception they registered it as a sudden feeling of their unsuitability and unworthiness. ... The disillusionment was not with the setting or the object but in a mysterious way with themselves.
> [Khan 1966, p. 75]

> The capacity for sexual intercourse and orgasm does not by any means guarantee the capacity for being maturely in love—nor does the capacity for a total object relation without the resolution of oedipal conflicts and the related freeing from sexual inhibition.
> [Kernberg 1974a, p. 212]

The next step in the hierarchy of love-related psychopathology is the characterological incapacity to remain in love. Individuals with this pathology seem quite capable of falling in love and might do so over and over again! They retain the capacity for bonding, erotic desire, and idealization of a love object. However, after an initial period of infatuation, their love begins to pale. They start to be vaguely uncomfortable in the relationship, questioning whether they really belong there. Defensive attempts to ward off this disturbing sentiment work only for a while. The dissatisfaction surfaces again, though its sources remain unclear. To convert this inner distress into a tangible interpersonal strife, blemishes and deficiencies are found in the love object. A paranoid situation now results, which, in a gesture of pseudo-magnanimity, is explained

away as a "poor match" between the two partners. The relationship comes to an end and, after a brief period of emotional relief,
the cycle repeats itself.

The dynamic factors underlying this phenomenology are complex and multileveled. Conflicts and deficits from various levels
usually coexist, fueling and/or defending against each other in
fluid dynamic patterns. Four nodal points in the hierarchy of conflicts contributing to this psychopathology are (1) a failed search
for a "transformational object" (Bollas 1979), (2) anxieties regarding fusion with the object (Mahler and Kaplan 1977, Mahler et al.
1975), (3) mobilization of aggression when a primitively idealized
object fails to live up to its promise (Kernberg 1974b), and (4) the
object's gradual acquisition of incestuous qualities and hence the
mobilization of oedipal guilt in the subject (Freud 1912a). These
dynamic patterns are not sharply demarcated from each other
and have many overlaps. Yet it is useful to consider them sepa-
rately so that the analyst's empathy is guided by a thorough knowledge of the psychological terrain as these difficulties enter the
transference–countertransference axis.

The first dynamic pertains to the search for a "transformational
object" (Bollas 1979) and a sense of failure in that search. A transformational object is the first object (usually the mother) and
is "experientially identified by the infant with the process of the
alteration of self experience" (p. 97). The mother is not yet recognized as having a separate existence but is felt as a process of transformation, and a trace of this feature persists in such object seeking in adult life. Bollas emphasizes that

> in adult life, the quest is not to possess the object; it is sought in
> order to surrender to it as a process that alters the self, where the
> subject-as-supplicant now feels himself to be the recipient of enviro-
> somatic caring, identified with metamorphoses of the self. . . . It
> is not an object relation that emerges from desire, but from a
> kind of proto-perceptual identification of the object with its
> active feature—the object as enviro-somatic transformer of the
> subject—and manifests itself in the person's search for an object
> (a person, place, event, ideology) that promises to transform the
> self. [pp. 97–98]

Bollas goes on to emphasize that such anticipation of being transformed fills "the subject with a reverential attitude toward the object, so that, even as the transformation of the self will not take place
on the scale it did during early life, the adult subject tends to nomi-
nate the object as sacred" (p. 99).

In the beginning of a love affair unconsciously seeking a transformational object, the object of one's adoration appears to
offer life-redeeming qualities. However, often that potential, even
to the extent it did actually exist in the object, wears off. To
begin with, the injured core of the self is not only seeking transformation but also revenge and is thus ambivalent and guilt-
ridden (Akhtar 1992b).[24] Besides drawing structural benefit from
the object, it also seeks to perpetuate the self-deprivation in an act
of sadomasochistic triumph over the object. Moreover, in engag-
ing the object successfully, these individuals begin to be uneasy
about having misrepresented their strengths, thus potentially
having oversold themselves. Dread at being discovered begins to
raise its head. Significantly, it is at the climax of the relationship
that such individuals

> become fearful, doubt themselves, become depressive, and start to
> withdraw. Their conscious affect was one of anxious concern for the
> situation or the person in terms of either their personal unsuitabil-
> ity or unworthiness. They tried sincerely to disillusion others about
> themselves and sought by every means to be got rid of, rejected, and
> abandoned. One felt the plan had changed inside them. The move-
> ment was now in the other direction. . . . To leave the situations and
> objects caused them genuine pain, remorse, and guilt. They felt,
> however, they had no option and so they became phobic and rejec-
> tive towards the object. [Khan 1966, pp. 73, 74]

While aggression toward the object is here a result of self-
defense, at other times such aggression is the primary source of
inability to remain in love.

---

[24]In a far-reaching critique of self psychology, Curtis (1983) has emphasized
this very point: unmet needs during development do not result in psychic gaps
or holes but in powerful affects, fantasies, and compensatory mental structures.

The second dynamic pertains to anxieties regarding fusion. Here intimacy threatens the boundaries of the self (Mahler and Kaplan 1977, Mahler et al. 1975), and being in love is experienced as a stressful situation (Gaoni 1985). A dread of surrender to "resourceless dependence" (Khan 1972) also lies at the core of this difficulty. The individual fears enslavement, even loss of identity, in intimacy and therefore withdraws from the relationship. However, aloneness also seems intolerable, so that the object is resought in a fluctuating pattern of closeness and distance (Akhtar 1992a, Escoll 1992). At other times, one object is dropped in favor of another, but the same conflict emerges sooner or later in that relationship as well. The descriptions of "ambitendency" (Mahler 1968), the "need–fear dilemma" (Burnham et al. 1969), and the "in and out programme" (Guntrip 1969) all speak to this very dynamic constellation, though from somewhat different theoretical perspectives.

The third dynamic contributing to the inability to remain in love has been described in detail by Kernberg (1984, 1995a). It involves an orally incorporative and narcissistic cycle of idealization, acquisition, and devaluation. Here the individual does not have a true object relationship with the person he claims to love. Instead, he seems to be relating to an externalized version of his own grandiose self and/or a primitively idealized part object. Such an individual usually presents with a narcissistic character structure and may show a driven sort of sexual promiscuity. He might reveal during analytic exploration

> a desperate search for human love, as if it were magically bound with body surfaces—breasts or penises or buttocks or vaginas. The endless, repetitive longing for such body surfaces may emerge, upon analysis, as a regressive fixation to split-off erogenous zones caused by the incapacity to establish a total object relation or object constancy (Arlow et al. 1968), a regression caused by the incapacity to tolerate ambivalence, the integration of love and hatred for the same object (in the last resort, mother). [Kernberg 1974b, p. 188]

As the actual qualities of the hitherto dimly perceived object begin to force themselves upon awareness, disappointment sets in.

Aggression is mobilized and love evaporates. Unable to tolerate ambivalence, the individual now finds the previously idealized object as "all bad." What was desperately sought is now vehemently rejected. The love affair breaks with much torment, at times, to both parties involved.

There is yet another source from which inability to remain in love can arise. This involves oedipal issues. After all, the particular love object has often been sought owing to its "oedipally optimal" distance (Akhtar 1992a, p. 35) from the primary love objects. However, as the romantic relationship deepens, the love object might come to acquire a greater oedipal significance. In other words, each partner now more prominently comes to psychically represent the desired but prohibited parent for the other. Erotic union within them becomes tantamount to incest![25] Castration anxiety gets mobilized and defensive operations centering upon repression result in the conscious self experience becoming devoid of erotic excitement. Love, which seems to have vanished from within the hitherto stable dyad (though most likely it has only gone underground), is now sought elsewhere.

FALLING IN LOVE WITH THE "WRONG" KINDS OF PEOPLE

> Closely akin . . . is the manifestation which I should like to call "neurotic exogamy." This occurs where a man experiences an insuperable aversion to any close relationship with a woman of his own people or nation. Or, to put it more correctly, of his mother's people. This is an indication of special measures taken to avoid the possibility of incest. [Abraham 1913a, pp. 48–49]

---

[25]Colarusso (1990) has recently highlighted how sexual relations in a married couple become oedipally recharged after childbirth. Ross (1996) also underscores the spoiling effect of the shadow of early parental imagos upon marital sexuality. However, long before such contemporary contributions, Horney (1928) had declared parental transferences in marriage to be the "fundamental problem of monogamy" (p. 323).

> The large wide-open eyes contain a hint of reproach.
> The gaze sinks deeply into me. She plays a fallen
> woman, the victim of a need for love that leads her
> repeatedly to villainous men who will use her and
> forsake her. She is stuck with her vulnerability, her
> hidden masochism, and I am stuck with my secret
> sadism. Across that gulf our glances meet, we recog-
> nize each other. We are a pair. [a character in *The
> Way Things Are*, Wheelis 1994, p. 86]

Closely related to the dynamic of the inability to remain in love
is the tendency to fall in love with the "wrong" kinds of people,
that is, prohibited and unavailable others, for example, those
much older or younger than oneself, blood relatives, and individuals who are already married or are otherwise "unsuitable in
reality" (Freud 1912a, p. 181). All of these stand, in the unconscious, for the oedipal objects. From this equation, these objects
draw their intense romantic appeal. Freud's (1910a) paper, "A
Special Type of Object Choice Made by Men" eloquently describes the male version of this syndrome. According to him, the
malady consists of two "necessary conditions for loving" (p. 166).
The first of these conditions is existence of an injured third party.
This requirement

> stipulates that the person in question shall never choose as his love
> object a woman who is disengaged—that is, an unmarried girl or
> an unattached married woman—but only one to whom another
> man can claim right of possession as her husband, fiance or friend.
> [p. 166]

The second condition involves the existence of at least a "faint
breath of scandal" (p. 166) about the woman's sexual behavior.
The fidelity and reliability of such a woman is thus open to question. Indeed, she might be overtly promiscuous. Freud went on to
state that men who make this sort of object choice display an extreme intensity in their longing and an unrelenting pattern of
repeating the same exact scenario again and again in their lives.
They feel a powerful urge to rescue the woman they love and feel
convinced that she is in need of them.

Freud traced the origins of this syndrome to the "parental complex" (p. 174) whereby the injured third party and the sexually tainted, unfaithful woman are none other than the father and the betraying mother of the night, respectively. Ten years later, Freud (1920b) demonstrated the occurrence of similar object choice in a homosexual girl. A more common female version of such "special type of choice" (Freud 1910a) is evident in the "other woman" (Akhtar 1985), that is, a single woman who is romantically involved, either repeatedly or on a sustained basis, with a married man. Here the oedipal wish for the father is poignantly coupled with the hateful competitiveness with the mother and the guilty masochism at the attempted (and partially actualized!) overthrow of the oedipal boundaries.

To the now well-recognized oedipal etiology of this syndrome, further impetus is occasionally given by preoedipal narcissistic and sadomasochistic trends. When this happens, the prohibited erotic longing acquires an even more pressured and despairing quality. In such cases, the chosen object not only meets the criteria outlined by Freud (1910a) but is realistically almost impossible to achieve, inappropriate in more ways than one (e.g., striking socioeconomic and intellectual difference), and/or more grossly "damaged"—to borrow a word from the novelist Josephine Hart (1991)—than merely having a sexually scandalous past. Many unhappy marriages owe their origin to a reckless enactment of rescue fantasies toward such a "debased" woman (Freud 1917b). In effect, then, while falling in love with the "wrong" kinds of people is seen mostly in association with a "higher level" (Kernberg 1970a) character organization especially in the form of a hysterical personality, its more devastating versions are found in borderline, narcissistic, and infantile personalities.

In the clinical situation, one mostly sees the relatively externalized portrayals of these difficulties with the patients endlessly talking about their rescue fantasies toward their love objects. In married male patients, a frequent manifestation is an extramarital affair with the wife consciously or unconsciously cast in the role of "madonna" and the mistress in the role of "whore." Often the developmentally earlier preoedipal splitting of the maternal imago into "good" and "bad" part representations fuels and complicates the situation. In female patients, at times, the core internal scenario gets mobilized in the treatment situation itself, giving rise to a powerful erotic attachment to the analyst. This, if receiving pre-oedipal currents, can give rise to "malignant erotic transference" (Akhtar 1994b), a matter closely related to the next psychopathological syndrome of love life.

INABILITY TO FALL OUT OF LOVE

> "Love addicts" [are] persons in whom the affection or the confirmation they receive from external objects plays the same role as food in the case of food addicts. Although they are unable to return love, they absolutely need an object by whom they feel loved, but only as an instrument to procure the condensed oral gratification. [Fenichel 1945, p. 382]

> The experiencing of hopelessness is . . . a part of normal development and is necessary for the attainment of a more reality-oriented sense of psychic self. [Schmale 1964, p. 300]

At first, the suggestion that the inability to fall out of love constitutes a psychopathological syndrome might appear strange. After all, is it not desirable for people to stay in love? A careful consideration, however, supports the validity of regarding a tenacious refusal to accept that one's love for someone is unreciprocated as psychopathological. Under normal circumstances,

> if love is unrequited, it tends gradually to decrease and come to an end. On a deeper level, unrequited love activates the defenses against the oedipal situation and promotes the working through of mourning the unattainable object. As such, unrequited love has a growth potential—in both childhood and adult life. [Kernberg et al. 1989, p. 190]

However, in neurotic, borderline, and potentially psychotic characters, "love" tends to intensify when it is not reciprocated. This is because such love is actually a demand for preoedipal acceptance, for preferred status, and for omnipotent control over the love object. Through all this, and more, the individual is attempting to ward off intense aggression from within, to stabilize a precarious instinctual economy, and to maintain structural integrity of his or her psyche. Lacking object constancy, such individuals are excessively dependent on external objects for the regulation of self-esteem and emotional well-being (see Chapter 1). They cling to the defensively idealized object and cannot tolerate frustration without regressing into murderous rage and/or suicidal despair. Individuals who remain tormented year after year by the memories of a failed romance suffer essentially from a similar difficulty.

Intense object addiction leading to pleading, coercion, and even stalking is another extreme behavioral manifestation of such impairment of object constancy. Its counterpart in the clinical situation is "malignant erotic transference" (Akhtar 1994b) characterized by (1) coercive demands for "love" and, at times, for sexual gratification; (2) an unmistakably hostile and controlling flavor to these demands; (3) the absence of erotic counterresonance in the therapist; and (4) the remarkable inconsolability of the patient. This syndrome, seen more frequently in women,[26] is most likely what Freud (1915a) had in mind when he mentioned "women of elemental passionateness who tolerate no surrogates" and "children of nature who refuse to accept the psychical in place of the material" (pp. 166–167). Important contributions to the understanding of this development in transference have also been made by Blum (1973), Eickhoff (1993), Joseph (1993), and Kernberg (1995a).

---

[26]The greater frequency of malignant erotic transference in women seems to have many explanations: (1) more intense reproaches in the female child toward the mother; (2) the extra burden on the female child's ego to mourn the "loss" of the penis; and (3) the actual experience, in the background of many such patients, of having been "picked up" by their fathers after being "dropped" by their mothers. This last factor, while saving the child from a schizoid or suicidal breakdown, robs her of a fundamental prototype of mourning; instead, she learns that what is lost ("all good" mother) can indeed be found (an overindulgent father). The fact that such rescues are usually quite instinctualized contributes to sadomasochistic sexual fantasies and a perverse defiance of oedipal limits in later adult life.

The fact that such rigid inability (or refusal) to accept the reality is a powerful defense against rage becomes evident when the patient verbally or implicitly declares, "Love me or I will kill myself," or even "Love me or I will kill you." Here, the fact that a combination of object coercion and primitive idealization is being employed as a last-ditch defense against profound, unneutralized aggression becomes nakedly apparent. It is as if the patient is saying, "Look, I am carrying a time bomb in my belly and your love can act as a safety catch that will keep it defused." The problem is clearly inside the patient, not in the interpersonal situation.

INABILITY TO FEEL LOVED

> Cynicism and asceticism appear to be the twin offspring of this temperament which demands a love from others which shall afford the givers no pleasure and which therefore is undeniably unselfish and "genuine." The cynic observes that amiable behavior brings pleasure and concludes that it is done for this reason. For him this is merely an inverted form of selfishness and hence worthless. . . . The ascetic, like the cynic, feels that love is not *real* if it is pleasurable. [Suttie 1935, p. 66]

> I don't allow for the fuzziness, the inexactness, of life, that it will never conform precisely to any pattern. I rule out error and laughter and slippage, and so take away hope for betterment, for decency. I want to pull them down into despair. My despair! That's it! If I can't make them love me . . . But they do! Clara loves me! What is it then? If I cannot make them find some way to relieve my fear so that I can accept love—that's it!—then I will drag them down into my vision of absolute, inescapable evil. How despicable I am! [a character in *The Way Things Are*, Wheelis 1994, p. 125]

It seems agreed upon that the capacity to fall and remain in love evolves gradually and from many ontogenetic sources. Less recognized is the fact that to feel loved has its own psychostructural prerequisites. According to Moore and Fine (1990), "self constancy and sound secondary narcissism are necessary in order to feel loved" (p. 113). In fact, many other ego capacities need to be in place for this experience to occur, including the capacities to (1) experience humility and gratitude; (2) recognize the value of the other, hence tolerate envy toward him or her; (3) renounce a cynical worldview and the masochistically tinged, deprived child representations of oneself associated with it; (4) relinquish infantile omnipotence and be satisfied with inner and outer life being "good enough" and therefore, by implication, imperfect; (5) psychically surrender to attachment, hence feel vulnerable to separation and loss; and (6) experience guilt, since some aggression toward the love object continues to emanate from within even under the best of circumstances. Many narcissistic, paranoid, and schizoid individuals lack these capacities and therefore cannot feel loved. In this context, the dark musings of Ben, the protagonist of Louis Begley's (1993) *The Man Who Was Late*, readily come to mind.

> Such as Veronique was, she made me happy as no one has except Rachel. Before she began to press me to act like a normal man, she made me a good deal happier. The poor dummy actually loved me. Rachel knew better: her idea was that, for a time, I could love her on a live-in basis. Probably that is all I am good for, although for a while, with Veronique, I made progress—I was beginning to be able to bear it, without wincing, when she was nice to me. [pp. 221–222]

To extend a popular psychoanalytic metaphor, individuals such as Ben do not lack mirrors but have impaired (or defensively compromised) visions! This prevents them from seeing their own libidinally invested reflections in others' loving and affirming behaviors toward them. They *are* loved but cannot allow themselves to *feel* loved.

A more problematic situation results when the inability to feel loved is accompanied by active attempts at rejecting, spoiling, and ruining the available libidinal supplies. This is most evident in individuals with "malignant narcissism" (Akhtar 1995a, Kernberg 1984, Rosenfeld 1971a). Such persons seek to destroy whatever love is offered to them in order to maintain a cold and contemptuous superiority over others. They mock loving and idealize hating. Consistently, they attempt to dehumanize, symbolically castrate, and destroy others. In becoming totally identified with the omnipotent destructive aspects of their selves and their internalized "bad" objects, they kill off their sane and loving self representations, which could develop attachment and dependence. The less disturbed among this group might rationalize their scornful attitude toward love as a culturally superior form of emotional reticence. They are often wistfully aware of their inner imprisonment but feel that there is little anybody (or they themselves) can do to unhinge this Faustian bondage.

Clinically, the inability to feel loved is seen more often in association with mild paranoid personalities. Here the deficient internalization of the comforting, constant mother is associated with a lack of ego integration, untamed infantile omnipotence, much sadomasochism, fragile self-esteem, and intense separation anxiety. In this context, Blum's (1981) concept of the "inconstant object" is highly pertinent. This refers to an ambivalently loved object that is felt to be both persecutory and needed. Such an object cannot be allowed to have an independent existence. The threat of betrayal by it must be tenaciously maintained. In a sense, this constant fear of abandonment is the aggressive reciprocal of "libidinal object constancy" (Mahler et al. 1975) and a desperate effort to preserve an illusory constant object while unremittingly fearing betrayal and loss. In the clinical setting, all this translates into a rigid paranoid transference, which secretly provides structural stability to the patient.[27]

CONCLUDING REMARKS

What is love? For most of mankind it has been a
sweet mystery whose presence was a miracle, whose
absence was a disaster. [Altman 1977, p. 35]

---

[27]In a related spirit, a character in Harold Pinter's *No Man's Land* (1975) says, "I have never been loved. From this I derive my strength." (p. 30)

> Structurally considered, love involves the id, ego, and superego. Parental love, approval, and comfort are internalized in the benign, mature superego, while a harsh, primitive superego impairs the ability to love and be loved. Love may be displaced from the original objects onto collective objects and causes; to religion; to artistic, intellectual, and athletic sublimations; to pets; and to highly personal interests. [Moore and Fine 1990, p. 114]

In the clinical situation, each psychopathological syndrome outlined above gives its own imprimatur to the evolving transference. The inability to fall in love manifests as a sustained detachment from the analyst or as an "as-if" (Deutsch 1942) sort of compliance with the treatment. The inability to remain in love leads to pronounced struggles around the inherent ambivalence resulting in marked fluctuations in the depth of attachment to the analyst or even a ruptured treatment. The tendency to fall in love with the wrong kinds of people underlies the traditionally understood oedipal erotic transference. The inability to fall out of love is associated with the more desperate and hostile "malignant erotic transference" (Akhtar 1994b). And the inability to feel loved emerges as a paranoid conviction of the analyst's lack of interest, if not dislike and hatred of the patient.

Such surgical separation of the phenomenological attributes and transference manifestations of the five syndromes, however, is more a matter of didactic necessity than an accurate reflection of clinical realities. In actuality, there is much overlap among these conditions. There is also a greater variability in their transference manifestations. Moreover, these five syndromes do not constitute an exhaustive list of psychopathological conditions involving love life. In focusing on phenomena encountered in psychotherapeutic and psychoanalytic practices, I have excluded the psychotic end of this spectrum. Prominent on this end are the "phantom lover syndrome" (Seeman 1978), erotomania proper (originally described by DeClerambault in 1942 and recently comprehensively reviewed by Segal 1989), and morbid jealousy of delusional proportions (see Mullen 1990 for a recent review of the pertinent literature).

Finally, while some of these syndromes (the first three, especially) do represent nodal points on a hierarchical continuum of psychopathology (Kernberg, 1974a,b, 1995a), the fact is that each of them contains deficits and conflicts from various developmental levels. The inability to fall in love, for instance, might represent the lack of activation of early psychophysical eroticism through a satisfying symbiotic experience, *and* a defense against unconscious envy of the love object, *and* even, at times, a pronounced inhibition resulting from intense castration anxiety. Similarly, the inability to remain in love might emanate from a futile search for a transformational object, anxieties regarding fusion with the love object, and/or conflicts related to narcissism, aggression, and the Oedipus complex. The implication of a developmental hierarchy in the various psychopathological entities outlined above, therefore, should not preclude attention to the multileveled nature of each syndrome itself. Keeping these caveats in mind while being aware of the pertinent psychopathological terrain will provide the analyst with the ego duality helpful in working with such patients. The analyst will possess both the inner resources for knowledgeable empathy and the capacity to be surprised by the patient's material.

Adding an element of surprise to this chapter itself, emphasizing the multifaceted nature of love, and celebrating its lyrical quality, I conclude with a poem of mine entitled "Through You."

I have known love
I have known what it is
To be yielding while still in command
To be demanding and yet be kind
To be sensuous while remaining restrained
To be inviting but only between the lines
To be apart yet not distant
To be close without getting intertwined
To be concerned though not intrusive
To be respectful but not in awe
To be childlike but not childish
To be generous without emptying the heart
All this I have known through you
Through you, my dear
I have known love.

4

HATRED

Hatred is a complex, characterologically anchored, chronic affective state that involves much cognitive elaboration and rationalization. Its manifestations are varied and include intricate disturbances of ego and superego functioning. Its primary aim is to destroy a specific object of unconscious fantasy and this object's conscious derivatives. This vengeful pursuit has a particular kind of stability to it. Indeed, the choice of the term *hatred* over the simpler *hate* serves to underscore the attribute of chronicity and stability of the phenomena involved. *Webster's New Universal Unabridged Dictionary* (1983) describes hate as a verb, hatred as a noun. The suffix *-red* comes from the old Anglo-Saxon *raeden* for signifying state or condition.

I begin my discussion by describing the various manifestations of hatred and distinguishing them from the related affects of rage, envy, and arrogance. Following this, I devote a brief section to the origins of hatred. Then, I comment on the sociocultural vicissitudes of hatred especially as these pertain to ethnic and racial prejudice and violence. Next, I focus on hatred in the clinical situation, highlighting its manifestations in the transference–countertransference axis. I then discuss the technical implications of these ideas and conclude with some remarks on aspects of hatred not covered in the preceding sections.

HATRED AND ITS MANIFESTATIONS

> Hatred for someone implies that the other person, through his cruelty or unkindness, is the cause of one's sufferings, that the latter are not self-imposed or in any way one's own fault. All the responsibility for the misery produced by unconscious guilt is thus displaced on to the other, supposedly cruel person, who is therefore heartily hated. [Jones 1928, p. 384]

> We hate people who, though very important to us, do *not* love us and refuse to become our cooperative partners despite our best efforts to win their affection. This stirs up in us all the bitter pains, sufferings, and anxieties of the past and we defend ourselves against their return by the *barrier of hatred*, by denying our need for those people and our dependence on them. [Balint 1952, p. 358, author's italics]

Hatred is the "core affect of aggression" (Kernberg 1995b) that angrily and relentlessly demands the destruction of a specific internal object and its externalized derivative forms. However, it is more than an affect. It is invariably accompanied by tenaciously held unconscious fantasies as well as distortions of ego and superego functioning. The unconscious fantasy underlying hatred consists of a belief that one has been wronged, betrayed, and mistreated by others. In the realm of the ego, there is a peculiar narrowing of cognitive functions that sharpens but distorts reasoning capacities and prevents the alteration of sadomasochistic beliefs by benevolent, corrective knowledge. Corruption of superego functioning is also associated with hatred. Common manifestations of this include blindness to ethical barriers in the path of one's destructive aims and ruthless exploitation and dehumanization of others. Such degradation can readily involve oneself if the self becomes inextricably identified with the hated object. Self-hatred can be evident in chronic low self-esteem, subtle or gross self-mutilation, somatization and hypochondria, and, of course, suicidal tendencies.

The manifestations of hatred vary depending on its intensity. At its extreme, hatred insists on the physical elimination, via murder, of the object. A lesser degree of hatred leads to a complete social ostracization of the object along with a ruthless erasure of its emotional importance to oneself. The object is allowed physical survival but is psychosocially killed. Physical abuse and psychological torture are next in the hierarchy of the clinical manifestations of hatred. It is at this step, so to speak, that hatred can become sexualized. Sadism and masochism appear on the psychic horizon.

> In contrast to the earlier, more encompassing form of hatred, sadism is characterized by the wish not to eliminate but to maintain the relationship with the hated object in an enactment of an object relationship between a sadistic agent and a paralyzed victim. The desire to inflict pain and pleasure in doing so are central here, representing an implicit condensation of aggression and libidinal excitement in inducing such suffering. [Kernberg 1992, p. 24]

At times, frank sexual excitement is enlisted for the purposes of undoing previous humiliation, trauma, and the resulting hate. Such hateful orgastic triumph over an object is implicit in certain crafty and greedy forms of seductiveness and explicit in sadomasochistic perversions (Stoller 1979). Indeed, sadomasochistic object relations in general and sadomasochistic sexuality in particular have much in common.

> Excitement, common to both, involves the ability to induce intense affective responses in another person against the other person's will; to feel in control, dominant, able to make another feel bad. Sadomasochistic excitement involves entering into what is ordinarily dangerous and forbidden: incestuous, exploitative, inappropriate, hurtful, infantile, regressive. The excitement is enhanced by the knowledge that it is wrong, destructive to oneself and the other, to give into regressive wishes to escape from autonomy by becoming embroiled with another in hostile, erotic contact. [Coen 1988, p. 58]

A less sexualized, milder form of hatred involves the desire to emotionally and/or intellectually dominate the object and, by its submission, to find "evidence" of one's libidinal freedom from it. If the object is totally under one's control, one's emotional dependence on it, and the conflicts emanating from such dependence, can be denied. Finally, a well-rationalized identification with a punitive superego might lead to a subtle form of hatred consisting of moralizing and constantly demonstrating one's ethical superiority over the object.

The manifestations of hatred can therefore be arranged on a hierarchical continuum of severity. Going from the most severe to the mildest form of manifest hatred, these include (1) physical annihilation, (2) psychosocial ostracization, (3) physical torture, (4) sadomasochistic sexuality, (5) psychological abuse, (6) emotional domination, (7) intellectual control, and (8) an unrelenting demonstration of one's moral superiority over the object. This continuum prompts us to look for potential correlations between degrees of hatred and levels of character organization.

In an attempt to clarify the relationship between the experience of hatred and personality types, Galdston (1987) proposed four categories of individuals: (1) those who cannot hate, (2) those who hate but cannot let go of their hatred, (3) those who hate but are not consciously aware of their hate, and (4) those who can hate and get over hating. The first group seems composed of weak, unentitled, schizoid, and "as-if" (H. Deutsch 1942) individuals who lack a "healthy capacity for indignation" (Ambassador Nathaniel Howell, personal communication, April 1996). The second (and perhaps the most hateful) group is composed of individuals with "the syndrome of malignant narcissism" (Kernberg 1989), paranoid personalities, and certain aggressive and sadistic antisocial characters. Borderline personalities, though given to frequent outbursts of anger, are not bitter and hateful on a sustained basis. The third group subsumes those with strong repressive barriers and reaction formations, most notably obsessive-compulsive individuals, though perhaps also certain depressive characters. The final group consists of relatively healthy individuals who possess the capacity for hatred under circumstances that truly warrant such reaction and the capacity to let go of the feeling when circumstances change. If this hierarchical arrangement (schizoid and as-if—paranoid and antisocial—obsessional and depressive—relatively normal) is sensible, then the question is, How can we help a given patient progress along this continuum? Before addressing this important technical question, however, it might be useful to further delineate the phenomena associated with hatred by distinguishing them from the related affects of rage, envy, and arrogance.

THE RELATIONSHIP OF HATRED WITH RAGE, ENVY, AND ARROGANCE

> Envy may be considered both a source of a primitive form of hatred, intimately linked with oral aggression, greed, and voracity, and a complication of the hatred that derives from the fixation to trauma. [Kernberg 1992, p. 25]

> Hate does not necessarily or immediately incite rage and, unlike the latter, seems to require an object. Both may be either acute or chronic, but hate tends to be more persistent and less episodic. It may be inferred from these considerations that in the adult it would be possible to have hate without overt rage and vice versa. [Blum 1997, p. 366]

Hatred differs from rage in important ways. Rage is ontogenetically primitive, hate is a later development[28] (Fenichel 1954, Jacobson 1953). Rage is acute, hatred chronic. Rage has disruptive effects on intellect while hatred might sharpen reasoning, though not without simultaneously narrowing its focus (Akhtar 1990b, Bollas 1992, Shapiro 1965). While both rage and hatred involve a conscious or unconscious fantasy involving a specific self and object relation, this fantasy is submerged in rage, more avail-

---

[28]While excessive hate might impede the acquisition of object constancy (Mahler et al. 1975), some object constancy is essential for experiencing the sustained affective state of hatred (Blum 1997, Galdston 1987).

able in hatred. Rage results from ego's conflict with an external object, hate from its conflict with an internal object. Rage pushes for immediate action. Hatred involves interposition of ideational process resulting in suppression of immediate muscular release (cf. Joseph Stalin's wry remark, "Revenge is best eaten cold!"). Rage comes and goes with the inciting event. Hatred simmers. Rage, attempting to modify the object's frustrating behavior, focuses upon the present. Hatred "dwells on the past, thinks of revenge in the future, and is not concerned with the present" (Pao 1965, p. 258). In this way, hatred comes to be a counterpart of idealization, which, only in the libidinal realm, robs the present by focusing on the past, in the form of inordinate nostalgia, or on the future, in the form of pathological optimism (see Chapter 7).

Rage and hatred differ in still other ways (Akhtar 1995c). Rage has no defensive purposes. Hatred frequently serves defensive aims against fear and guilt (Jones 1928), dependent longings (Fairbairn 1940, Hill 1938), repressed grief and separation anxiety (Searles 1956, 1962), and dread of psychotic decompensation (Gabbard, in Winer 1994). Rage has little long-term adaptive purpose. Hatred, in linking past and future, establishes a sense of continuity and might contribute to a person's identity. Finally, rage, in aiming to eliminate a source of irritation, unshackles the self from the object. Hatred, in contrast, places the individual in a state of psychic bondage:

> If he remains close to the object, he may betray his hatred and provoke the wrath of the object, who could crush him. On the other hand, if he attempts to avoid the hated object, he is denying himself needed libidinal supplies. Caught in a dilemma, the hater feels trapped. [Pao 1965, pp. 258–59]

Milan Kundera, the renowned novelist, has summarized the situation thus: "Hate traps us by binding us too tightly to our adversary" (1990, p. 24). Indeed, hatred might become an ego-syntonic basis of object relations much as a tormented, yet stable, tie to a frustrating object is the basis for certain masochistic characters (Berliner 1958).

Hatred also has a close relationship with envy. This emanates from the fact that during early infancy the source of psychic gratification and frustration is one and the same, namely the breast (and subsequently, the mother as a whole object). In other words, the obstacle to gratification is the same as the origin of gratification. Under such circumstances, the baby experiences any frustration as a deliberate withholding on the part of the breast (mother) and as a result, develops intense wishes to both greedily incorporate it (her) as well as vengefully destroy it. This pressure to spoil and destroy the very object that is secretly admired and needed for psychic survival lies at the root of envy. Interestingly, then, envy is consciously a source of hatred while unconsciously it is a form of hatred. It involves hostility toward someone perceived as possessing and teasingly withholding something highly desirable. The greater the envy, the more likely is an actual perception of the envied person as one who possesses the desirable qualities. The perception of one's own lack of desirable attributes reflects the poorly developed and experientially atrophied pertinent ego functions. It also gives testimony to self-hatred, which attacks and destroys one's goodness and compromises the capacity to recognize whatever good does survive within oneself.

Destruction of one's mental capacities at the hands of self-hatred also underlies the attitude of arrogance. If hate is intense and the moral dictates are to be kind no matter what, then one possible outcome is the denial of hatred by destroying all awareness of the affect and transforming its aggressive potential into action. Such defensive action obliterates cognitive functioning and leads to the syndrome of arrogance, curiosity, and pseudo-stupidity (Bion 1957). Arrogance results from narrow-mindedness in the realm of feeling and perception. This, in turn, is caused by the hostile obliteration of the concept of whole objects and their replacement by dehumanized figures toward whom malice can be directed without empathy and remorse (Brenman 1985). The hateful devaluation of the object is accompanied by a heightening of secondary narcissism and this also contributes to arrogance. A peculiarly naive curiosity about others paradoxically accompanies such dehumanization. However, this curiosity does not express

genuine wishes to understand others. Rather it reflects the puzzle-
ment about others' motivations on the part of an individual who
has little knowledge of his own intrapsychic life. Pseudo-stupidity,
the third feature of this syndrome, is a consequence of the mas-
sive tendency toward projection and the resulting inability to
internalize new knowledge. An individual with pseudo-stupidity
feels immensely surprised when his hostile acts are found as such
by others. He is also unable to alter his paranoid views in the light
of new knowledge. Together, arrogance, curiosity, and pseudo-
stupidity give rise to a clinical picture of a mindless certainty, omnipotence, and intellectual smugness. The attitude of omnipotence, which almost invariably characterizes intense hatred, also
emanates from a total identification with a harsh and punitive
superego. This brings us to the ontogenetic roots of hatred.

ORIGINS OF HATRED

> The ego hates, abhors and pursues with intent to
> destroy all objects which are a source of unplea-
> surable feeling for it, without taking into account
> whether they mean a frustration of sexual satisfac-
> tion or of the satisfaction of self-preservative needs.
> [Freud 1915b, p. 138]

> Hate, I regard not as a primal independent instinct,
> but as a development or intensification of separation-
> anxiety which in turn is roused by a threat against
> love. It is the maximal ultimate appeal in the child's
> power—the most difficult for the adult to ignore.
> [Suttie 1935, p. 31]

Any search for the origins of hatred must accommodate the pertinent heuristic conceptualizations as well as empirical observations
in this realm. On the conceptual level, one needs to consider the
diverse theoretical views regarding aggression itself since hatred
is the core affect of aggression. On the empirical level, one should
note the role of childhood trauma, neglect, and abuse, since a
history of such sources of unpleasure is invariably associated with
adult clinical syndromes of hatred.

Beginning at the conceptual level, one notes that there are five different theoretical positions regarding the nature and origins of aggression (see Chapter 2). One extreme, pioneered by Freud (1920a) in *Beyond the Pleasure Principle* and adhered to by Ferenczi (1929), Klein (1933, 1948), Menninger (1938), Eissler (1971), and Rosenfeld (1971b), holds steadfastly to the concept of death instinct and posits aggression to be a destructive outward deflection of such a self-annihilating instinctual substrate. The other extreme is represented by Suttie (1935), Fairbairn (1943, 1944), Guntrip (1969, 1971), and Kohut (1972, 1977), who have dissociated themselves from the instinctual basis of human motivation altogether. While their view does allow for innate assertiveness, which under the influence of frustration might turn into destructiveness, it rules out innate destructiveness in no uncertain terms.

Between these extremes lie three other views that reject the death instinct but adhere to the instinct theory, viewing aggression as one of the two basic instinctual drives. The first of these three views regards the aim of aggression to be variable though mainly involving destruction. It sees the infant's motility, activity, and assertion as emanating from a noninstinctual energy source to which neutralization of instinctual aggression might also contribute. This is the position of Anna Freud (1963, 1972), Hartmann and colleagues (1949), Waelder (1956), and Brenner (1971, 1982). The second position extends the scope of the instinctual aggression to include infantile activity, assertion, and attempts at mastery. It considers both nondestructive and destructive aggression to be fueled from the same energy source. Moreover, it emphasizes that hostile destruction is only elicited by unpleasure. This is the position taken implicitly by Winnicott (1950) and explicitly by Parens (1973, 1979). Finally, the third position excludes nondestructive activity from aggression and presents a view of drives different from that traditionally held. It proposes that early pleasurable and unpleasurable affects (emanating from the evocation of hard-wired potentials by neonatal object relations) gradually consolidate into the libidinal and aggressive drives that subsequently become supraordinate motivational systems. This is the theoretical stance of Kernberg (1982a, 1992, 1995b).

At the risk of oversimplification and overlooking the hybrid notions (Kernberg 1992, Parens 1979, Stechler 1987) in this realm, the five theories can be grouped into two broad categories.[29] One (Fairbairn 1943, Freud 1915b, Kohut 1977, Winnicott 1950) regards it as a trait acquired as a result of environmental failures and intrusions; the other (Brenner 1971, Freud 1920a, Klein 1933) proposes destructiveness to be inherent to human nature. The first group of theories implies hatred to be a new and pathological development altogether, while the second group implies it to be a remnant of the original infantile destructiveness. The first group of theories suggests that hatred develops because the growing child cannot find the love and care needed for his growth. The second group suggests that hatred persists into adulthood because it has not been tamed by love,[30] metabolized through mourning, and sublimated via ego's interventions. The first set of theories does not pay attention to the constitutionally determined variations among individuals in this regard; the second set does. However, both sets of theories ultimately end up with infantile and childhood frustration as the root of hatred. Since some frustration is unavoidable in childhood, some hate too becomes developmentally inevitable. Painful awareness of separateness from the primary love object and the associated loss of infantile omnipotence especially generate hatred. However, in its more pathological and clinically relevant form, hatred emanates from trauma more severe than such ordinary childhood frustrations.

Indeed, recent research (Paris 1994, Perry and Herman 1993, Stone 1989) has demonstrated the high prevalence of profound neglect as well as physical and sexual abuse in the childhood background of those filled with rage and hatred. Reconstructive data

---

[29]In light of the many theoretical positions taken by Freud regarding aggression (see Chapter 2 for details), it is not surprising that he represents *both* these views. In his first dual instinct theory (1915b), aggression was largely a subsidiary and reactive manifestation of self-preservative instinct. In his second dual instinct theory (1920a), aggression came to be viewed as an outward deflection of the self-threatening death instinct.

[30]Freud's comment that "hate, as a relation to objects, is older than love" (1915b, p. 139) is pertinent in this context.

from psychoanalytic treatment of such individuals confirms this (Blum 1981, Pine 1995). Shengold (1989) has simply but poignantly summarized this situation and I quote him at length.

> Some of the stories that patients tell about their parents and childhood could make the psychiatrist weep: my father beat us so badly he broke bones; my mother put lye in my halfwit brother's oatmeal; my mother kept the bedroom door open when she brought men home for sex; my stepfather took baths with me and taught me to suck him off, and when I told my mother she slapped me and called me a liar. Sometimes the accusations do not primarily concern beatings and sexual abuse but hatred and mental torture; or they are about complete indifference, neglect, and desertion. They present parents who are psychotic or psychopathic or alcoholic. Love and empathy are described as never or only intermittently present—cold indifference or destructive hatred reigns. Often one hears of a kind of brainwashing, a cultivation of denial by the parents that makes the child doubt the evidence of his or her own senses and memory. [pp. 14–15]

Together, the three elements outlined here (abuse, lack of empathy, and brainwashing) have a profoundly destructive effect on the growing child's mind. The extreme unpleasure associated with such experiences turns healthy aggression into rage and hatred (Parens 1979, 1995) with a specific self-object relation getting fixated at the base of this hostile destructiveness. This involves the picture of a frustrated and anguished self relating to a powerful, withholding, sadistic object. There also occurs an unconscious identification with both victim and victimizer. This leads to

> an intensification of the actual relationship with the frustrating object, that is, an increased dependency in reality on the hated object in order to influence, control, punish, or transform it into a good object, and, at the same time, the unconscious tendency to repeat the relationship with the hated object with role reversals, becoming the hateful object dominating, teasing, frustrating, and mistreating another object onto which the self-representation has been projected. [Kernberg 1995b, p. 68]

Hatred offers the hope of reversal of suffering and thus acquires an addictive quality. The individual so driven treats others badly because he feels he was himself treated badly. There is a total identification with the aggressor. Such individuals thus become both victims and victimizers. "As victimizer, they cannot live without their victim—the projected, persecuted self; as victim, they remain attached to their persecutors internally and sometimes, in behavior shocking to an observer, externally as well" (Kernberg 1992, p. 28).

Such scenarios can, at times, transcend the intrapsychic and interpersonal worlds of individuals. Finding commonality of cause with others and with the intoxicating sanction of a group, the victim–victimizer hatred can spill into ethnic, racial, national, and international affairs.

SOCIOCULTURAL VICISSITUDES

The most gruesome human destructiveness is encountered not in the form of wild, regressive, and primitive behavior, but in the form of orderly and organized activities in which the perpetrators' destructiveness is alloyed with absolutarian convictions about their greatness and with their devotion to archaic omnipotent figures. [Kohut 1972, p. 378]

When love and hate clash, either we feel guilt and make reparation, or we are persecuted by guilt. To avoid either consequence, we can pervert the truth, draw strength from a good object and feel free to practise cruelty in the name of goodness. It is as though we omnipotently hijack human righteousness and conduct cruelty in the name of justice. [Brenman 1985, p. 274]

Processes involved in group hatred have both similarities and differences with the individual psychodynamics described above. Like individual hatred with a trauma in its background, group hatred is also founded upon hurtful historical events. Like individual hatred, group hatred is also accompanied by memory alterations. Individuals traumatized as children either remember their childhoods selectively (emphasizing its painful aspects) or feel unsure about the actuality of traumatic events due to the "gaslighting" by the parents who denied what was occurring. Groups show the phenomenon of "chosen trauma" (Volkan 1988), whereby a historical injustice of the past is given exalted status and meanings far beyond its original implications. This "memory" is then used to rationalize a sense of victimization and the consequent victimizing of other groups upon whom victim representation of the original group is projected. Also, like individual hatred, group hatred can acquire a tenaciously driven quality with all the elements of the compulsion to repeat.

However, there are certain specific aspects to group hatred. First and foremost is the fact that the group's collective conscience sweeps away previous rules and regulations and substitutes its own moral values (Freud 1921). There is thus a surrender of personal superego on the altar of group approval. Second, there is the important role of the group leader. Almost invariably, such an individual is narcissistic,[31] charismatic, and capable of exerting a powerful fascinating effect (see Olden 1941 in this regard) on others. Through his oratory and actions, the leader appeals to the group members' infantile hunger for acceptance, love, and narcissistic supplies. He evokes "chosen glories" (Volkan 1988), that is, exaggerated accounts of past achievements of the group. He offers the promise of a new family, placing himself in the father's role. He allows hitherto prohibited gratifications and encourages the shifting of aggression toward those outside the group. This enhances group cohesion,[32] which, in turn, strengthens the leader's hold on the group. He comes to exert a hypnotic influence on his followers by diminishing their shame and guilt, increasing their nar-

---

[31]Freud's (1931b) description of the narcissistic type includes the statement that such people are "especially suited to act as a support for others, to take on the role of leaders and to give a fresh stimulus to cultural development or to damage the established state of affairs (p. 218).

[32]See in this context Loewenberg's (1995) astute observations on the psychodynamics of nationalism. His book also offers a most searching analysis of racial and religious prejudice in today's world.

cissism, and facilitating the projection of their own sense of inferiority on outsiders. In doing so, the "destructive pied piper" (Blum 1995, p. 18) permits and promotes prejudice, hatred, and even violence toward the debased outsiders. Third, there is a peculiarly regressive pull to the collective power of the group, which drowns the individual identities of its members. This regression also accounts for the intensification of affects and inhibition of intellect, the two cardinal features of group psychology according to Freud (1921). Not surprisingly, under such circumstances, individual members lose their previous sense of right and wrong as well. Feeling righteous and even victims themselves, the group members now proceed to treat others with prejudice. In times of external threat and/or economic distress, the group regression can be much greater and utilized by the leader for his own narcissistic purposes. Now the group, feeling itself a victim, begins to victimize others. The oppressed of yesterday have become the oppressors of today. The consequences of this occurrence at the group level can be lacerating and frequently leads to an "inevitable dance with death" (Neubauer 1995, p. 160). No less bloody is the enactment of this complex victim–victimizer drama in the clinical situation.

HATRED IN TRANSFERENCE
AND COUNTERTRANSFERENCE

The conscious aim of vengeance is retribution, punishment, and a longed-for state of peace. . . . Unconsciously the aim of the vengeful individual is to hide a more disastrous damage to the ego, a damage experienced during the earliest years of life and underlying the specific injuries of which he complains. In this sense the act of revenge is a defense mechanism whose function is to conceal the deepest traumata of childhood. [Socarides 1966, pp. 358–359]

A countertransference-experience which has been long-lasting in my work with one patient after another is a guilty sense of not being fully committed, inwardly, to my functional role of the patient's thera-

HATRED

pist, despite my maintenance of all the outward trap-
pings of therapeutic devotion. [Searles 1986,
pp. 212–213]

Individuals who are filled with hatred tend to exhaust the endur-
ance of the analyst. By silently ignoring the analyst, lying to him,
flatly dismissing his interventions, mocking his office decor, dis-
paraging his physical appearance, questioning his manner of
dressing, making phone calls to him at predictably inconvenient
hours, and directly or indirectly ridiculing his accent, ethnicity,
or race, these patients sooner or later get their analysts to feel angry
and spiteful toward them. Such "inductive conduct" (Maltsberger
and Buie 1974, p. 626) strains the analyst's work ego and begins
to flood it with unneutralized aggression. Hatred in transference
thus finds its counterpart in the form of countertransference hatred.

Transference Hatred

In considering transference hatred, it is important to keep in mind
that hatred can exist without overt rage and rage without sustained
hatred. Another important variable is the degree to which hatred
is acknowledged as emanating from within oneself versus the extent to which it is split-off, disavowed, and deposited into others
by means of projection and projective identification. Moreover,
there is no such thing as pure hatred or pure love. Their admixture is invariable and, in accordance with the "principle of multiple function" (Waelder 1936), it contains and expresses many
issues at the same time. Also to be considered is whether the hatred
expressed by the patient represents a true, core issue or a defensive maneuver to keep other distressing affects and fantasies in
check. To be sure, the two formulations cannot be surgically separated, and yet the empathic discernment of which agenda has
experiential and communicative priority is important.

It is with such caveats that one can talk of specific transference
constellations associated with hatred. Essentially, there are three
configurations, namely schizoid transference, psychopathic transference, and paranoid transference. *Schizoid transference* is characterized by an attitude of tenacious withdrawal, which, in the set-

ting of devoted attendance of sessions, can be quite striking. The patient comes regularly, often rushing and a bit late. He gives an appearance of being eager and motivated. Yet, from the beginning of the hour or after a few superficial associations, the patient falls silent. This silence often turns out to be intractable. It is almost as if the patient has actually disappeared, leaving an empty shell in his place. Often the patient feels that his mind has gone blank. When he does talk, spontaneously or at the encouragement of the analyst, his associations do not spiral downward into psychic depth. There remains a brittle, guarded, and factual quality to them. While mildly dysphoric, the patient generally appears free of anxiety. However, the absence of anxiety is apparent only because

> it is kept latent by the particular method of dispersal. The feeling of being disintegrated, of being unable to experience emotions, of losing one's objects, is in fact the equivalent of anxiety. This becomes clearer when advances in synthesis have been made. The great relief which a patient then experiences derives from a feeling that his inner and outer worlds have not only come more together but back to life again. At such moments it appears in retrospect that when emotions were lacking, relations were vague and uncertain and parts of the personality were felt to be lost, everything seemed to be dead. All this is the equivalent of anxiety of a very serious nature. [Klein 1946, p. 21]

The mind-numbing, frustrating, and maddening impact of such tenacious silences is usually not in the patient's awareness. The fact that he has placed the analyst in a straitjacket of technical helplessness remains unknown to the patient, whose cognitive functions are destroyed by hatred. Not infrequently, this transference is associated with experience of oneself and the analyst as inanimate objects. This emanates from the transferential re-creation of early childhood experiences of having frequently being treated as a mere thing by an enraged parent, who himself or herself lost the quality of being human at those times.

> The quality of the rage is such that the child feels distanced from the mother she knew, as though the mother has forgotten that the

child is her child. None of the softening of anger that love would bring, or even that personal connection would bring, is experienced as present at these moments. [Pine 1995, p. 125]

Defensive distortions of early parental images also contribute to the nonhumanness of the experience. "The fantasy of an inhuman, disconnected parent wards off the child's terror and rage at a parent experienced as malevolent" (Lafarge 1995, p. 769). It is a way to manage the pain of a deeply and constantly frustrating object relationship. Often the experience of one's own and the analyst's nonhumanness is associated with lying and distorting the information presented to the analyst. Lafarge has called this type of transference the "psychopathic-unreal" transference to distinguish it from a related second constellation she describes as the "psychopathic-paranoid" transference. In my scheme, however, her first category is a hybrid between the schizoid and psychopathic transferences, and her second category is divisible into the psychopathic and paranoid transferences.

Psychopathic transference (Kernberg 1992) is characterized by the patient's deliberate deceptiveness with the therapist, so that he will be misled in assessing the patient's actual and psychic reality. This deceptiveness may include withholding information, lying, or, more frequently, telling half-truths. The projection of such dishonesty on the analyst leads the patient to experience his analyst as dishonest. At times, the patient's entire personality does not succumb to such deceptiveness and paranoia (Kernberg 1992). In a small and helplessly sequestered part of himself, the patient continues to experience a desire for honesty. O'Shaughnessy's (1990) ironic comment pertains to this very state of affairs: "I think there is one thing in the liar's favor: since he knows he lies, he knows also that there could be truthful object relations" (p. 194).

With tactful but firm confrontation of the patient's deceptiveness and a consistently interpretive approach toward the tendency to keep parts of oneself hidden, greater integration of personality can be achieved. Often this results in the clinical situation going from the frying pan into the fire. The "quieter" psychopathic transferences give way to loud, noisier *paranoid transference.* While this sequence is common, it should be acknowledged that some patients manifest paranoid transference from the very beginning of their treatment.

Such a transference involves the patient's conviction that the analyst dislikes or even hates him. Specific elaborations of this basic theme, derived from real and imagined insults and injuries of childhood, fill the sessions. The patient distorts the reality of what the analyst says or does and can seriously jeopardize the therapeutic relationship. His belief is tenacious and remains unaffected by knowledge (see Britton 1995 in this regard). Such paranoid transferences are characterized by primitive aggression accompanying highly aggressive part-object relations that are split off from the patient's idealized self and object representations. The impact of such intense hostility on the analyst's work ego is not insignificant. Indeed, paranoid transferences can readily mobilize hatred in the analyst. This can result from schizoid and psychopathic transferences, too, but the development of countertransference hatred in such circumstances is somewhat slower.

Countertransference Hatred

The countertransference experience of hatred contains elements of both aversion and malice, though one of these aspects might be more conscious than the other. Aversion leads to the wish to withdraw from the patient and abandon him. Malice leads to cruel impulses toward the patient, manifesting as sarcasm, inflexibility, and even directly hurtful actions. At first, these feelings are mild and fleeting. As the treatment proceeds, however, they become deeper and more sustained. Viewing himself as a compassionate and caring individual, the analyst is vulnerable to mobilize unconscious defenses against such countertransference experience.

Maltsberger and Buie (1974) have outlined five such defensive postures: (1) *Repression*: This might give rise to lack of interest in working with the patient, chronic boredom, excessive daydreaming during the sessions, frequent and obvious looking at the clock, and, worse still, forgetting the patient's appointments. (2) *Turning against the self*: The analyst using this defense becomes doubtful about his skills, excessively self-critical, and masochistically submissive to the patient. This last mentioned tendency is more marked in those analysts who are characterologically prone to guilt and self-punishment. (3) *Reaction formation*: The analyst using reaction formation might become excessively helpful ("pitiless hospitality" in Salman Rushdie's terms!) with omnipotent rescue fantasies and unrealistic interventions in the patient's real life. The defensive nature of such therapeutic zeal is betrayed not only by their anxious rigidity but often by their results as well. (4) *Projection*: Here the analyst begins to dread that the patient will commit suicide. "This kind of preoccupation is usually accompanied by some degree of fear (the consequence of projected malice), and with a degree of aversion, i.e., the patient seems abominable" (Maltsberger and Buie 1974, p. 629). (5) *Distortion and denial of reality for validation of countertransference hatred*: In order to rationalize his hatred, the analyst might distort clinical facts and ignore important information. As a result, he might transfer, prematurely discharge, or altogether abandon the patient.

Such reactions are of course problematic and, one hopes, do not occur very often. More frequent, or at least more desirable, is that the analyst does not bury his hatred deep into his unconscious but lets it emerge into his conscious awareness. While this does not eliminate the deleterious impact of this hatred on his analytic ego altogether, it does permit him to work his way through this difficult experience. At worst, the analyst continues to oscillate between emotionally giving up on the patient and attempting to resolve the patient's hatred analytically. Indeed, these oscillations may reflect "a reasonable compromise formation that permits the therapist to step back and evaluate the effects of his various interventions and gives him some breathing space before he returns to an active interpretive stance" (Kernberg 1992, p. 31).

Handled this way, the experience of countertransference hatred can be highly informative to the analyst. The analyst's felt torment[33] gets gradually translated into a fuller understanding of the patient's inner world (and behind that, the patient's childhood family relationships). Searles (1986) has put the salutory effect of such working through into words most clearly by stating that he

> cannot overemphasize the enormously treatment-facilitating value, as well as the comforting and liberating value for the therapist personally, of his locating where this or that tormenting or otherwise upsetting countertransference reaction links up with the patient's heretofore-unconscious and unclarified *transference*-reactions to him. [p. 214, author's italics]

The discernment of such correlation between the transference and countertransference hatred is an integral part of the analytic treatment of individuals with severe hatred.

TECHNICAL IMPLICATIONS

> The unconscious feeling that parts of the self are unknown increases the urge for integration. The need for integration, moreover, derives from the unconscious knowledge that hate can only be mitigated by love; and if the two are kept apart, this mitigation cannot succeed. In spite of this urge, integration always implies pain, because the split-off hate and its consequences are extremely painful to face. [Klein 1960, p. 274]

> Sometimes the split takes the form of one part of the ego standing aside as if observing all that is going on between the analyst and the other part of the patient and destructively preventing real contact being made using various methods of avoidance and evasion. [Joseph 1975, p. 48]

---

[33]I have elsewhere (Akhtar 1995b) discussed the beneficial role of self care, self-education, self-scrutiny, and self-analysis in the management of intense feelings on the analyst's part.

On the one hand, to suggest that hatred (or any particular affective state, for that matter) requires specific ways of handling goes against the technical grain of psychoanalysis. After all, the aim in psychoanalytic listening involves "not directing one's notice to anything in particular" (Freud 1912c, p. 111) and dealing with all material alike. On the other hand, there is also a legacy of "strategy" (Levy 1987) in psychoanalysis that dictates measured, deliberate tracks of interventions in certain circumstances. Moreover, in dealing with intensely hateful patients, one is often in the realm of psychoanalytic psychotherapy rather than psychoanalysis proper anyway.

Besides this tension, there is the schism between the "classic" and "romantic" visions (Strenger 1989) of psychoanalysis that yields differing views of hatred and its technical handling. In the "classic" view, embodied in the writings of Klein (1946) and Kernberg (1991a, 1992, 1995b), transference hatred is based on the activation of a highly instinctualized, aggressively laden, specific object relationship. The patient hates what he also seeks from the therapist: unlimited love and unwavering dedication to him. The patient also hates (because he deeply envies it) the therapist's inner world of good objects manifest in his peace, creativity, and patience. In addition, the patient employs defenses against the awareness of pleasure in his hatred and, at times, against even the existence of hatred in him. In the "romantic" view, embodied in the writings of Winnicott (1949, 1956) and Kohut (1972, 1977), transference hatred is based on the patient's feeling retraumatized in a therapeutic setting that has failed, at least in that particular moment, to meet his striving to feel understood and his need for a strong, idealizable parental figure as a source of strength. The patient hates the interpretive deconstruction of his wholesome movement toward the analyst, finding it painfully similar to the disregard of his childhood affectionate leanings by his parents. Indeed, the patient might learn to use distance, and, to wit, even hatred itself, as a defense against such anaclitic longings.

These two views of transference hatred, not surprisingly, lead to technical stances that emphasize either the interpretive approach to *defenses against hatred* and its real or imagined origins or an affirmative approach that takes into account the *defensive functions of hatred* while empathically "holding" and gently reconstructing the childhood scenarios of pain that fuel the hatred. To be sure, an exclusive allegiance to one or the other model misses the mark since the clinical material almost invariably reflects both sides of the story. The *schizoid transference* reflects a hostile erasure of relatedness as well as a loving protection of the analyst from one's malevolent inner contents. The *psychopathic transference* reflects a clever spoiling of intimacy as well as a desperate search for an undisturbed bond with the analyst. The *paranoid transference* reflects a mistrustful attack upon the analyst as well as a fierce clinging to him for reliable unreliability. Patients' communications therefore always warrant a multifaceted attention. The integrative approach that results from such attention is what I will now attempt to highlight. I will use Kernberg's (1992, 1995b) technical recommendations as a point of didactic departure. I opt for this strategy largely owing to the fact that Kernberg has provided perhaps the most influential and comprehensive guidelines in this realm.

Approaching specific technical interventions to the treatment of individuals with intense hatred, Kernberg (1995b) makes the following seven suggestions: (1) assess the realistic risks of unleashing destructive forces from within the patient and the possibility of their being contained by the patient's ego and the therapeutic frame; (2) judiciously use various auxiliary measures, including a firm initial contract (Kernberg et al. 1989, Yeomans et al. 1992), to structure the treatment in order to minimize risks to the patient, therapist, and others; (3) diagnose secondary defenses against hatred and consistently interpret them, with full awareness that such interventions might shift a quiet psychopathic transference (involving deceptiveness, dishonesty, and deliberate withholding of information) to a more heated paranoid one; (4) help the patient become aware of his pleasure in hatred, thus seeking to render it ego-dystonic; (5) interpret the patient's paranoid reaction including acknowledging the incompatible views of "reality" held by the patient and the therapist; (6) identify, circumscribe, and tolerate such a "psychotic nucleus" in the transference before attempting to resolve it interpretively; and (7) interpret, in relatively traditional manner, the guilt-ridden depressive transferences that emerge after the resolution of paranoid transferences.

Kernberg's focus is on interpretation and the ancillary measures he suggests are intended to sustain this unmasking interpretive enterprise. His approach is steadfastly consistent with his theory and unwaveringly "classic" (Strenger 1989), despite its overtones of much activity on the therapist's part. However, while emphasizing the necessity to discern defenses *against* hatred, Kernberg does not pay adequate attention to the alternate formulation, that is, the defensive functions *of* hatred (e.g., against dependent longings in the transference). And, while in his phenomenological outline he notes the characterological anchoring of hatred, he does not address the adaptive aspect of transference hatred. The issue, I must emphasize, is not whether hatred in transference is an activation of an early victim–victimizer relationship (however distorted by fantasy) *or* is itself a defense against "the dread to resourceless dependence" (Khan 1972). It is not an either/or situation since "in the flow and flux of analytic material we are always in the world of 'both/and'" (Wallerstein 1983, p. 31). Kernberg's consistent focus on the first formulation is admirable. His omission of the second one is questionable.

Similarly, in his emphasis on interpretation, Kernberg seems to minimize the analyst's other functions. Here I have the role of the "holding environment" (Winnicott 1960) in mind. While Kernberg does acknowledge the need of structuring the treatment, his concern is more about the realistic risks and not on the psychic containment and metabolism of the patient's hatred by the analyst (see the elaboration of technical consequences of the "holding environment" concept in (Akhtar 1992b, Lewin and Schulz 1992, Modell 1976). Kernberg also does not discern the unconscious hope inherent in the patient's hatred, a hope that the analyst will survive his attacks and, in doing so, detoxify his relentless need for revenge. I have elsewhere (Akhtar 1998) provided clinical material to highlight the importance of the analyst's reverie in the discernment of such paradoxes. Also pertinent in this context is Pao's (1965) observation that "when a patient allows himself to reveal his affective state, the patient is more committed to attempting a constructive personality change" (p. 263). This vector of the patient's communication is not adequately recognized in Kernberg's approach.

Moreover, in recommending consistent interpretation, Kernberg seems to overlook the fact that the patient in the throes of intense hatred does not actually have a reasonable portion of his ego allied with the analyst. The patient is neither able nor receptive to the interpretive undertaking. "When deeply regressed, the patient cannot identify the analyst or appreciate his point of view anymore than the fetus or newly born can sympathize with the mother" (Winnicott 1947, p. 202).

Kernberg also does not address the fact that, at times, a patient's expression of hatred might actually be a developmental milestone, achieved for the first time during the analytic situation; this is most likely the case with individuals in Galdston's (1987) category of "those who cannot hate." Kramer (1987) has made a similar point about the emergence of a sense of entitlement for the first time during analysis. Under such circumstances, a quick effort at interpretive deconstruction is perhaps not the most suitable element of technique. More helpful, at first, is a "developmental interpretation" (Abrams 1978) that supports and helps structuralize the resumption of hitherto thwarted initiatives in the patient. Putting all this together, it appears that Kernberg's interpretive stance might crowd the psychic space for containment, holding, validating, affirming, and development-facilitating interventions. (To be sure, some other analysts, for example, Balint, Winnicott, and Kohut, tend to lean too heavily in the opposite direction.) Once again, it is not an "either/or" argument but a "both/and" plea. A synthesis of the two technical stances does seem warranted (see also Akhtar 1995d,e).

A similar broad-mindedness is needed in conceptualizing the hatred experienced by the analyst. Kernberg traces its origin to the patient's assault and to his use of splitting and projective identification. In other words, the hatred felt by the analyst is actually the patient's hatred. I agree with this formulation but, seeing additional possibilities, find it restrictive. Coltart addresses this very issue.

> The belief that whatever happens in the psychoanalytic process is a result of something emanating from the patient, which is then projected into the analyst, has contributed to the creation of a distinctively stagnant psychoanalytic product: the "you-mean-me" interpretation. . . . "You-mean-me" interpretations automatically refer everything that the patient says to a comment about the analyst. Such comments are then said to be "transference-interpretations." In fact they represent a certain paranoid position on the part of the analyst, systematized and presented under the useful disguise of good, "depressive" "maternal" work. [Coltart, in Kohon 1986, p. 72]

Clearly, the therapist's hatred could arise from sources other than the patient's projections of their hateful self and object representations. His own conflicts, independent of those of the patient, might generate hatred in him. Marked actual differences in ethical and political spheres between the two parties also can actually or defensively be stirred up in the analyst, causing him to experience hatred. Finally, since hatred is not always pathological (Kernberg 1992) the therapist's hatred of his patient might also (either totally or in part) be at times rational. Indeed, Winnicott (1947) not only speaks of the therapist's justified hatred but also of the technical implications of such conceptualization. He proposes that

> in certain stages of certain analyses the analyst's hate is actually sought by the patient, and what is then needed is hate that is objective. If the patient seeks objective or justified hate he must be able to reach it, else he cannot feel he can reach objective love. [p. 199]

Winnicott bases this technical stance on his sense that a growing child can only believe in being loved after reaching being hated; here, he echoes Freud's (1913b) statement that "in the order of development hate is the precursor of love" (p. 325). Winnicott goes on to raise the matter of disclosure[34] of the analyst's hate to the patient.

> This is obviously a matter fraught with danger, and it needs the most careful timing. But I believe an analysis is incomplete if even towards the end it has not been possible for the analyst to tell the patient what he, the analyst, did unbeknown for the patient whilst he was ill, in the early stages. Until this interpretation is made the patient is kept to some extent in the position of infant—one who cannot understand what he owes to his mother. [p. 202]

The omission of the therapist's objective hatred and its ultimate revelation, guided by considerations of optimal distance (Akhtar 1992a, Bouvet 1958, Escoll 1992) and tact (Poland 1975), is noticeable in Kernberg's technical recommendations. Risking the "sin of repetition" (Kiell 1988, p. 2), I emphasize that the technical notions I have tried to highlight here are additive, *not* alternative, to what Kernberg suggests. The view of the patient's hatred as an activation of an early object relationship, the conceptualization of the therapist's hatred as a countertransference response, and the consistent focus on interpretation are enriched, not impoverished, by comparable attention to the defensive and adaptive aspects of the patient's hatred, the objective nature of the analyst's hatred, and the role of noninterpretive interventions during the treatment.

CONCLUDING REMARKS

> The different outcome in each individual is in the
> main the product of two varying factors: the strength
> of love and hate tendencies (the emotional forces

---

[34]Blum (1997) has recently raised questions about Winnicott's recommendation. His critique, especially of the handling of the particular case on which Winnicott's views are based, is well reasoned. Nonetheless, I believe that while the particular clinical example used by Winnicott might not have been the best for the purpose, the idea he was proposing does have merit.

in each of us) and the influence of environment
throughout life on each of us, these two factors
being in constant interaction from birth till death.
[Riviere 1937, p. 169]

While the preceding sections have addressed many significant
matters pertaining to hatred, three areas remain unaddressed. First,
there seems to be a lack of consensus regarding the degree of fixity or stability to hatred. While most contemporary analysts (Blum
1997, Kernberg 1992) emphasize the sustained nature of hatred,
Anna Freud (1972) held a different stance. She felt that while
libidinal aims are specific to the drive, aggressive aims associate
themselves with varying purposes. She also distinguished the two
drives in regard to the objects. Libidinal development proceeds
from a need-satisfying object through intermediate steps to object
constancy but aggression does not take this step toward sustained
commitment. The seemingly "fixed hate" (A. Freud 1972, p. 165)
of the paranoic is actually a vicissitude of libido rather than of
aggression.[35] According to Anna Freud, a good lover is faithful, a
good hater promiscuous.[36] How is this observation to be integrated
with the contemporary view of hatred as closely tied to a specific
object representation? Clearly, more thought is needed in this
realm.

Second, the antagonistic relationship between hatred and forgiveness needs to be fleshed out. Are there intermediary stages between the two extremes? Are there traumas that are unforgettable

---

[35]Blum's (1981) concept of the "inconstant object" is a contemporary elaboration of this "fixed hate" theme. It refers to an ambivalently loved object that is
felt as both persecutory and needed. It cannot be allowed to have a separate
existence. The threat of betrayal by it must be tenaciously maintained. In a sense,
such constant fear of persecution is the reciprocal of libidinal object constancy
and a desperate effort to preserve an illusory constant object.

[36]A social observation supporting the promiscuous nature of hatred is that
individuals with pronounced anti-Semitism also despise other ethnic minorities
(Adorno and Frenkel-Brunswick 1950). Significantly, a replication of this American study in India (Varma et al. 1973) revealed similar results regarding the
distribution of anti-Muslim attitudes.

and yet do not fuel sustained hatred? With what affects are they associated? What is the impact of hatred on memory and how do alterations in memory of past "reality" facilitate a move toward mourning, acceptance, and forgiveness? Kafka's (1992) view that we repeat not what we have repressed and cannot remember but what we remember in a particular rigid way is pertinent here. The technical implication of this proposal is that in order to overcome hatred we do not need recall of what has been forgotten but an amplification and revision of what is remembered. Volkan's (1987b, 1988) psychopolitical observations are also along the same lines. Rudolph and Rudolph (1993), in contrast, argue that memories of old hurts are often dredged up to create "ancient hatreds" out of contemporary socioeconomic conflicts.

In either case, the question remains as to how "unforgivable" traumas can be transformed into "nearly forgivable" or even "forgivable" traumas. Discussing this matter in a different context, I have suggested that acknowledgment, apology, and material and/or emotional reparation from the perpetrator *and* some taking of revenge by the victim helps in furthering the mourning of a very severe trauma (Akhtar 1995c). Revenge, though "politically incorrect," puts the victim's ego in an active position and changes the libido-aggression balance in the self-object relationship. The victim no longer remains passive, pure, and innocent, the perpetrator no longer the sole cruel party. These shifts succeed in reducing hatred, at times to the extent of permitting forgiveness. More clinical and sociological data, however, is needed to confirm or refute these hypotheses.

Finally, there is the issue of the so-called normal hatred. Kernberg (1992, 1995b), for one, states that hatred is not always pathological and, in those with normal superego integration, it "bridges over to the sublimatory function of courageous aggressive assertion in the service of commitment to ideals and ethical systems" (1992, p. 25). Others (e.g., Horowitz, in Winer 1994, Winnicott 1947) agree with the concept of "normal hatred." Indeed, Thomas Carlyle (1795–1881) cheerily quipped about "a healthy hatred of scoundrels," and Freud's lifelong "need for an enemy" (Gay 1988, p. 396) underscored the existential value of such hatred. Long

before both of them, Aristotle had already voiced a similar sentiment: "To enjoy the things we ought and to hate the things we
ought has the greatest bearing on excellent character" (Bartlett
1980, p. 87). More recently, Blum (1997) has observed that the
capacity to hate may facilitate self-assertion and individuation.
When not excessive and when not responded to by the caregiver's
counterhate, hatred can subserve the developmental process.

More clarity, however, is needed here. What really are the characteristics of this so-called normal hatred? Is the incapacity to feel
it pathological? Are there cross-cultural variations of it? Are there
developmental phases (e.g., adolescence) when hatred is more
"normal" than at other times (e.g., latency)? Winnicott (1947) does
talk about the structure-building role of objective hatred between
parents and children, but we need to know more about this "good
enough hate" (Harvey Rich, personal communication, December
1994)!

Actually more conceptual rigor and clinical documentation is
required in all three areas mentioned above, namely the fixity
or fluidity of hatred, the antagonistic relationship between hatred
and forgiveness, and the concept of normal hatred. With this I
come back full circle to the phenomenology, origins, and psychodynamics of hatred and to reiterate these issues now in an extremely
condensed form, I conclude with a brief quote from an unlikely
source. This quotation captures the complexity of the phenomena
under consideration. It hints at the traumatic origins of hatred, its
powerful rationalizations, the accompanying ego and superego
distortions, the mechanisms of splitting and projective identification, the affective and cognitive hell of paranoia, and the ultimately
self-destructive results of hatred. It was spoken by the late Richard
Nixon on August 9, 1974, the day he resigned in disgrace from the
presidency of the United States. Nixon said: "Others may hate you.
Those who hate you don't win unless you hate them. And then you
destroy yourself."

Part III

FRICTIONS

5

KOHUT
VERSUS KERNBERG

In a paper that is now considered a psychoanalytic classic, Stone (1954) discussed the "widening scope" of indications for psychoanalysis. He offered profound clinical insights regarding the rule of abstinence, resemblance as a necessary condition for transference development, variable degrees of deprivation in the analytic situation, modifications of technique with borderline cases, and, finally, legitimate transference gratifications to prevent undesirable severe regressions in sicker patients. Stone emphasized the need for detailed history taking and for carefully observing the patient's reactions to the examiner during the assessment of analyzability. He stated that psychoanalytic treatment should be supported by painstaking diagnosis and should not be used for "trivial or incipient or reactive illness, or in persons with feeble personality resources" (p. 593). However, he also emphasized that

> psychoanalysis may legitimately be invoked, and indeed *should* be invoked, for many very ill people, of good personality resources, who are probably inaccessible to cure by other methods, who are willing to accept the long travail of analysis, without guarantees of success. There is always a possibility of helping, where all other measures

fail. With the progressive understanding of the actions of psychotherapeutic admixtures or of large-scale "parameters" in the psychoanalytic method, now so largely intuitive in their application, we can
hope such successes will be more frequent. [pp. 593–594, italics
added]

Since the publication of Stone's paper in 1954, many outstanding psychoanalysts have enriched our understanding of this
widening scope of psychoanalysis. Two investigators who are the
most prominent, most theoretically influential, and, in some
ways, the most controversial in this group are Kohut and Kernberg.
Together, they have provided the much-needed rejuvenating stimulus to American psychoanalysis that had begun to experience
"a diminution of scientific productivity and a loss of intellectual
excitement" (Cooper 1983, p. 4). Both have occupied prominent
positions in the American and international psychoanalytic organizations. Both are regarded as enthusiastic teachers and charismatic lecturers. Both have presented significant emendations
of classical theory and in doing so have gathered followers and
opponents. Both have been, at various times, viewed as having fos-
tered cult-like social phenomena within the scientific community
of psychoanalysts and other mental health professionals (Calef and
Weinshel 1979, Cooper 1988). Both have addressed matters of
central concern to the British object relations theorists. Both, therefore, directly or indirectly, have spurred the current American
interest in examining the contributions of Klein, Fairbairn, Winnicott, Guntrip, Balint, and others. Both have made contributions
that extend beyond the restricted clinical domain. Both have written about aspects of "normal" psychology. Kohut has written of
appreciation of music (1957, Kohut and Levarie 1950), creativity
(1976), humor (1971, 1977), group psychology (1976), charisma
(1976), and wisdom (1971); Kernberg, of mature love (1976),
aging (1977a), leadership patterns (1978a, 1980), regression in
groups and organizations (1978a, 1980). Finally, both have stimulated work in applied psychoanalysis especially in the psychoanalytic
study of sociopolitical conflicts (GAP report 1978, Volkan 1980,
1986, Zonis 1980).

Despite these remarkable similarities, fundamental differences exist in the depth psychologies of Kohut and Kernberg. These differences are evident in their views on personality development, origins of psychopathology, and the nature of curative factors in psychoanalysis. The degree of their allegiance to general psychiatry is not the same, and they occupy different positions vis-à-vis "mainstream" psychoanalysis. In addition, they display a markedly different attitude toward the theoretical contributions of others. These three areas of difference—relationship to psychiatry, regard for others' contributions, and proximity to the classical theory—are amply exemplified (see Akhtar and Thomson 1982) in their writings on narcissistic personality disorder.

RELATIONSHIP TO GENERAL PSYCHIATRY

> Psychoanalysis, as a theory, research method, and more of treatment constitutes a major sector of the mental health field in general and psychiatry in particular. Its sector lies mainly in the psychological sphere and offers to psychiatry a theory basic to the understanding of psychopathology and psychotherapy. [Reiser, quoted in Altshuler 1979, p. 157]

> Recall that it was Freud himself who speculated (on clinical, psychological grounds) about the probable existence of sexual hormones, before they were generally discovered! Psychoanalysis has always had a place in the neuroscientific revolution. [Levin 1995, p. 539]

When 138 national psychiatric experts were asked (Strauss et al. 1984) to identify the top ten publications during 1970–1980 that they regarded to be seminal or of lasting value, their list included Kohut's two monographs (1971, 1977) and Kernberg's two collections of paper (1975b, 1976). As the article reporting this opinion survey was entitled "The Cutting Edge in Psychiatry" and as it appeared in the foremost psychiatric journal in the country, it is tempting to assume that Kohut and Kernberg have a similarly close relationship to psychiatry, and that the impact of their work on the field of general psychiatry is comparable. A closer inspection of their respective contributions, however, reveals the contrary.

Kohut (1971) specifically disavows "the traditional medical aim of achieving a diagnosis in which a disease entity is identified by clusters of recurring manifestations" (pp. 15–16). He declares his theory and the methods emanating from it to be "psychology through and through" (1982, p. 399). Kohut maintains the traditional psychoanalytic caution about psychiatric nosology. In the case of narcissistic personality disorder, for instance, he emphasizes that "the crucial diagnostic criterion is based not only on the evaluation of the presenting symptomatology or even of the life history, but on the nature of the spontaneously developing transference" (1971, p. 23). He places great emphasis on the analyst's empathic immersion in his patients' subjectivity, and his self psychology is devoted, almost in its entirety, to the elucidation of the narcissistic transferences and their ontogenetic antecedents in faulty parental empathy.

Kohut expresses much trepidation regarding psychoanalytic characterology as well. When he does describe various types of narcissistic personalities (Kohut and Wolf 1978), he uses labels that differ from customary psychiatric terminology. He does not attempt to correlate the merger-hungry and contact-shunning types, for instance, with borderline and schizoid personality disorders, respectively, thus missing an opportunity for his nosological eloquence to have a psychiatric counterpart. Moreover, Kohut is visibly less interested in the more severe end of the narcissistic-borderline spectrum. And, on the only occasion in his three monographs that he does mention medication, Kohut (1984) regards its mode of action as predominantly through its symbolic meanings to the patient.

Kohut's participation in the forums and publications of academic psychiatry is also minimal. A quick glance at the indexes of the *American Journal of Psychiatry* and *Archives of General Psychiatry* reveals no contribution from Kohut over the last thirty years (1951–1981) of his professional life. Finally, though Kohut was an enthusiastic teacher and an outstanding lecturer, he seldom participated in the annual American Psychiatric Association (APA) conventions and similar major psychiatric conferences (Paul Fink, personal communication).

In contrast, Kernberg has maintained a close affiliation with academic psychiatry. He is among the contributors (Kernberg 1975a) to the widely read *Comprehensive Textbook of Psychiatry-II* (Freedman et al. 1975). He participated editorially in the *American Psychiatric Association's 1982 Annual Review* (Grinspoon 1982) of psychiatry. His work, often in the form of collaborative participation in empirical research, has appeared in major psychiatric journals, for example, *Archives of General Psychiatry* (Koenigsberg et al. 1983), *Journal of Nervous and Mental Disease* (Kernberg et al. 1981), and the *American Journal of Psychiatry* (Selzer et al. 1987). In addition, Kernberg has frequently presented his ideas at the yearly APA conventions. He is a frequent examiner for the American Board of Psychiatry and Neurology. He reviews papers for the *American Journal of Psychiatry* and has published book reviews in that journal (e.g., Kernberg, 1988).

Kernberg's clinical concerns also overlap with those of general psychiatrists: borderline personality organization (1967); clinical features of narcissistic personality disorder (1974c); normal psychology of aging (1977a); diagnosis, prognosis, and intensive treatment of schizophrenic patients (1977b); distinctions between adolescent identity crisis and borderline identity diffusion (1978b); refinement of diagnostic interviewing techniques (1981); supportive psychotherapy (1982b); hospital management of patients with severe character pathology (1976, 1984); evaluation and management of chronically suicidal patients (1984); and the establishment of initial therapeutic contract with borderline patients (Selzer et al. 1987).[37]

---

[37]This last mentioned work has been extended to form a monograph (Kernberg et al. 1989) and has also spurred another book on this subject (Yeomans et al. 1992).

Kernberg's nosologic terminology frequently matches customary psychiatric language. When he uses a term differently from its
current psychiatric usage, he clarifies his stance. This is manifest
in his distinguishing between *hysterical* and *histrionic* personalities
(Kernberg 1985); even his adopting the *histrionic* label for what he
would have earlier (Kernberg 1967) referred to as "infantile" personality is accommodation to the mainstream psychiatric nosology.
On the other hand, he unhesitatingly points out omissions of entities he deems valid, for example, hypomanic (Akhtar 1988a) and
as-if (Deutsch 1942) personalities, from the current "official" psychiatric classification. Rather than summarily ignoring *DSM-III*
(American Psychiatric Association 1980) a document with pervasive impact on general psychiatry, Kernberg (1984) critically evalu-
ates it. Finally, he includes psychotropic medications, and even
electroconvulsive therapy (ECT), as valid treatment modalities, the
effect of which he does not readily reduce to their symbolically encoded significance alone.

The degree to which Kohut's and Kernberg's work has been
assimilated by general psychiatrists also varies. Kohut's self psychology has been the subject of a lead article (Baker and Baker 1987)
in the official APA journal. Kernberg's work has not warranted such
en bloc introduction, perhaps because it has already become more
diffusely assimilated. Blashfield and McElroy (1987), for instance,
report that Kernberg is the second most frequently cited author
and the most frequently cited psychoanalyst in the current psychiatric literature on personality disorders.

In summary, Kohut and Kernberg seem to occupy considerably
different positions vis-à-vis mainstream academic psychiatry. Kohut
has little to do with the forums, perspectives, terminology, and
preoccupations of general psychiatry, whereas Kernberg is intimately involved with all these aspects. A brief digression, however,
is necessary before discussing whether this difference has affected
the psychoanalytic aspect of Kohut's and Kernberg's work. The
relationship between academic psychiatry and psychoanalysis has
been, since Freud's day, a confusing and ambiguous one. Freud's
alienation from academic medicine and its complex historical rea-

sons have been amply documented (Jones 1953). Less well re-membered is Freud's (1919) recommendation that psychoanaly-sis should play a prominent role in medical school curricula. He stated that teaching psychoanalysis to medical students would im-press upon them "the significance of mental factors in the differ-ent vital functions as well as in illnesses and their treatment" and would afford them "a preparation for the study of psychiatry" (pp. 171–172). Although Freud emphasized that such a didactic curriculum would not equip general psychiatrists to practice clini-cal psychoanalysis, he believed an important purpose would still be served if they learned "something about psychoanalysis and something *from* it" (p. 173).

Since Freud made his comments, much literature has accumu-lated underscoring the importance of psychoanalysts' involve-ment in academic psychiatry (Altshuler 1979, A. Freud 1966, Gitelson 1962a, Meissner 1976, Potter and Klein 1951, Strassman et al. 1976). Most authors agree that a continued involvement of psychoanalysts in academic psychiatry is indeed desirable.[38] Ana-lysts provide a balanced ambience in the departments of psychia-try and, in their teaching role, serve as significant professional ego ideals for psychiatric residents. Such involvement positively influences the latters' applying for psychoanalytic training (Strass-man et al. 1976). Even the residents who choose nonanalytic careers find it valuable to be exposed to teachers who can help them connect their patients' manifest symptomatology with its underlying unconscious motivations. This involvement enhances their capacity for clinical understanding and wins informed friends for psychoanalysis within psychiatry at large. These con-siderations have acquired even greater importance in the current climate of narrow biological overenthusiasm in psychiatry and the dwindling candidate pool for psychoanalytic training. Active in-

---

[38]This is not to deny that significant practical barriers may exist for a practic-ing psychoanalyst to establish or maintain an academic career in psychiatry. That these barriers come from both the analytic institutes and the medical schools is recognized by many prominent psychoanalysts (Altshuler 1979).

volvement with psychiatric departments does pose challenging demands for psychoanalysts, but the potential impact they thus have on future professionals may outweigh the sacrifices and hardships involved.

Another question that has received less attention, however, needs to be answered before one wholeheartedly endorses continued psychiatric involvement on the psychoanalyst's part. This question pertains to the impact a general psychiatric involvement has on the psychoanalyst's analytic work ego.[39] On one hand, it can be argued that the ideal for which a psychoanalyst should strive is exclusive dedication to psychoanalytic practice and teaching. Such focused immersion, the argument continues, is the best way to sharpen one's analytic work ego, avoid nosological superficialities, strengthen theoretical rigor, and maintain professional identity as a psychoanalyst. On the other hand, it can be argued that seeing a large number of patients, providing consultation to people with varying degrees and types of psychopathology, interacting with medical colleagues, and remaining open to challenges to psychoanalysis from newer developments in psychiatry may widen the psychoanalyst's perspective. Whether such a broadening of perspective strengthens or weakens the analyst's analytic identity would then depend on a complex set of factors, which may range beyond merely his psychiatric involvement. These factors may include, among others, the genuineness of his interest in psychoanalysis to begin with, his maintenance of an analytic practice, and, above all, his self-analyzing capacity.

Returning from this digression specifically to Kohut and Kernberg, one would think that if involvement in psychiatry were indeed detrimental to an analyst's dedication to psychoanalysis, Kernberg would suffer more. Kohut's work would deepen its anchor in psychoanalytic theory, and Kernberg's approach would loosen its moorings, become detached from depth psychology. Actually, the opposite seems to be the case. However, before dis-

---

[39]The lively and informative dialogue between Charles Brenner and Robert Michels during the 1987 fall meetings of the American Psychoanalytic Association in New York sharply elucidated the two sides of this argument.

cussing their positions vis-à-vis classical theory and technique, I will highlight their attitudes toward the significant, related contributions of other psychoanalysts.

REGARD FOR THE THEORETICAL CONTRIBUTIONS OF PREDECESSORS AND CONTEMPORARIES

> The theoretical model he has developed often strikingly resembles the work of other relational model theorists. These similarities are never openly addressed or considered by Kohut, who presents himself as if he were working in a vacuum, continually breaking new ground. [Greenberg and Mitchell 1983, p. 366]

> Kernberg has created the most comprehensive object relations theory of development, psychopathology, and treatment yet developed. . . . No other theorist has succeeded so well in synthesizing the work of Jacobson, Mahler, and Klein and in integrating object relations theory with the structural concepts and technical principles of ego psychology. [Summers 1994, pp. 237–238]

Kohut has been criticized repeatedly for not acknowledging antecedent theoretical ideas that are reflected in his self psychology (Bacal 1987, Rothstein 1980, Stein 1979). I myself have earlier elaborated this tendency in Kohut's writings (Akhtar 1988b). He implies originality in presenting ideas that clearly existed in earlier literature. For instance, in emphasizing the powerful impact of maternal care on the developing psychic structure of the child, Kohut disregards Freud's deep awareness of this matter. Not only did Freud (1923) recognize the significance of the real nature of early objects to the development of ego, he also explicitly emphasized the "mother's importance, unique, without parallel, established unalterably for a whole lifetime as the first and strongest love-object and as the prototype of all later love relations—for both sexes" (Freud 1940, p. 188). Kohut does not acknowledge Freud's profound statement. He also ignores Hartmann (1939, 1952a), who had further highlighted the complex interplay of instinctual drives and early object relationships underlying ego development. Even more striking in this context is Kohut's stance toward Mahler's work. In his first monograph (1971), Kohut condemns Mahler with faint praise and then dismisses her developmental observations as belonging in a sociobiological framework outside "the core area of psychoanalytic metapsychology" (p. 219). In his second monograph (1977), the acknowledgment of Mahler's work is limited to the mention of her name in the book's preface. The entire body of research on separation-individuation (Mahler 1968, 1972a,b,c, Mahler et al. 1975) is thus ignored, and so is its careful elaboration of the importance of the "optimal emotional availability" (Mahler 1972a, p. 410) of the mother to her growing infant.

Kohut's disregard of earlier contributions is even more evident when it comes to British object relations theorists: Fairbairn, Winnicott, Guntrip, and Balint. Fairbairn is not widely read in this country, and under different circumstances his omission might have gone unnoticed. Kohut's conceptual debt to Fairbairn, however, is greater than can be comfortably denied. Robbins (1980), in a paper suggesting that the current Kernberg–Kohut controversy is an outgrowth of the earlier Klein–Fairbairn schism, lists the similarities between Fairbairn and Kohut. Both underemphasize the pleasure principle and instinctual drives, especially inborn aggression. Both regard a pristine, whole self to exist from the beginning, and both view its growth to depend more on satisfactory object relations than on libidinal gratification. Both believe that disappointments in the primary object lead to regressive autoerotic fragmentation and drive supremacy. Both view regression as a separate pathway, not a reversal of developmental steps previously taken. Moreover, as Bacal (1987) points out, Kohut's (1977) description of "self-state dreams" (p. 109)—dreams that are not wish fulfillments but straightforward depictions of the current psychological condition of the self—is a near replica of Fairbairn's (1944) earlier concept of "state-of-affairs dreams." In view of these remarkable similarities, it is disturbing to note the absence of Fairbairn's (1952a) work from all three Kohut monographs (1971, 1977, 1984).

Winnicott receives a similar treatment. His concepts of "true" and "false" selves (Winnicott 1960a) closely parallel Kohut's notions (1977) of the joyful "nuclear self" and the "compensatory structures" elaborated to mask defects in the self. Winnicott suggests that the "false self" is a caretaker of the withdrawn "true self" and that it searches for optimal human circumstances in which the latter may come into its own. Kohut attributes a similar function to drive activity in general; drives are enlisted in an attempt to bring about a selfobject relationship that would repair the injured self. Both Winnicott (1965) and Kohut (1977) see psychopathology as a result of environmental failure. Both emphasize the "holding" rather than psychosexual gratification aspect of the maternal care. Even the mirror metaphor popularized by Kohut was mentioned earlier by Winnicott (1967); he describes the role the mother plays in mirroring the child's self to the child and the deleterious effects of chronically deficient mirroring on the child's growing personality. Finally, Kohut (1977) suggests that the mother not only needs to enthusiastically reflect her growing child's grandiosity, but also to gradually shift her responsiveness to increasingly age-specific tasks and skills. Winnicott (1953) similarly states that the "mother's main task (next to providing opportunity for illusion) is disillusionment" (p. 95; author's parenthesis). Despite these overlaps in their outlook, Kohut makes no mention of Winnicott except in an inconsequential footnote in his 1971 monograph.

Guntrip is not even mentioned, though there are many similarities (Bacal 1987) between his and Kohut's views. Guntrip's (1969) description of the fundamental human anxiety as the fear of the loss of ego itself is akin to Kohut's (1977) later description of the "disintegration anxiety" (p. 104) or the feared anticipation of the breakup of the self. Guntrip, like Kohut, speaks of the self as the most meaningful psychic constellation. Moreover, both of them suggest that instinctual conflicts are themselves defenses against more basic, self-related anxieties. Finally, Guntrip's theory of therapy, with its emphasis on regrowth of the personal self, is strikingly similar to Kohut's view in this regard.

Kohut's attitude toward Balint is a curious one. In his 1971 monograph, he dissociated himself from Balint's views. He stated that he wished to "remain faithful to the classical formulation" of primary narcissism and could not impute to "the very young child . . . the capacity for even rudimentary forms of object-love" (p. 220). Kohut was thus criticizing Balint's (1937) concept of "primary love." However, as Bacal (1987) has convincingly argued, "primary love" is not really an object-instinctual concept at all and is in essence similar to Kohut's (1977) own later formulation of infantile selfobject tie. One therefore expected that, in his second monograph, Kohut would reassess Balint and discuss what now appeared to be a great similarity between their ontogenetic formulations. He does not do so.[40]

Kohut also ignores those contemporary investigators who present evidence contradictory to his theses. Certain aspects of Mahler's work and the object relations theories of Jacobson (1964) and Kernberg (1975b, 1976) belong in this category of omissions. Finally, Kohut makes little effort to correlate his developmental scheme with the data of infant observational research. He barely mentions Spitz (1965) and completely ignores Bergman and Escalona (1949), Lustman (1956), Thomas et al. (1963, 1968), Emde et al. (1976), and Stern (1976), to name just a few. Some of these data could put to considerable test the purely environmental view of the development of self and its psychopathology as espoused by Kohut and his followers.

Kernberg's theoretical formulations and suggested treatment techniques have also had their share of critical evaluation and disagreements (Atkin 1975, Calef and Weinshel 1979, Holzman 1976, Klein and Tribich 1981, Segal 1981). While many of Kernberg's critics disagree with his interpretation of earlier literature, not one has suggested that he does not pay enough attention to others' contributions. Calef and Weinshel (1979), even in their pervasive disagreement with Kernberg, acknowledge that he has attempted to incorporate the views of "object relations theory, Kleinian theory, ego psychology theory, the developmental approach, Bionian theory, and probably others as well" (p. 473). Brenner

---

[40]For a more sympathetic comment upon the Balint–Kohut connection, see Ornstein (1992).

(1976a) states that Kernberg, as compared with other object relations theorists is "the most scientifically conscientious." Klein and Tribich (1981), while sharply questioning some of Kernberg's interpretations of the earlier literature, implicitly acknowledge that he has extensively cited Freud, Hartmann, Jacobson, Fairbairn, Guntrip, Bowlby, and Winnicott, among others. The only omission they find is Balint. However, their review does not include Kernberg's 1980 book, which does refer to Balint's contributions in a meaningful way.

Kernberg (1980) openly acknowledges his conceptual gratitude to his predecessors. He states that "some of Fairbairn's ideas have contributed to my own thinking"[41] (p. 68) and that Jacobson's work (1964) has had a "profound influence" (p. 85) on his theoretical formulations. This willingness to acknowledge important others while maintaining a thoughtful distance is evident in Kernberg's having provided detailed, separate evaluations of Klein's, Fairbairn's, and Jacobson's theoretical achievements. Moreover, he has attempted to correlate his own reconstructive hypotheses with Mahler's developmental theory (Kernberg 1980) and his metapsychological formulations regarding instincts and affects with new findings in such fields as ethology, neurophysiology, general learning theory, and psychophysiology of affect (Kernberg 1976). It therefore appears that when it comes to others' contributions, Kernberg shows much greater acknowledgment and gratitude than does Kohut. Ironically, Kernberg (1975b) even acknowledges that he has borrowed the term *grandiose self* from Kohut, although he uses it with a different etiologi-

---

[41]Fairbairn has influenced Kohut and Kernberg in different ways. Kohut (1977) has elaborated on Fairbairn's (1952a) environmental or "external" emphasis, that is, the actual role of early caregivers, minimization of the pleasure principle, a view of aggression as only a reaction to frustration, and consideration of drives and the Oedipus complex as strategies for maintaining a cohesive self. Kernberg (1975b, 1976, 1980), on the other hand, has been more influenced by Fairbairn's (1944, 1952a) endopsychic or "internal" focus, that is, the early dyadic internalizations, mechanism of splitting and the necessary coexistence of self and object representations in early internalizations.

cal formulation. This brings us to a comparison of their respective positions regarding classical psychoanalysis.

RELATIONSHIP TO
MAINSTREAM PSYCHOANALYSIS

> As did Adler, Rank, and Jung before him, for example, Kohut has renamed his depth psychology, reassessed the value system and scientific status of psychoanalysis, redefined the psychic elements of interest to depth psychology, and revised the technical procedures of the treatment of patients. [Cooper 1983, p. 8]

> Kernberg has devoted a great deal of effort to positioning himself within the evolving tradition of the drive/structure model. [Greenberg and Mitchell 1983, p. 327]

Kohut's involvement with classical psychoanalysis can be divided into three phases: the "classical" phase, the "transitional" phase, and the "radical" phase. In the first phase, he operated within the bounds of the classical theory. His technique was directed by its framework, and he made significant contributions (Kohut 1957, 1964, Kohut and Levarie 1950) from within this perspective. Kohut was recognized as an outstanding teacher and clinician. He vigorously participated in the activities of the American Psychoanalytic Association and was elected its president in 1964. He also served as vice president of the International Psychoanalytic Association from 1965 to 1973 and as vice president of the Sigmund Freud Archives from 1971 to 1981. Then, he gradually began to question the theory and technique of classical psychoanalysis.

A transitional phase of Kohut's theory building followed, culminating in the publication of his 1971 monograph. The innovations introduced there by Kohut were still, though with already palpable conceptual discomfort, within the framework of classical drive theory. The concept of "narcissistic libido" (Kohut 1971), for instance, was, on the one hand, an accommodation to the classical drive model and, on the other, a significant departure from it.

It invokes such concepts as narcissism, libido, and cathexis, and quantitative, economic factors, while at the same time bifurcating Freud's libido theory into two independent developmental lines, one leading to object love and the other to healthy self-regard. This transitional phase constituted what Kohut (1977) later referred to as "psychology of the self in the narrow sense of the term" (p. 207). It regarded the self as content of the mental apparatus, that is, as mental representations within the id, ego, and superego.

The transitional phase was followed by the final, "radical" phase, in which Kohut (1977) proposed the self psychology in its "broad sense" (p. 207), that is, in a sense that views the self as a superordinate constellation with the drives and defenses of its constituents. With this shift, Kohut's language also underwent a noticeable change. What he had earlier termed grandiose self, idealized parent imago, transmuting internalization, and narcissistic transferences (Kohut 1971), now became nuclear goals, nuclear ambitions, selective inclusion, and selfobject transferences (Kohut 1977). Narcissism became synonymous with self; the tripartite structure was discarded, and, as Rothstein (1980) points out, "analysis" (Kohut 1971) became "restoration" (Kohut 1977). The tone of his last paper (Kohut 1982), with pervasive first-person beginnings, poignant feelings of his having struggled more or less alone, haughty dismissal of the influential theoretician Hartmann, portrayal of instinctual drive as a "vague and insipid biological concept" (p. 401), and a desire for "decisive scientific action" (p. 398), befits more a pioneer of a new school rather than a major collaborator with psychoanalysis.[42] Kohut's break with classical theory here is clearly in sight. "Self psychology has freed itself from the distorted view of psychological man espoused by traditional analysis" (Kohut 1982, p. 402).[43]

---

[42]The prose of this paper has an almost uncanny and, given its contents, ironical resemblance to Freud's style of writing.

[43]Five years before this triumphant declaration, Kohut (1977) had reproached Schafer, whose theoretical contributions he praised, for not taking into account "the need for gradualness in theory change if the psychoanaltyic 'group self' is to be preserved" (p. 85). Could it be that Kohut was, at the same time, restraining his own pioneering spirit?

Kernberg's relationship with mainstream psychoanalysis is less surgically divisible into phases, although it appears that he has followed an opposite trajectory from Kohut. Initially, he was regarded as somewhat of an "outsider"[44] who was presenting a "loose theoretical amalgam [which] does conceptual violence both to the old theory and the new product" (Calef and Weinshel 1979, p. 473). His theory was criticized for glossing over thought processes in psychic life (Holzman 1976). His nosological clarifications were regarded as unrealistically precise (Segal 1981) and "atomistic distinctions" (Calef and Weinshel 1979, p. 477). He was seen as blurring the distinction between psychoanalysis and psychotherapy, overemphasizing the role of pregenital factors, especially pregenital aggression, and giving undue importance to "the real activity and care of the early introjected objects in toto, particularly the mother" (Calef and Weinshel 1979, p. 488).[45] With the passage of time, which diluted the impact of his introducing some Kleinian concepts into the mainstream theory, and also with Kernberg's (1975a, 1979, 1980) thorough presentations of his agreements and disagreements with his predecessors and contemporaries, as well

---

[44]Kernberg's having been trained in Chile and thus not having "grown" in organized American psychoanalysis may also have facilitated this impression.

[45]Kernberg's harshest critics (Klein and Tribich 1981), on the other hand, state that "his object-relations theory is essentially oblivious to the infant's external world" (p. 31). How can these two diametrically opposed interpretations of Kernberg's position be reconciled? In my opinion, while Kernberg's focus is on endopsychic structures, he overlooks neither the constitutional nor the environmental roots of their development and distortion in health and psychopathology. Two quotations from his ample elaboration of this matter illustrate my point. Writing about pregenital aggression, Kernberg (1976) states,

> The inborn determinants of economic factors (that is, the intensity of the affective, behavioral, and other neurophysiological components which enter into aggressively determined internalized object relations, and general affective and cognitive thresholds) *together with* environmental influences crucially contribute to the organization of the aggressive drive. [p. 118, italics added]

Or, "excessive aggression may stem *both* from a constitutionally determined intensity of aggressive drives or from severe early frustration" (Kernberg 1975b, p. 28, italics added).

as with his increasing attention to the complex interplay of drives, affects, ego capacities, and maturational factors in early structure formation (Kernberg 1976, 1985), he came to be regarded as more of an "insider." For many years, Kernberg served as associate editor of the *Journal of the American Psychoanalytic Association,* and in 1996 he was elected president of the International Psychoanalytic Association; both achievements clearly indicate that he is regarded highly by prominent mainstream psychoanalysts.[46] Indeed, "there is probably no psychoanalytic author more widely read or quoted in the world today" (Wallerstein 1986, p. 711) both within and outside of specifically psychoanalytic circles, than Kernberg. Wallerstein (1986) believes that Kernberg's secure eminence in this regard is, in part, because he

> has not encouraged a revisionist movement in the sense of a new "school" or new (and different) overall psychology for psychoanalysis, nor has one developed in the sense, for example, that Kohut's self psychology has become a new psychology confronting psychoanalysis with a different overall mental paradigm. Kernberg has unswervingly seen his contribution as squarely within the edifice of classical psychoanalysis, trying to integrate two of its major emphases, the American ego-psychological and the British object-relational, within one coherent schema to be sure, but in that sense only additive and synthesizing, not divisive or cultish. And here history seems to have borne him out and allayed the concern expressed seven years ago by Calef and Weinshel. [p. 714]

It is with such a historical backdrop that a comparison of Kohut's and Kernberg's respective positions regarding major concepts of classical psychoanalysis is most useful. Such a comparison should ideally include their respective views on a variety of theoretical and

---

[46]A similar reconciliatory stance toward the latter-day Kohut also is already in evidence (Bacal 1987, Bach 1985, Pine 1985, Wallerstein 1983). This is not only a reflection on the contemporary vulnerability of the psychoanalytic profession, which can ill afford further splits within its ranks, but, on the positive side, shows a spirit of greater flexibility and maturation within psychoanalytic theorizing.

technical matters. Since such an all-encompassing review is not possible here, I will select only two matters to compare the views of Kohut and Kernberg: the concept of conflict and the Oedipus complex. I will discuss their technical contributions in the section on narcissistic personality, below.

Conflict

Intrapsychic conflict is central to the structural model of the mind, and psychoanalysis has prototypically been a psychology of conflict. In Kris's (1947) famous aphoristic definition, the subject matter of psychoanalysis is nothing but "human behavior viewed as conflict" (p. 6). Brenner (1976b, 1982) provides a more current, detailed statement of the same fundamental theme, and there remains a broad consensus among psychoanalysts that the concept of conflict is basic to the understanding and treatment of psychopathology. The inevitability, even desirability, of frustration and conflict in the maturation and development of the self is also a view peacefully adhered to by most analysts.

In contrast, Kohut's self psychology proposes that, under optimal circumstances, the origins of the self are free of conflict.[47] Moreover, Kohut (Kohut and Wolf 1978) suggests that the "primary disturbances of the self," including psychoses, borderline states, narcissistic behavior disorders, and narcissistic personality disorders, are not manifestations of intrapsychic conflict but of a state of psychological deficit. Such a stance, besides causing a major rupture in the historical continuity of the psychoanalytic emphasis on conflict from Freud to Brenner, also leaves many of Kohut's own clini-

---

[47]Among Kohut's followers, Tolpin (1980) makes this point most emphatically. She distinguishes "Mahler's baby" from "Kohut's baby" (p. 51) and suggests that while Mahler viewed conflict to be inherent in psychic development and growth of the child, Kohut proposed that, given optimal parental responsiveness, the growing child is internally conflict-free. In this view, any conflict experienced during development is already pathological. Clearly, this position is fundamentally different from the traditional psychoanalytic viewpoint in which Mahler's theory is deeply anchored.

cal observations unexplained. For instance, is there no potential conflict between grandiose and idealizing aspirations? Do the grandiose beliefs about the self not contradict the more realistic, conscious assessments of the self? Does the patient not experience any tension between his narcissistic wishes and his later-acquired moral prohibitions? If the "contact-shunning" personalities (Kohut and Wolf 1978) avoid social interaction out of fear of their intense longings, then are their need for others and their avoidance of them not in conflict with each other?[48] One possible reason for the negation of conflict by Kohut's self psychology may be that the word *conflict* is being extremely narrowly defined. Almost exclusively (Kohut 1977), an intrapsychic conflict is equated with a structural or intersystemic conflict. This overlooks other varieties of intrapsychic conflicts. There is intrapsychic conflict (A. Freud 1965) between different instinctual tendencies or conflicted ego impulses or contradictory identifications in the superego. There is also object relations conflict (Dorpat 1976), which involves a less differentiated psychic structure that is antecedent to id-ego-superego differentiation. The subject with an object relations conflict experiences the conflict as between his own wishes and his internalized representations of another person's values. This is in contrast to a person with a structural conflict, who experiences both vectors of the quandary as belonging to his own self. This manner of conceptualizing various types of intrapsychic conflict is consonant with the hierarchical model of mind proposed by Gedo and Goldberg

---

[48]Such a clarifying attempt can be derided as phenomenological hair-splitting and taking the word *conflict* too literally. It could appear to ignore that psychoanalytic thought has been moving in the direction of a more object relations type of theory in keeping with our greater understanding of the initial dyad and its many reverberations, and that there is, as a consequence, a kind of political conservative vs. progressive aspect to the conflict–deficit debate. "Conflict" has come to stand for oedipal, neurotic conflict and not an internal psychic struggle alone, and "deficit" implies preoedipal or dyadic, while not excluding the existence of intrapsychic struggle of forces. It should therefore be emphasized that the choice here to sharply define the word *conflict* is purposive and not based on ignorance of its unfortunate, political buzz-word significance.

(1973). Their design allows for a tripartite model at a higher developmental level and an object relations model at a lower developmental level. This view is also supported by Greenspan's (1977) correlation of "internal object constancy" (Mahler and Furer 1968) with structural conflicts and lack of such constancy with object relations conflicts.

Kohut, however, insists on a conflict-deficit dichotomy. This "puzzling and . . . fundamentally unhelpful" (Wallerstein 1983, p. 37) dichotomy has led to the creation of the reified psychological postulates of the "tragic man" and the "guilty man" (Kohut 1977). "Tragic man" is a person with a psychological deficit, who is struggling to maintain cohesion of his fragmenting self, and "guilty man" refers to one battling with his prohibited sexual and aggressive longings. This dichotomy, however, leads to an artificial separation of preoedipal and oedipal development. I have suggested elsewhere (Akhtar 1984b) that the tragic man is no less guilty than guilty man; the tragic man's guilt emanates from his pregenital sadism toward the parental objects and from a sense of having taken too much from the mother and depleted her. Similarly, the guilty man is no less tragic than the tragic man insofar as the source of his guilt is his incestuous and patricidal fantasies (but not acts), wishes that emanated from within him with the unfolding of a constitutional blueprint beyond his control, and a family structure not of his choosing. What is more tragic than to punish oneself for one's own thoughts? The artificial dichotomy of the tragic man and the guilty man oversimplifies human experience, ignores genetic spirality, overlooks the "principle of multiple function" (Waelder 1936), and produces unnecessary and unfortunate duplicity in psychoanalytic technique.

In contrast to Kohut, Kernberg does not posit a deficit-conflict dichotomy. He regards the classical structural neuroses as a symptomatic counterpart of the "higher level" character organization where "defensive operations against unconscious *conflicts* center on repression" (Kernberg 1976, p. 143, italics added). On the "lower level" too, that is, among people in the borderline range of psychopathology, Kernberg (1970a) sees the compromised ego capacities to be the result of an intrasystemic conflict. This is the conflict of ambivalence whereby predominantly aggressively derived self and object representations are defensively kept apart from libidinally derived self and object representations in order to protect a safe ego core and to avoid the anxiety emanating from the potential destruction of any internalized goodness. Such conditions, according to Kernberg (1976), are characterized by a "pathological condensation of pregenital and genital *conflicts* with predominance of pregenital aggression" (p. 146, italics added). Also, in accordance with classical psychoanalytic perspective, Kernberg regards intrapsychic conflict as a necessary and inevitable aspect of mental life and not merely an unfortunate by-product of faulty parental responsiveness to the growing child. However, it is simplistic to leave things at this level alone. The fact remains that conflict, defined as the dynamic struggle of internal forces, is clearly evident in Kohut's descriptions of patients; and deficit, defined as inadequacy of libidinal internalizations, is implicit in Kernberg's portrayal of severe character pathology. This is not surprising. Indeed this is to be expected since

in the flow and flux of analytic clinical material we are always in the world of "both/and." We deal constantly, and in turn, both with the oedipal where there is a coherent self, and the preoedipal, where there may not yet be; with defensive regressions and with developmental arrests; with defensive transferences and defensive resistances and with recreations of earlier traumatic and traumatized states. [Wallerstein 1983, p. 31]

Since this is true, what is all the fuss about? I believe that it has to do with whether intrapsychic conflict is seen as primary and hence causative of whatever deficits or defects might exist in a given psychic structure or whether a primary deficit model is proposed that pushes intrapsychic conflict aside, rendering it only an epiphenomenon. Kernberg's views belong in the first category, and Kohut's in the second. The former fits in better without the usual understanding of psychoanalytic theory and practice.

The Oedipus Complex

During his "classical" phase, Kohut accepted the traditional view of the nature and significance of the Oedipus complex. In his "transitional" phase, too, he retained a significant place for oedipal conflicts, though he separated narcissistic libido from object libido and assigned narcissistic issues a parallel, equal importance. In a clinically astute observation Kohut (1971) emphasized that the

> following relationships may exist between the phallic-oedipal structures in which the child's wounded narcissism plays only a secondary role, and the narcissistic structures (phallic and prephallic) which are the leading pathogenic determinants of a narcissistic transference. (1) Either (a) the narcissistic or (b) the object-transference pathology is clearly predominant; (2) a dominant narcissistic fixation coexists with an important object-transference pathology; (3) a manifestly narcissistic disorder hides a nuclear oedipal conflict; and (4) a narcissistic personality disorder is covered by manifestly oedipal structures. [pp. 154–155]

Kohut suggested that late in the analysis of even the narcissistic pathology, an oedipal situation may emerge that "must be dealt with analytically as in the case of a typical primary transference neurosis" (p. 155). Later, Kohut (1977) added that such oedipal constellations were a result of a consolidation of the self never before achieved. They were therefore "new, . . . not a transference repetition" (p. 228). Reconstructing from the joy of his patients in arriving at such an experience, Kohut portrayed the childhood oedipal phase itself in a glowing manner. However, this positive emphasis led him to locate the origin of oedipal conflict differently from classical theory. The conflict does not originate in the child's stimulating, contradictory, and unrealistic strivings themselves. It results from unempathic parents who see the constituents of the child's oedipal aspirations in isolation and therefore cause their intensification. A second departure from classical theory was Kohut's related proposal that "the Oedipus complex of classical analysis that we take to be a ubiquitous human experience is . . . already the manifestation of a pathological development" (p. 246).

Moreover, with his progressive move toward self psychology, Kohut's view of the Oedipus complex became increasingly "sanitized." Little mention is found in his writings of penis, vagina, urinary stream pleasure, infantile theories of childbirth, penis envy, primal scene, castration fears, and the like. Most important, Kohut's approach to the oedipal phase does not genuinely recognize the triadic, as against dyadic, nature of relationships typical of this phase. Even the Odysseus myth, which Kohut (1982) finally proposed as the centerpiece of his theory and by which he wished to replace the centrality of the Oedipus complex, is essentially a dyadic parable.

Kernberg, in contrast, recognizes the Oedipus complex as a landmark developmental event. Although his interest is clearly in the "prehistory of the Oedipus complex" (Freud 1925), Kernberg does not question the essential nature of the conflict as portrayed by classical psychoanalysis. His classification of character pathology (1970a) includes a category of "higher level" organization displaying solely or predominantly oedipal-phase conflicts. This group of disorders, including hysterical, obsessional, and some depressive-masochistic personalities, is seen by Kernberg as an ego-syntonic counterpart to the respective, classical symptom neuroses. Kernberg (1978b, 1980) discusses the vicissitudes of oedipal resurgence during adolescence and during middle age. Finally, in his descriptions of borderline and narcissistic characters, Kernberg (1967, 1975b) emphasizes the pathognomonic condensation of oedipal and pre-oedipal conflicts under the overriding influence of pregenital aggression. He points out that intense oedipal strivings may prematurely develop in a child to deny frustrated oral dependent needs. Kernberg emphasizes that such development powerfully reinforces oedipal fears by pregenital fears of the mother. Under these circumstances, a positive Oedipus complex is seriously interfered with. Adult sexuality is then characterized by either sexualized dependency or prominent negative oedipal trends. These manifest in greedy promiscuity and orally derived homosexuality among men, and, among women, in an intensified penis envy, flight into promiscuity to deny penis envy, or a sexualized search for the gratification of oral needs from an idealized mother, leading to homosexuality. Obviously, the differences Kohut and Kernberg have in their views of the Oedipus complex reflect their overall positions vis-à-vis classical psychoanalysis. These differences are further manifested in their approach to narcissistic personality disorder.

VIEWS ON THE NARCISSISTIC PERSONALITY

> Many analysts feel that the contributions of Kernberg and Kohut are significant and creative as well as contradictory. Analysts attempt to integrate and preserve the contributions of both authors. Yet each seems limited in certain respects, and that the two are often contradictory contributes to confusion. [Rothstein 1978, p. 904]

> Both Kernberg and Kohut agree on the importance of maternal responsiveness and warmth for the development of healthy self-representations. Kernberg, however, places far greater emphasis on the pathological role of rage in the genesis of narcissistic pathology. [Cooper 1984, p. 45]

Phenomenology

Kohut (1971) emphasizes that the diagnosis of narcissistic personality depends less on observable behavior than on the spontaneously evolving mirror and idealizing transferences during the psychoanalytic treatment of such patients. However, he does acknowledge that a person with a narcissistic personality disorder frequently presents the following clinical features:

(1) in the sexual sphere: perverse fantasies, lack of interest in sex; (2) in the social sphere: work inhibitions, inability to form and maintain significant relationships, delinquent activities; (3) in his manifest personality features: lack of humor, lack of empathy for other people's needs and feelings, lack of a sense of proportion, tendency towards attacks of uncontrolled rage, pathological lying; and (4) in the psychosomatic sphere: hypochondriacal preoccupa-

tions with physical and mental health, vegetative disturbances in various organ systems. [p. 23]

Although profoundly angry reactions had been associated with narcissistic personality by many earlier observers (e.g., Nemiah 1961, Reich 1933), Kohut (1972) describes such a tendency in eloquent detail. The central features of narcissistic rage are the need for revenge—the undoing of hurt by whatever means—and a compulsion in this pursuit, with utter disregard for reasonable limits. The irrationality of this vengeful attitude is frightening because reasoning is not only intact but sharpened. Another affective feature, in the description of which Kohut anticipated Grunberger (1975), Bach (1977), and Svrakic (1985), involves the narcissistic person's tendency toward hypomanic exaltation. Kohut portrayed it as an anxious excitement, sometimes associated with trancelike ecstasy and near-religious feelings of transcendence. This emotion is often precipitated by favorable occurrences in reality that stir up the narcissist's as yet untamed exhibitionism and flood his psyche with archaic grandiosity.

Kohut (Kohut and Wolf 1978) describes five types of narcissistic personalities: (1) mirror-hungry personalities, who are impelled to display themselves and to seek others' admiration to combat their inner sense of worthlessness; (2) ideal-hungry personalities, who chronically search for others whom they can admire for their power and prestige and from whom they can draw emotional sustenance; (3) alter-ego personalities, who need a relationship with someone who conforms to their own values and thus confirms their inner reality; (4) merger-hungry personalities, who seek to control others in an enactment of their need for inner structure; and (5) contact-shunning personalities, who avoid social contact out of a fear of the intensity of their need for attachment and love. While this classification is didactically appealing, it leaves many questions open. First, Kohut and Wolf (1978), after describing the first three of these narcissistic types, make a puzzling and unexplained turnabout and state, "They should, in general, not be considered as forms of psychopathology but rather as variants of the normal human personality" (p. 422). Second, whether these are to be considered separate types or facets of a unitary syndrome remains unsettled at this particular time. After all, what actuarial data exist to support subclassification within a syndrome that itself remains disputed and unsettled for many practitioners in the field? Third, Kohut and Wolf do not comment on the fact that their "merger-hungry" and "contact-shunning" types overlap borderline and schizoid personalities, respectively, and thus miss an opportunity for psychoanalytic-psychiatric linkage. Finally, while they state that the relationships established by mirror-hungry, ideal-hungry, and alter-ego hungry do not last long, they do not address the issue of aggression, which spoils these initially blissful unions.

Kernberg (1975b, 1976) portrays people with narcissistic personality disorder as displaying excessive self-absorption, intense ambition, grandiosity, overdependence on tributes from others, and an unremitting need for power, brilliance, and beauty. He emphasizes the pathology of the inner worlds of such persons. This manifests in their shallow emotional life, defective empathy, inability to love, and peculiar inability to experience sadness and mournful longing when facing separation and loss. Kernberg also points out that the narcissistic person lacks genuine sublimations; his work is in the service of exhibitionism and self-esteem regulation, done in order to receive praise. In addition, there are associated superego defects and a tendency toward corruptibility and cutting ethical corners.

Kernberg's description of the narcissistic personality differs from that of Kohut in four ways. First, he emphasizes the paranoid substrate of the syndrome and hence regards mistrust, hunger, rage, and guilt about this rage (Kernberg 1975b) as the basic cause of the self-inflation and not merely reactive phenomena, as Kohut proposes. Second, he gives a special place to the chronic envy that underlies the narcissistic person's seeming scorn for others. Indeed, Kernberg considers defenses against such envy, particularly devaluation, omnipotent control, and narcissistic withdrawal, a major aspect of the clinical picture of narcissistic personality disorder. Third, Kernberg, in his usual attitude of rapprochement with general psychiatry, provides a diagnosis of narcissistic personality that differentiates it from other personality disorders. Among these he includes borderline and antisocial personalities on the one hand, and obsessional and hysterical personalities on the other hand. Finally, unlike Kohut, Kernberg does not attribute the middle-aged narcissist's denial of his age-specific limitations and his envy of younger generations to a failure in achieving his true destiny. Instead, he suggests that this deterioration of the narcissist's internal world is yet another step in the repeating cycles of "wants, temporary idealizations, greedy incorporation, and the disappearance of supplies by spoiling, disappointing, and devaluation" (Kernberg 1980, p. 138).

Pathogenesis and Metapsychology

Kohut (1971) sees narcissistic disorder, or the primary disturbance of the self (Kohut 1977), as originating in faulty parental empathy with the growing child. The disorder is regarded as a developmental arrest in which archaic grandiosity and the need for idealization have failed to be subsumed under phase-specific, mature psychic functioning. Deficient maternal mirroring and traumatic ruptures of parental idealizations lead to a failure of "transmuting internalization" (Kohut 1971). The resulting clinical picture depends on the extent to which these structures are experientially felt, repressed, split off, or acted out.

In his theoretically "transitional" phase Kohut (1971) separated narcissism from the developmental line of drive-based object relations. He saw oedipal issues, and the structural neuroses consequent upon them, as having a sequential relation to the narcissistic sector and its pathology. However, such a separation left theoretical loopholes. Greenberg and Mitchell (1983) point out, for instance, that Kohut's distinction between narcissistic disorders and structural neuroses stemming from instinctual conflicts

> seems fundamentally contradicted by Kohut's formulations concerning the development of self. If drives are disintegration products reflecting a breakdown of primary relational configurations, how can "structural neuroses" contain at one and the same time no self pathology and conflicts concerning drives, which by definition reflect severe self pathology? [p. 359]

In his radical phase, that is, in the development of self psychology in its broad sense, Kohut (1977) maintained his essential thesis that the disorder is a result of deficient parental empathy. However, this time Kohut attempted a more far-reaching revision of classical metapsychology. He totally minimized the significance of instinctual drives and, as described earlier, placed the Oedipus complex in a context completely different from its classical view. The problem with Kohut's view of the genesis of the narcissistic personality disorder is its undue, single-minded emphasis on one etiological factor, namely deficient maternal empathy. Indeed, Kohut (1977) proposes that the mothers of these patients suffer from a specific "pathogenic personality disorder"[49] (p. 189). However, if this is true, why do all children of the same mother not have narcissistic personalities? Even in the realm of parental influence, Kohut's self psychology does not do justice to "the spectrum of mothering and fathering experiences by patients who have narcissistic disorders" (Rothstein 1980, p. 431). Almost totally ignored are the role that patient's gender, birth order, special endowments, parental overvaluation, and the child's own primary process distortions of the real objects play in the genesis of the disorder.

Kernberg, on the other hand, does not propose a separate line of development of narcissism. He sees the narcissistic personality not as a form of developmental arrest, but as specific pathological formation to begin with. Kernberg posits that narcissistic patients do not suffer from an absence of certain structures in the ego and superego, but from the presence of pathological primitive structures. He differentiates the normal narcissism of children, which he believes retains a realistic quality, from the early development of pathological narcissism, which creates fantastically grandiose fantasies (Kernberg 1975b). He believes that narcissistic patients were treated by their parents in a cold, even spiteful, but nonetheless special manner. In

---

[49]Not only is this reminiscent (Wallerstein 1983) of the now disproven "schizophrenogenic mother" concept, it also reveals a curious contradiction in Kohut's approach to nosology. On the one hand, he hesitates to diagnose patients from their symptoms and histories alone; on the other hand, he "diagnoses" their mothers from second-hand data!

addition, the quality of their early introjections was altered by age-specific misperceptions as well as by paranoid distortions of parental figures due to their own aggression toward their parents. Using Kohut's term with a different structural formulation, Kernberg proposes that the *grandiose self* is formed by a fusion of aspects of the real self, the idealized self, and an idealized object representation. Associated with such fusion, which permits a greater overall cohesion than is evidenced in borderline pathology, is the disowning through splitting of the needy-hungry self representations, the depriving object representations, and the rage, envy, and fear that bind them together.

Such a state of affairs, Kernberg further posits, leads to a condensation of preoedipal and oedipal conflicts under the overriding influence of pregenital, especially oral, aggression. This has deleterious effects on the oedipal experience[50] and on the salutary identifications that, under ordinary circumstances, should follow from its resolution. These effects include intense castration anxiety, on the one hand, and an orally derived greedy promiscuity and perverse tendencies on the other.

In summary, the differences between Kohut's and Kernberg's views of narcissism involve (1) its separateness versus its necessary relationship with object relations, (2) a developmental-arrest versus a pathological-formation view of the grandiose self, (3) the reactive versus the fundamental substrate view of aggression, and (4) the relative importance of the Oedipus complex in pathological narcissism. These differences affect the treatment techniques suggested by Kohut and Kernberg.

Treatment Technique

The treatment of the narcissistic personality proposed by Kohut is psychoanalysis. However, his version of psychoanalysis is clearly different from that which is commonly understood. Kohut's (1971,

---

[50]That narcissistic pathology may result from predominantly oedipal conflicts is held neither by Kernberg nor by Kohut. However, other investigators (Rothstein 1979, Spruiell 1975) do hint at such a possibility.

1977) approach aims at permitting the full-blown development of narcissistic transferences with the activation of either unfulfilled mirroring or idealizing selfobject needs. The implication is that such transference itself completes a halted development. A second suggested step is to interpret to the patient that his grandiosity or idealizing needs were once phase appropriate and that it was lack of environmental provision that led them to persist as such. The patient's rage, if it erupts in the treatment, is interpreted as an understandable response to the (inevitable) empathic failures of the analyst. Such an experience is reconstructed backwards to similar experiences caused by faulty parental empathy during childhood. The entire approach is anchored in the analyst's empathic immersion in his patient's subjective experience, which is regarded as a replica of the patient's childhood experience. Kohut (1984) summarized his view of the curative factors in psychoanalysis when he stated,

> Psychoanalysis cures by the laying down of psychic structure. And how does this accretion of psychological structure take place? The most general self psychological answer to this . . . question is also simple: psychological structure is laid down (a) via optimal frustration and (b) in consequence of optimal frustration, via transmuting internalization. . . . A good analysis, we believe, leads to a cure only by its employment, in countless repetitions, of the basic therapeutic unit of understanding and explaining, that is, via interpretation, the analyst's only active function in the analytic process. [pp. 98, 209]

Despite this statement about interpretation, a reading of Kohut's (1977) second monograph leaves one with the impression that the treatment he proposes differs from traditional psychoanalysis in significant ways. There is an overemphasis on the reparative function of the analyst and the role of empathy. In the usual understanding of analytic work, empathy is a prerequisite, and not a replacement, for interpretation. Moreover, there are limits to empathically derived knowledge (Wallerstein 1983). I have elsewhere (Akhtar 1984b) summarized the potentially problematic consequences of overemphasis on empathy. These include (1) overvaluation of the person of the analyst; (2) erroneous data emanating from the subjectivity of the analyst and not the patient's material; (3) a shift in responsibility for therapeutic difficulties from patient's intrapsychic resistances to the countertransference of the analyst; (4) a negation of the limits of empathically derived knowledge; and (5) in a totally empathic atmosphere, the splitting off of aggression and its discharge outside the treatment hours.

There are other differences in Kohut's technique and traditional psychoanalysis. Drive-related fantasies are regarded as regressive products of a fragmenting self. The unity of self-knowledge and cure is denied. Dreams are often interpreted on a manifest level with little need for associative material. Negative transference is viewed as a result of countertransference blocks. Reconstructions often are linear, with an implied absolute parallelism between the transference recapitulations and childhood experience, taking no account of unconscious memory distortion in this regard.

Kernberg (1976), on the other hand, emphasizes that narcissistic transferences are a multilayered structure, which includes early wishes, defenses, real experiences, and unconscious distortions of them. He states that the

> patient's disappointments in the analyst reveal not only fantasied— or real—frustrations in the transference: they also reveal dramatically the total devaluation of the transference object for the slightest reason and, thus, the intense overwhelming nature of the aggression against the object. . . . "Disappointment reactions" in these cases reflect conflicts about aggression *as well as* libidinal strivings. . . . The narcissistic transference, in other words, first activates past defenses against deeper relationships with the parents, and only then the real past relationships with them. [p. 263, italics added]

Kernberg's view is in greater accordance with the "principle of multiple function" (Waelder 1936), and, in its regard for the complex, multifactorial nature of transference manifestations, is more consonant with the usual analytic approach. He agrees with Kohut that most narcissistic patients should be treated by psychoanalysis and that it is important to permit a full development of their transferences. However, he does not regard their rage reactions as re-active to the analyst's empathic failure. Indeed, he proposes a full exploration, interpretation, and working-through of negative trans-ference to be the only way to diminish the patient's envy and re-solve his pathological grandiose self. Kernberg (1976) also suggests that the positive (libidinal) aspects of the patient's experience should also be addressed since

> focusing on such remnants as exist of a capacity for love and object investment, and for realistic appreciation of the analyst's efforts, prevents an almost exclusive focus on the latent negative transfer-ence, which can be misinterpreted by the patient as the psycho-analyst's conviction that the patient is "all bad." [p. 263]

Kernberg also regards the analysis of oedipal issues as an impor-tant second step in the treatment, which by the time these issues occupy the center stage should proceed in a fashion increasingly closer to the standard classical analysis of a neurotic patient. Fi-nally, Kernberg does not suggest a different technique of dream interpretation and regards empathy as only a tool, not a replace-ment for interpretation and working through.

SUMMARY AND CONCLUSIONS

> During the past two decades the work of Kohut and Kernberg has been crucial in the United States in focusing our attention on issues of the self and the necessity for an understanding of the many dimen-sions of narcissism if we are to achieve an analytic comprehension of the difficult character disorders. [Cooper 1989, p. 542]

This comparison of Kohut and Kernberg reveals important simi-larities and yet profound differences between them. Among their similarities are their influential positions in the field of psychoanaly-sis, their rejuvenating stimulus to psychoanalytic theorizing, their enrichment of our understanding of patients who belong in the "widening scope" (Stone 1954) of psychoanalysis, the interest they have stimulated in the study of British object relations theorists, the psychoanalytic studies of sociopolitical process they have spurred, and their enhancement of our technical skills, especially in the psychoanalytic treatment of narcissistic characters.

Kohut's and Kernberg's differences are no less numerous or impressive. Kohut rejects the medical model of diagnosis and regards general psychiatry as a potential threat to psychoanalysis; Kernberg maintains a close affiliation with the language, preoccupations, and organized forums of general psychiatry. Kohut ignores others' contributions even though his own contributions are only "original in emphasis, not in substance" (Rothstein 1980, p. 426); Kernberg profusely cites others, including Kohut, and openly acknowledges his conceptual debt to his predecessors. Kohut began his theorizing within the confines of classical psychoanalysis and then went through a transitional phase where he began to question the traditional approach. In his final theorizing, Kohut disputed even such core psychoanalytic concepts as conflict, drives, the Oedipus complex, and interpretation and insight as the fundamental curative factors in psychoanalysis; Kernberg, in contrast, has progressively moved toward mainstream psychoanalytic theory while constructing conceptual bridges between contemporary ego psychology and British object relations theory. Kernberg's contributions are additive; Kohut's potentially divisive. Kohut and Kernberg clearly differ in their conceptualization of narcissistic personality disorder. Kohut eschews descriptive diagnosis and considers spontaneously unfolding transferences as the only reliable tool in diagnosis; Kernberg provides detailed behavioral descriptions of such patients and regards descriptive diagnosis as complementary to the psychodynamic formulation. Kohut sees the etiology of the disorder in parental empathic failure, leading to a developmental arrest upon archaic forms of grandiosity and self-esteem regulation; Kernberg regards such pathological grandiosity to have developed as a defense against paranoid anxieties consequent to splitting and projection of aggressive self and object representations with secondary distortions of the Oedipus complex. Kohut emphasizes the reparative function of the analyst in the psychoanalytic treatment of narcissistic personality;

Kernberg steadfastly underscores the interpretative function of the analyst. Kohut emphasizes empathy as a therapeutic tool; Kernberg regards it as a technical necessity for interpretation. Kohut makes reductionistic, linear reconstructions of childhood traumata from patients' conscious recall; Kernberg posits that narcissistic transferences activate at first the past defenses against deeper relationships with parents and only then the real past relationships. Kohut appears to decode dreams from manifest content and does not provide adequate associative material to substantiate his conclusions; Kernberg proposes no deviation from traditional technique in the handling of dreams. When rage appears in treatment, Kohut views it as reactive to empathic failures of the analyst that reactivate similarly traumatizing experiences from the past; Kernberg views pregenital aggression as the basic, inciting agent against which the grandiose self is built as a defense. His suggested technique insists upon a thorough interpretation of negative transference developments in their defensive as well as recapitulation aspects.

Though not addressed here, other differences exist between the views of Kohut and Kernberg. Most important among them is the implications of their theories for their respective views of fundamental human nature. For Kohut, man is born whole, full of potential, even happy and eager to joyfully actualize the blueprint of his destiny. If he is unhappy, it is because of environmental failure. All his conflicts are the end result of unfortunate, tragic disorganization caused by lack of parental empathy. For Kernberg, conflict is embedded in normal development. Lifelong struggle with intrapsychic and reality conflicts is unavoidable. There is no escape from aggression, both from within and from without. Life, comprising the constant reactivations of the infantile conflicts as well as renewed challenges posed by reality, however, is still interesting and has the potential for that greatest of human experiences, love. But even love can never be totally free of early transferences. Need the reader be reminded that Kernberg's view of human nature is closer to what the founder of psychoanalysis envisioned?

6

NEEDS VERSUS
WISHES

A wish is the paradigmatic motivational concept in psychoanalysis. Derivative and disguised versions of infantile, contradictory, prohibited, and unrealistic wishes as well as defenses against them form the experiential nexus of the analytic material. The conceptual centrality of such wish-defense juxtaposition is underscored in Kris's (1947) well-known statement that the subject matter of psychoanalysis is nothing but "human behavior viewed as conflict" (p. 6). Brenner (1976b, 1982) provides a more current, detailed, and pure statement of the same fundamental theme, and there exists a broad consensus among psychoanalysts that the wish-defense (or wish-wish) conflict is basic to the understanding and treatment of psychopathology.

The evolution of this ideational mainstream, however, has not precluded an alternate model of psychopathology and human motivation. This is the so-called deficit model with its attendant emphasis upon thwarted developmental needs instead of repressed prohibited wishes. While vociferously brought to the attention of North American psychoanalysts by the emergence of self psychology (Kohut 1977, 1982, 1984, Kohut and Wolf 1978, Wolf 1988), the cardinal features of this model (e.g., deficit, need, affirmation)

have existed in psychoanalysis from its beginning. Indeed, in one
form or another, this disharmony between conflict and deficit
models runs through the early Freud–Ferenczi debates, the
Klein–Balint schism in England, and the current Kernberg–Kohut
controversy in the United States. Significantly, while attempts have
been made to bridge the gap between the two models and their
technical implications (Killingmo 1989, Strenger 1989), none has
focused on the need-wish distinction that characterizes the two
paradigms at their motivational base.[51] This chapter seeks to fill
this lacuna in the psychoanalytic literature.

In this chapter, I delineate the concept of a psychological need
and discuss its distinction from a wish. I begin by summarizing Freud's
views on the topic. Then I elucidate the pertinent concepts in the
subsequent psychoanalytic literature. I synthesize this literature,
delineate certain specific psychological needs, and note the potential pitfalls in such conceptualization. Then I highlight the implications of recognizing these needs for the psychoanalytic technique.
Having discussed the phenomenological and technical aspects, I
return to Freud and conclude with a brief theoretical postscript.

FREUD'S VIEWS
ON THE NEED-WISH DISTINCTION

> If someone's need for love is not entirely satisfied
> by reality, he is bound to approach every new per-
> son whom he meets with libidinal anticipatory ideas.
> [Freud 1912b, p. 100]

---

[51]The major psychoanalytic glossaries (Laplanche and Pontalis 1973, Moore
and Fine 1968, 1990, Rycroft 1968) neither address this distinction nor contain
the definition of a psychological need. The only exception is Eidelberg's (1968)
encyclopedia, which does contain entries on "instinctual need" (p. 200) and "narcissistic need" (p. 260). The former is defined as a tension caused by an instinctual "drive," the latter, curiously, a "wish" for additional libidinal cathexis. While
these definitions shed little light on the need-wish distinction, the fact that "need"
is used in both an instinctual and a relational context is significant. In the subsequent literature, the latter connotation seems to gain even more prominence.

> We do not say of objects which serve the interests of
> self-preservation that we *love* them; we emphasize that
> we *need* them. [Freud 1915b, p. 137, author's italics]

> I cannot think of any need in childhood as strong
> as the need for a father's protection. [Freud 1930,
> p. 72]

Freud used the word *need* in four different ways. The first and best known was in the form of "instinctual need" (Freud 1900, p. 585, 1926, p. 139, 1930, p. 132). This concept is the cornerstone of his theory of motivation, portrayed as even more fundamental than "wish" (*wunsch*). This distinction was most clear in his explication of the dream theory. Freud (1900) referred to an experience of satisfaction after which the mnemic image of a perception remains associated

> with the memory-trace of the excitation produced by the *need*. As a
> result of the link that has been established, next time this need arises
> a psychical impulse will seek to re-cathect the mnemic image of the
> perception and revoke the perception itself, that is to say to re-
> establish the situation of the original satisfaction. An impulse of this
> kind is what we call a *wish*. [pp. 565–566, italics mine]

Freud thus distinguished between a need and a wish. Need arose from an inner tension and was the "psychical representative of the stimuli originating from within the organism" (1915d, p. 121). Wish, in contrast, was indissolubly bound to the memory traces of a previous gratification. Need was the more basic motivation, while wish was contingent upon a need; a wish could hardly emerge without a need at its foundation. Also, Freud implied that a need could not be repressed while a wish was subject to repression (Harold Blum, personal communication, 1993).

Freud's second use of the word *need* referred to certain strivings of the ego. Among these he mentioned the ego's "inborn need for established causes" (1908, p. 212) as well as its "need for projection" (1911b, p. 63). Noticeable here is that the ego's autonomous strivings as well as its defensive efforts to protect itself from uncomfortable impulses, affects, and fantasies are accorded a "need" status. Freud's third usage of the word *need* was in connection with psychopathology and included not only the celebrated "need for punishment" (first mentioned in 1918 but not elaborated fully until 1924), but the "need for an unfulfilled wish" (1900, p. 148), the "need for a sexually debased object" (1912a, p. 185), the "need for illness" (1923, p. 49), the "need for expiation" (1927, p. 183), and the "masochistic need for suffering" (1937a, p. 265). The tenacity of these psychic requirements and the destabilizing effects of their nonfulfillment led Freud to designate them as "needs." The fourth and the final context of Freud's use of the word *need* was a developmental one. Freud referred to the child's "need for help" (1909a, p. 47), "need for affection" (1905c, p. 227, 1914, p. 165), and "need for a father's protection" (1930, p. 72). Unlike the later "relational" theorists, however, Freud traced these clearly psychological needs to the vicissitudes of man's biological givens. He noted that since the human infant was born so helpless,

> the dangers of the external world have a greater importance for it, so that the value of the object which can alone protect it against them and take the place of its former intra-uterine life is enormously enhanced. The biological factor, then, establishes the earliest situations of danger and creates the need to be loved which will accompany the child through the rest of its life. [1926, p. 155]

Since Freud viewed *instinctual* need as a *psychical* representative and the need for *love* as emanating from a *biological* factor, it is not surprising that he employed the same German word, *Bedurfnis*, for needs that range widely in their closeness to somatic origins ("instinctual need") on the one hand and experiential derivations ("need for a sexually debased object") on the other. Thus, regardless of its origin, if a requirement seemed obligatory for mental sustenance and stability, Freud called it a need. This stance is also discernible in a revealing statement he made about his own nature: "An intimate friend and a hated enemy have always been necessary requirements of my emotional life" (1900, quoted by Gay, 1988, p. 55).

Such "necessary requirements" seem to have a link with another one of Freud's (1905c, 1909b, 1915b) concepts, namely that of "ego instincts." These were seen to serve "self-preservative" (1909c, p. 44), "self seeking" (1908, p. 212), and "self subsisting" (1930, p. 122) aims. The prefix *self* in this context is usually taken to mean bodily self and it certainly does have that connotation. However, it also includes the psychic self. Thus the aims of ego instincts were also "psychically self preservative" and "psychically self seeking" and in this fashion, conceptually very close to the concept of needs.[52]

I shall return to this point toward the end of the chapter. For now, I wish to sum up by saying that Freud's views of "need" (1) hold it as a more basic motivational vector than wish, (2) regard the obligatory nature of the requirement as its central defining feature, (3) contain both id and ego origins of needs, (4) allow for ubiquitous as well as idiosyncratic needs, and (5) include developmentally necessary and pathological needs in their descriptions. This complex tapestry of Freud's contributions was to be explicated by his followers, with some focusing on one aspect, some on another.

SUBSEQUENT CONTRIBUTIONS

One thing in all this has very special relevance. This has to do with the immature ego—rendered strong by the mother's adapting well enough to the baby's *needs*. This is not to be lost in the concept of her satisfaction of the baby's instinctual drives. [Winnicott 1969a, p. 242, author's italics]

---

[52]An unmistakable echo of these ideas can be found in Maslow's (1968, 1970) hierarchy of human needs. He categorized them into *deficiency needs*, which must be met before any possibility of transcending them can be envisioned, and *growth needs* which propel the person toward wholeness and self-actualization. Needs for love and affection belong to the first group, needs for freedom, goodness, and justice to the second group. The two sets of needs might exist in harmony or conflict with each other.

> During the entire practicing subphase, mother con-
> tinues to be needed as a stable point, a "home base"
> to fulfill the need for refueling through physical
> contact. [Mahler et al. 1975, p. 69]

Freud's early followers continued to use the word *need* occasionally, without much effort at distinguishing it from a *wish*. His phrase,
"the need for punishment," especially gained wide currency and
received contributions from Nunberg (1926), Reich (1928),
Fenichel (1928), and Alexander (1929), among others. Aside from
an occasional endorsement of its origin in the endogenous and
experience-unrelated force of the death instinct (Alexander 1929),
little in these contributions answered the question as to why such
pursuit of suffering should not be called a "wish."

The word *need* kept appearing in other contexts as well, though,
once again, with little attempt at its definition. In the phenomenological realm, patients' "need to be kept" (Sandford 1952),
"need to be an only child" (Romm 1955), "need to be pregnant"
(Lerner et al. 1967), and "need-fear dilemma" (Burnham et al.
1969) were described. In the developmental realm, one came
across expressions such as the child's "need to retain the symbiotic situation" (Jacobson 1964), "need for tactile stimulation"
(Shevrin and Povl 1965), "need for company" (A. Freud 1965),
"need for phallic reinforcement" (Sperling 1967), "symbiotic
need" (Savitt 1969), "need for optimal maternal availability"
(Mahler et al. 1975), "need for dialogue" (Nickman 1985), and
"need for a caretaking other" (A. Bergman 1996). In the realm
of applied psychoanalysis, the term appeared in connection with
the human "need for decoration" (Harnik 1932), "need to know"
(Emch 1944, Steinberg 1993), and "need to have enemies and
allies" (Volkan 1988). While the needs mentioned here were all
implied to be ubiquitous and structure-sustaining, the focus of
this literature was elsewhere. The word *need* was used as if its meaning is self-evident.

In all fairness, however, it should be acknowledged that the
developmental literature was perhaps not so nonchalant about
this issue. Indeed, it is among the more focused contributions
to the concept of need, which includes the views of (1) early meta-

psychologists, (2) child analysts and developmentalists of various persuasions, (3) British analysts of the independent tradition, and (4) their American counterparts, the self psychologists.[53]

Metapsychologists

Prominent among the first set of contributions are those made by Nunberg (1931), Hartmann (1939, 1964), Rapaport (1960a), Schur (1966), and G. Klein (1976). Nunberg (1931) championed the concept of a "primary need for causality" (p. 126), though he seemed ambivalent about its origins. On the one hand, by adding the modifier "primary," he implied that this need had an origin independent of instincts. On the other hand, committed to the instinct theory and writing before Hartmann's (1939) introduction of "autonomous ego functions," he felt compelled to deduce that "in the need for causality the binding (synthetic) tendency of Eros reveals itself in a sublimated form in the ego" (p. 127). To be sure, the matter is not one of either/or. The human epistemophilic tendency—"the need to know" (Steinberg 1993)—is multidetermined, drawing its sources from sexual and aggressive drives as well as from the conflict-free sphere of ego functions.

Other concepts introduced by Hartmann (1939, 1964) were also pertinent, albeit indirectly, to the need-wish distinction. His proposal that the human infant is born in a state of preparedness for an "average expectable environment" that evokes and facilitates healthy adaptation contained the notion of developmental needs (more specifically delineated by child analysts later on). His concept of "change of function," too, was useful in this context. It provided a basis for understanding how wishes arising within the matrix of early object relations can, owing to their intensification for whatever reason, come to acquire a need-like, imperative quality (see Edgcumbe and Burgner 1972). Finally, his underscoring the

---

[53]To a large extent, these groupings are artificial. After all, many developmentally inclined contributors discuss metapsychological issues, many members of the British independent tradition were child analysts, and so on. Categorizing the literature in this fashion is largely for didactic ease.

autonomous nature of ego's tendency toward rationalization and intellectualization highlighted the primary aspect of Nunberg's (1931) basically instinctual "need for causality."

Aiming at further elucidation of the instinct-ego balance in the motivation of human behavior, Rapaport (1960a) began by distinguishing between "causes" and "motivations." He noted that while all motivations were causes, not all causes were motivations; causes could arise from external reality, defenses against motivation, nonmotivated internal states, serendipity, and so on. Motivations, in contrast, displayed preemptoriness, cyclicity, and a certain selectiveness of objects. Rapaport emphasized that psychoanalytic theory of motivation

> must distinguish between instinctual drive motivations, motivations derived from and dependent upon instinctual drive motivations, and motivations autonomous from instinctual drive motivations, whether they are derived from instinctual drives or are of a different origin. (1960a, p. 854)

Rapaport stated that derivative motivations arise as a consequence of defenses (e.g., altruism from countercathexis of aggression) and are themselves subject to defensive alterations. He also described "quasi-need types of motivations . . . which are selective but are of a low, yet discernible, degree of preemptoriness, cyclicity, and displaceability" (pp. 865, 866) as well as "reality-attuned, autonomous motivations" (p. 867) with no instinctual basis. The first of these notions was later developed by Modell (1975) in his concept of "quieter instincts" that account for attachment and object relations. The second notion prepared the ground for conceptualization of ego needs in the child developmental literature.

Before going to that body of work, however, the views of Schur (1966) and G. Klein (1976) must be considered. Schur, following Hartmann (1939), placed the emergence of psychic intentionality at about 3 months of age. Until then memory traces were not adequately laid down and it was not proper to speak of wishes, since these emanate from remembered experiences. Schur stressed the difference between the "physiological concept 'need' and the psychological concept 'wish'" (p. 68), leaving little conceptual space for a purely psychological need. Yet, he also stated that the early "id-drives-striving-demands-derivates, whatever we may call them (I purposely avoid the term *wishes* before discussing the essential meaning of this crucial concept), *need* an object for their gratification" (p. 47, italics added). To be sure, this use can be viewed as merely colloquial. However, it also leaves the door open for the concept of a psychological need.

Far from such ambivalence, G. Klein (1976) openly embraced the concept of need on a psychological level. He advocated replacing the language of energic forces by the language of activity, relationships, and values. This perspective gave the word *need* a special meaning.

> A need is a state of thwarted tendency. It is misleading to picture such an active but interrupted tendency as an impersonal energic concentration separated from the ego. The need is an ego-world relationship in a state of active but aborted actualization. When the tendency is lived out, so to speak, when it is unimpededly realized, we do not speak of it as a need. Only when such a directional tendency is blocked in its course do we have a need. [p. 97]

Fulfillment of needs results not only in pleasure, according to Klein, but also in ego strengthening. Moreover, need-type motivations also arise from the search for vital pleasures besides libidinal gratification. These include needs for pleasure in pleasing, pleasure in effectiveness, and pleasure in synthesis. Extending the Freudian pleasure principle to such ego activities and emphasizing the inevitably object-related significance of all motivation, Klein presented a novel view of psychological needs.

Infant and Child Developmental Researchers

The second set of contributions to the concept of psychic needs comes from analysts involved in child analysis and analytically informed infant and child observation (Edgcumbe and Burgner 1972, A. Freud 1965, Furman 1987, Lichtenberg 1989, Lichtenberg et al. 1992, Mahler 1968, Mahler et al. 1975, Parens 1987, Spitz 1957). Spitz (1957) emphasized that it is misleading to speak of a wish in the neonatal context. Psychic volition is nonexistent in the first weeks of life and the baby's search for drive gratification—manifested through the scanning behavior of the rooting reflex—emanates from a phylogenetically determined "prototype for the reality principle" (p. 91). Thus, Spitz not only underscored the instinctual bases of early object relations, he implied that reality oriented needs precede wishes; an object needs to be found before it can be wished for.

A. Freud (1965) specifically distinguished the infantile stage of "need-satisfying" relationship to the object. Such a relationship exists for the infant only at times of need and ceases to exist when needs are satisfied. While the infant's bodily needs were at the center of her conceptualizations here, Anna Freud also spoke of the baby's "imperative desires" (p. 65), a designation that could imply psychological needs. In a developmentally later context, she did speak of the "child's *need* for company" and the "*need* to be loved" (1965, p. 40, italics mine). Here the instinctual foundation of the need concept is relegated to the background; these needs appear largely psychological. This stance is also evident in her speaking of "patterns of identification which are *needed* for building up an independent structure" (1965, p. 46, italics mine).

Similar self-building and self-stabilizing needs are found sprinkled in the developmental observations of Mahler (Mahler 1968, Mahler et al. 1975). She noted that during the symbiotic phase the infant begins to perceive need satisfaction as coming from outside and turns libidinally toward that source. In a telling move linking the need-wish concepts, Mahler stated that once such object tie is established, "the need gradually becomes a wish" (Mahler et al. 1975, p. 46). She delineated further psychic needs that have to be met for the child to acquire a separate and unique sense of selfhood. She emphasized that while "the lion's part of adaptation must come from the pliable, unformed infant . . . there must be a measure of adaptation on the mother's part too" (Mahler et al. 1975, p. 63). The latter provides the psychic requirements for the child's growth. These requirements or needs include the following: the infant's need for mutual cuing with mother during the symbiotic phase; the need for the mother's tolerance, encour-

agement, and indeed pleasure in his or her rudimentary exploration during the differentiation subphase; the need for the mother's
letting go and yet remaining available for emotional refueling
during the practicing subphase; the need for the mother's resilience and giving the child "a gentle push, an encouragement towards independence" (p. 79) during the rapprochement subphase.
The shift of need concept from the cauldron of instincts to the
chamber of object relations is evident here.

Edgcumbe and Burgner (1972), in discussing the concepts of
need-satisfaction and need-satisfying relationships, also moved in
this direction. They advocated reserving the term *need-satisfying
relationship* to "a *mode* of relating" (p. 300, author's italics) whereby
the relationship revolves around the functions performed by the
object and not the object itself. They distinguish between "self-
preservative needs, sexual and aggressive drive pressures, and various requirements of the developing ego," acknowledging that such
distinctions are difficult since "emotional requirements can, and
do, become as imperative as instinctual needs and pressures"
(p. 301). Indeed, they conclude that "primary biological needs,
drive pressures, and ego requirements" all "may legitimately be
termed needs" (p. 309).

A similar biopsychosocial overlap in the concept of "needs" is
evident in Furman's (1987) work. She spoke of the child's "innate
need for safety" (p. 287), which, only after a prolonged period of
parental know-how of meeting it, gives way to a properly developed
wish to take care of oneself. She notes that the parents' most helpful attitude to their child's needs is respect. The focus of her
attention seemed to be on the child's physical needs (e.g., sleep,
food), but she also mentioned the child's needs for quiet holding,
for company, for feeling loved, and for receiving support in want-
ing to be independent.

Parens (1987) also highlighted the developing child's needs.
Among these he included the child's "need for help," "need for
autonomy," "need for limits," and "need to be held" (pp. 31, 39,
57, 186), both physically and psychologically. Parens noted that
frustrated needs simply do not go away; they clamor for gratification and foster a greater degree of neediness.

The concept of psychological needs then found a most thorough exponent in Lichtenberg (1989, Lichtenberg et al. 1992). He posited that motivation emanates from five systems designed to promote the fulfillment and regulation of basic human needs.

> Each motivational system is a psychological entity (with probable neurophysiological correlates). Each is built around a fundamental need. Each is based on behaviors clearly observable, beginning in the neonatal period. The five motivational systems are: (1) the need for psychic regulation of physiological requirements, (2) the need for attachment-affiliation, (3) the need for exploration and assertion, (4) the need to react aversively through antagonism or withdrawal, and (5) the need for sensual enjoyment and sexual excitement. [1989, p. 1]

Lichtenberg emphatically distinguished needs from wishes, reserving the former term for "basic requirements" and the latter for "symbolic representations of aims and goals" (p. 17). Needs are closer to the neurobiological base, wishes to the experiential repertoire. Needs and wishes may coincide or may oppose each other. Lichtenberg stated that when these fundamental needs are met, the result is a feeling of self-cohesion. When these needs are not met, the individual experiences a sense of disturbed cohesion.

The British Independent Analysts

The analysts of the British independent tradition also focused heavily upon psychic needs. While the contributions of Fairbairn (1944, 1952a), Balint (1959, 1968), and Winnicott (1960b,c, 1962) are well known in this context, it was actually Suttie,[54] who first placed needs at the center of the psychoanalytic theory of motivation. As early as 1935, Suttie stated that he was "introducing the

---

[54]Bacal and Newman (1990) note that "among the pioneers of the object relations perspective, no one is more remarkable nor unsung than Ian Suttie" (p. 5). Citing Brome (1982) as their source, they suggest that while Suttie published his major works in the mid-1930s, he had already elaborated a substantial object relations approach in an unpublished paper in 1923.

conception of an innate need-for-companionship which is the infant's only way of self-preservation. This need, I put in the place of the Freudian Libido, and regard it as genetically independent of genital appetite" (p. 6).

Fairbairn's (1944, 1952a) subsequent declaration that "libido is primarily object-seeking," Balint's (1959, 1968) notion of "primary love," and Winnicott's (1960b) concept of "ego-needs" are all in the spirit of Suttie's (1935) "innate need for companionship." Balint (1968) delineated the human need for "harmony with one's environment" and outlined technical guidelines for handling the patient desperately seeking such harmony in the analytic situation. Winnicott (1960d), who saw himself as "the leading figure in the movement towards a recognition of *need satisfaction* as earlier and more fundamental than wish fulfillment" (pp. 471–472, author's italics), emphatically distinguished between "ego needs and id needs" (1960a, p. 141). He noted that a mother's satisfying her baby's instinctual drives is not the same as meeting his or her ego needs. Indeed, it is possible to "gratify an oral drive and by so doing to violate the infant's ego function" (Winnicott 1962, p. 57). Winnicott emphasized that the instinctual drives are not, psychologically speaking, internal to the early infant. Only gradually does the infant's ego develop the capacity to experience the id demands as emanating from within the self. Until then, "the word 'need' has significance . . . [and the] word 'wish' is out of place as it belongs to sophistication that is not to be assumed at this stage of immaturity" (Winnicott 1956, p. 256). He emphasized that

> a mother must fail in satisfying instinctual demands, but she may completely succeed in not "letting the infant down," *in catering for ego needs*, until such a time as the infant may have an introjected ego-supportive mother, and may be old enough to maintain this introjection in spite of failures of ego support in the actual environment. [p. 312, author's italics]

Winnicott (1956) noted that the proper attitude toward unmet needs of childhood was the provision of an environment that gives the individual a new opportunity for ego-relatedness. This therapeutic orientation was further elaborated by the exponents of his work including Guntrip (1969), Khan (1974, 1983), and Casement (1991). The last mentioned most clearly reiterated the distinction "between 'libidinal demands,' which cannot be gratified in any analytic psychotherapy without risking a serious disturbance of the analytic process, and 'needs' which cannot be frustrated without preventing growth" (pp. 273–274).

Casement (1991) outlined the needs of childhood that seem most relevant to psychoanalysis. He noted that

> an infant needs to be securely held; needs to have the consistent care of a mother (or mother substitute) who has an empathic understanding of the infant's various indications of what is needed; needs to be fed but also to be given space in which to find the breast that feeds; needs a mother who can tolerate being "used" . . . needs a mother who can intuitively accept the infant's initially "omnipotent" control of her; . . . needs a mother who is at first able to be maximally available to her infant but who becomes progressively less available and less controlled by the infant's demands. [p. 276]

As children grow, they also need their parents to find their oedipal temptation and rivalry manageable. They need to discover that their blossoming sexuality is healthy. Also, during various stages of development, especially adolescence, they need to be able to confront their parents and have the latter "survive" such confrontation (see Blos 1967, and Ehrlich 1993). Drawing parallels between childhood needs and the needs of patients in analysis, Casement noted that all patients need to feel securely held, consistently and reliably treated, and have the analyst "survive" their aggressive demands. In addition, some patients "need to be allowed to establish a provisional omnipotence over the analyst" (1991, p. 277) while others need a sense of space that protects them from his impingements.

Self Psychologists

A similar empathic attention to psychic needs emanating from developmental arrests characterized Kohut's (1971) delineation of mirroring and idealizing transferences. Positing the origin of excessive narcissism in the unmet childhood needs for being mirrored and for finding one's parents admirable, Kohut proposed an empathic-affirmative, as against interpretive, approach to the transferences of these patients. His initial formulations accorded such developmental needs a parallel status to the instinctual drives from various psychosexual phases. Later, however, he derided instinctual drive as a "vague and insipid concept" (Kohut 1982, p. 401). His views, now organized under the rubric of "self psychology," began to portray psychosexual conflicts and their attendant wish-defense struggles as disintegration products of an unempathically treated self (see Chapter 5 for an elucidation of the different phases in Kohut's theorizing). He theorized that the growing self requires certain kinds of input from objects to achieve and maintain its cohesion and vitality. These "selfobject experiences" (Kohut 1977) essentially involved one's being recognized and accepted and having the opportunity to bask in the strength of parents and parent substitutes.

Kohut (1984) later pointed out that the need for such experiences is not restricted to early development but remains throughout life. The exponents of his ideas expanded on this theme and added to the types of selfobject experiences that are needed for the establishment and maintenance of a cohesive, energetic, and balanced self. According to Wolf (1994), these experiences meet (1) the need to feel alikeness with peers, (2) the need to test oneself out against some benign opposition, (3) the need to feel successful in bringing about the desired results of one's actions, and (4) the need to have the experience that the caregivers are affectively attuned to the dynamic shifts in one's inner state.

Summary

The needs delineated by the child development researchers, British independent analysts, and self psychologists show a striking overlap. Together, the three sources emphasize the growth facilitating and psychic-self preservatory nature of these needs. While the innate origins of these needs is recognized, their instinctual substrate, underscored by the metapsychologists, is either minimized or rejected. Instinctual needs, it seems, have gradually been replaced by relational needs, and the source of needs has shifted from the id to the ego. This move reflects the overall direction of psychoanalytic theorizing away from a biological-mechanistic model to a purely psychological-relational one.

However, attempts at categorically separating the two models risk overlooking two very important matters. First, Freud himself worked on the levels of both the biological-mechanistic abstraction and the personal-object related observation. His "case histories, whether clinical or in the realm of applied analysis, hardly rely on tension reduction as an explanatory construct. . . . The individuals he writes about are motivated by wishes, desires, and a striving towards objects" (Richards 1996, p. 78). Even in the specific context of needs, Freud's conceptualizations were supple rather than rigid. He used the word *need* at one time to denote concepts that were more innate and biological and at another time to describe those that were more experientially derived. Moreover, he invariably saw the somatic and psychic as coexistent. To portray Freud's stance as lopsided does injustice to the complexity of his thought. Second, the either/or portrayal of needs and wishes, implicit in some of the literature covered, tends to create an artificial split between body and mind, between experiential matrix and internal fantasy life, and between the growth-promoting psychological requirements and an individual's specific ways of seeking and metabolizing those experiences. In contrast, the comprehensive, contemporary psychoanalytic approach to these matters is biopsychosocial, taking the bodily foundations, the intrapsychic fantasy elaborations, and the environmental input into account without assigning motivational primacy to any single factor once for all (Richards 1996). It is only with such an orientation that any attempt at further synthesis of this literature can yield useful results.

SYNTHESIS, CAVEATS, AND BEYOND

Concern with clarification of terms is unpopular among psychoanalysts and rare in psychoanalytic writing. This is partly due to Freud's example. Semantics could hardly be the concern of the great explorer, and some inconsistency in the usage of words may well be considered the prerogative of

> genius. It is a different matter when a generation
> or two of scientists assume a similar prerogative. . . .
> Since scientific communication is impaired by am-
> biguity of meaning, the need for clarification has
> become urgent. [Hartmann et al. 1946, pp. 27, 28]

> Classical analysis does not, in the manner of the inter-
> personal tradition, impute superordinate status to
> the quest (or drive) for relational intimacy, but it
> does not thereby devalue it. For classical analysis, the
> need for intimacy is simply one of the many driving
> forces suffused with unconscious wishes and fears;
> it is a need that can be satisfied only when one's sense
> of morality, the resources of reality, and the affects
> that accompany intimacy are taken into account.
> [Richards 1996, p. 79]

Having reviewed the concept of psychological needs in the writings of Freud and of subsequent analysts (ego psychologists, British independent analysts, developmentalists of various persuasions, and self psychologists), we are now prepared to bring their common elements together and develop a proper definition of *need*. However, before doing so, it seems worthwhile to take a look at two other sources[55] that almost always have something instructive

---

[55]Still other sources enrich the understanding of need-wish distinction. These sources are both "psychoanalysis-near" and "psychoanalysis-distant." Prominent in the former category are Fromm's (1950) sociologically inclined concepts of basic human needs (e.g., rootedness, relatedness, transcendence) and Bowlby's (1969, 1973, 1980) ethologically informed observations on human attachment and the associated needs (e.g., the need for a "secure base"). Prominent in the latter category are the fields of economics and philosophy. Within economics, one can find the suggestion (Marx 1867; see also Galbraith 1971, Heller 1976) that a deliberately engineered exaltation of human wishes into false needs is a typical maneuver of the capitalistic, free market system. Within philosophy, one can locate discussions of the need-wish distinction in both Western and Eastern traditions. The perception of the analogues of "need" in Western thought from the Greeks to the present philosophical systems have been traced by Springborg (1981). In the East, various ascetic orders seek to reduce human desire to its minimum, relegating many needs to a wish status. Gandhi (1940), in his attempts to become "absolutely passion-free," concluded: "I must reduce myself to zero" (pp. 504, 505).

to offer: English language and the human body (Akhtar 1994a).
The distinction between needs and wishes is actually quite clear in
the English language. Webster defines *need* as "necessity, compulsion . . . a lack of something useful . . . a condition in which there
is a deficiency of something" and *wish* as "to desire, to long for, to
want" (Webster 1983). Differences become readily apparent. Need
is portrayed as contingent upon lack, wish is not. Need is mostly
described as a noun, wish is mostly described as a verb. Need is
portrayed as pressing ("compulsion"), wish has no such qualifiers.
Indeed the synonyms for need in Webster are "exigency, emergency, strait, extremity, necessity, distress," even "destitution, pov-
erty, indigence (and) penury."

For understanding the need-wish distinction, the human body,
too, is an informative source. Examples of its wishes include a soft
mattress to sleep on, vanilla ice cream, a particular type of toilet,
sex with a specific individual. Examples of its needs include the
requirements of oxygen, sleep, food, elimination, and release
from sexual tension. Once again, the distinction is apparent.
Needs are universal, wishes idiosyncratic. Deprivation of the
body's needs causes structural damage, frustration of its wishes
does not.

Equipped with this psychoanalytic, linguistic, and somatic the-
saurus, one might define *need* in the psychic realm as the requirement that (1) arises from a sense of lack or deficit, mentalized as
a consequence of ego inability in the face of instinctual pressure
or real or imagined external attacks; (2) is not experience-bound
but common to all human beings; (3) if fulfilled, helps in the development and sustenance of mind; (4) if unfulfilled, results in a
simple, urgent, monotonous and repetitive demand, the not meeting of which leads to the structural disintegration of the mind.
Being contingent on lack and possessing a preservative/restorative
potential vis-à-vis psychic structure lends *need* yet another quality,
namely (5) a certain freedom from intentionality, conferring upon
it an aura of justifiability.

A need, thus defined, has complex relationships with the concept of a wish. The two concepts exist on a somewhat different level
of abstraction. Need arises from lack and leads to yearning. Wish,

in contrast, is an individual's specific way of fulfilling his needs. Need is universal, wish is experience-bound; wish invariably has "a uniquely personal history, a uniquely personal form, and a uniquely personal content" (Brenner 1982, p. 22). Need, unlike a wish, is not subject to repression. Also, a wish can be replaced by another wish, but a need cannot be replaced by another need. A need is psychically represented (via a demand) only when it is not fulfilled. A wish, in contrast, has a persistent psychic representation with memory, fantasy, and associated affect.[56] Frustration of a wish causes dynamic shifts and compromise formations. Frustration of a need results in urgent demands which, if unmet, are followed by a structural regression. Needs and wishes can be in harmony such as in the desire to sleep, to have sexual gratification, or to be recognized and affirmed by one's love objects. Or, they can be in opposition to each other such as in "a toddler's wish to follow a lost ball into the street and yet need protective restraint" (Lichtenberg 1992, p. 112) or a patient's wish to have sex with the analyst while having the need to be frustrated in this pursuit.

While the need-wish distinction is easy at such a gross level,[57] it no longer remains so during the ebb and flow of the analytic process. Many unanswered questions then surface. First, is the need-wish distinction to be made phenomenologically? To do so seems prob-

---

[56]Such conceptualization overlaps with the Lacanian distinction between need, demand, and desire. According to Lacan (1958), "need" is an intermittent organic tension while "demand" is its articulation in language. However, in seeking need satisfaction, demand also seeks the object's love. Need and demand therefore become split, leaving an insatiable leftover called "desire." Desire is "neither the appetite for satisfaction, nor the demand for love, but the difference that results from this abstraction of the first from the second" (Lacan 1958, p. 287).

[57]This is also evident in the decision that the patient needs analysis. Under ideal circumstances, he or she also has a wish for it. In the absence of such a wish, the analyst's interventions are directed at helping the patient understand the reasons behind his inability to wish for the help he or she actually needs (Rothstein 1995). When, however, the patient expresses a wish for undergoing analysis while the analyst feels that the patient does not need it, the latter's interventions are directed toward helping the patient decipher the reasons for the wish for what he or she does not need.

lematic. An inordinately entitled, narcissistic patient might experience his wishes as pressing needs. A masochistic patient, with a pronounced ascetic bent, might deride his needs as mere wishes. Yet
another individual, lacking a sense of healthy entitlement, might seek
refuge from anticipated rejection by labeling all his desires needs
and none of them wishes; after all, having needs carries a lesser burden of intentionality. Phenomenology, therefore, does not seem a
reliable guide here, but what is the alternative?

Second, are needs and wishes as distinct in adult life as they
perhaps might be during childhood? It seems that in the course
of development, needs and wishes become intricately condensed
with each other. Hartmann's (1964) warning regarding the
"genetic fallacy" must be heeded here. The surgical separation of
needs and wishes also runs contrary to the "principle of multiple
function" (Waelder 1936), a central tenet of psychoanalytic theorizing. In clinical situations, therefore, the need-wish distinction
might have to be a relative one at best. Some fantasy, some desire,
some yearning of a patient might be viewed as predominantly need-
based and others predominantly wish-based but each as containing both need and wish elements. For instance, a narcissistic
patient's idealization of his analyst would be viewed as containing both his continued need for an admirable parent and a defensive wish to ward off aggression against the undeniably imperfect
analyst. A schizoid patient's withdrawal would be viewed as manifesting both his need to protect himself from the intimacy of the
transference relationship and his wish to arouse curiosity and a
rescue effort on the part of the analyst.

Finally, how does one respond to adult patients whose developmental needs have remained unmet during formative years? After
all, such real or imagined deprivations do not result in psychic gaps
or holes but in compensatory structures involving powerful affects
and fantasies (Curtis 1983). A "therapist of supply" (Killingmo
1989, p. 76) cannot simply fill such lacunae by kindness toward the
patient. The patient's rage over unmet needs and guilt over this
rage are also activated in the transference and fiercely combat
benevolent attempts at solace.

With such caveats in mind, one may synthesize the literature reviewed and propose six basic psychological needs. These needs, while not free from wish-defense elements, do warrant a recognition in their own right. Their existence in the human psyche is ubiquitous, though the degree of their overtness and the manner in which they are met varies from culture to culture. Regardless of such variations, these needs have to be met for healthy psychic development to take place and for relationships, including marriage, to survive. They also have to be met for the analytic work to take hold and continue in an optimal fashion. These needs are (1) the need for one's physical needs to be deemed legitimate; (2) the need for identity, recognition, and affirmation; (3) the need for interpersonal and intrapsychic boundaries; (4) the need for knowing and understanding causes of events; (5) the need for optimal emotional availability of a love object (in the clinical situation, the analyst); and (6) the need for a resilient responsiveness on the part of one's love objects (in the clinical situation, the analyst) under special circumstances. I will now briefly comment upon the technical implications of these six needs.

TECHNICAL IMPLICATIONS

The ultimate need in every case, of course, is the gaining of insight with growing appreciation and apprehension of reality. But on the way to this many of these severely ill patients have other needs which have to be met; if they are not met analysis becomes impossible. [Little 1957, p. 241]

On the part of the analyst, the meeting of unmet needs in analysis is usually more incidental than deliberate. The analyst, by sticking to his/her analytic task, provides the patient with opportunities for finding what is needed—that is unconsciously looked for. The patient's experience of finding what is needed within the analytic relationship may then

> contribute deeply, but often silently and unseen,
> towards eventual therapeutic change. [Casement
> 1991, pp. 289–290]

Under ordinary circumstances, these six psychological needs are met during analysis without any deliberate effort on the analyst's part. Indeed, these needs become apparent only when the analytic process begins to falter as a consequence of their not having been met. Both these points should become highlighted in the following discussion of the technical issues involved.

The Need for One's Physical Needs to be Deemed Legitimate

While Freud's (1909b) feeding the Rat Man is viewed as a striking exception, the fact remains that all analysts take care of certain basic physical needs of their patients. They provide them a comfortable couch, a noise-free office, and, in most cases, access to a restroom. To an analysand experiencing postural unease due to advanced pregnancy, they might offer an extra pillow. They arrange the lighting of their office so as to prevent visual discomfort to the recumbent patient. More important, when such physical provisions are threatened, they attempt to restore them, though without overlooking the meanings of their intervention to the patient.

A Vignette from My Own Analysis

Once during a late afternoon session in my analysis,[58] I was made uncomfortable when the rays of the setting sun found their way, through the slightly open blinds of a window, straight to my eyes. I shielded my eyes with my hand and kept talking, albeit a bit distractedly. Noticing this, my analyst got up from his chair, walked

---

[58]In citing vignettes from my own analysis, I am breaking from tradition, which, with the exception of some analysands of Freud and a few contemporary analysts (e.g., Hurwitz 1986, Simon 1993), has relegated the description of such experiences to informal banter among analysts, much to the loss of literature on psychoanalytic technique.

up to the window, and pulled the blinds closed. As he did this, he said, "I notice that the sunlight is troubling you and I am wondering as to what has prevented you from saying something about it or asking me to pull the blinds shut?" By the time he finished speaking, he was already back in his chair.

This shows that the meeting of physical needs does not preclude an investigative stance toward the analysand's anxieties, wishes, and defenses involving such needs. The analyst, of course, has the option for a direct inquiry such as above or a silent scanning of the patient's associative material following such gratification.

Case 1

Some years ago, I had moved into a new office. An analysand with known psychosomatic sensitivity to fresh paint started to sneeze and cough badly during her second session in the new office. Knowing that the hallway water fountains were not yet functional, she asked me where she could get some water to drink. I told her that she could step out and I would instruct my secretary on the intercom to give her a paper cup, which she could take to the ladies room to get some water. The patient went out and returned within a few minutes. She mumbled "thanks" and resumed the chain of thought she was pursuing earlier. I listened to the material carefully, wondering if any overt or covert reference to my intervention would appear. None did. During the next couple of sessions, I silently looked for any reference to my intervention but did not find it.

Clearly, it can be asserted that had I asked directly I would have found something of significance. Perhaps. On the other hand, could that not be induced or iatrogenic material? More important, I believe that not to give her an opportunity to drink water would have rendered me realistically intrusive and hence transferentially unusable. What is of even greater significance in such instances is not the meeting of the physical need per se but its recognition as being legitimate. This meets the more basic, psychological need for such biological dignity.

The Need for Identity, Recognition, and Affirmation

While undergoing the potentially regressive and destabilizing pro-
cedure of psychoanalysis, patients need to retain their identity at
all times. In the treatment of analyzable cases with a higher level
character organization (Kernberg 1970a) and a solid identity
(Akhtar and Samuel 1996, Erikson 1959), this issue does not surface at all. The regressive emergence of sequestered, repressed, and
unmetabolized self representations (and their defensive deploy-
ments within the transference–countertransference axis) does not
alter the patient's core self-experience. In sicker patients, however,
breaches in self-cohesion (including those affecting the temporal
continuity of self-experience) might have to be mended by the
analyst's occasional demonstration of his "remembering" who the
patient is day after day and by his "bridging interventions" (Akhtar
1995a, p. 150) that synthesize contradictory self representations
and their associated affects together. Closely associated with the
maintenance of identity is the patient's need to be recognized—
both literally (for instance, upon the analyst's opening the office
door each time, as well as in a chance encounter outside the office) and metaphorically—as uniquely himself or herself. Warmth,
conveying a sense of familiarity and affiliation, and not gushing
enthusiasm, is what is at issue here. The analyst's continued acknowledgment of the patient's adult identity during moments of
regression is a related point of technique.

Affirmation is also a part of this need. Patients need to feel understood (Balint 1968, Casement 1991, Kohut 1977) before they can
utilize the analyst's understanding of them for understanding themselves. They need to feel that their psychological experience is valid.
The issue here is the "realness" of the patient's subjective experience (Killingmo 1989, Schwaber 1983a,b) and not the veracity of
their reports of external events.[59] Meeting this need of the patient

---

[59]In certain cases of childhood sexual abuse (Kramer 1991) and sadistic control leading to "soul murder" (Shengold 1989), the analyst might indeed have
to confirm the reality of such events. However, the patient's need for such veri-
fication must at first be explored and the results of the analyst's intervention
analytically managed.

becomes evident in the analyst's greater regard for the patient's conscious material including his or her rationalizations. The analyst does not view them as merely defensive but also as the patient's healthy strivings to understand psychological events (Hartmann 1939).

This emphasis on the ego side of the needs to be mirrored and affirmed should not make one forget that such needs are inevitably condensed with psychosexual wishes and unconscious fantasies.

Case 2

This concern was most evident in the statement of a narcissistic man who, as a child, had been unempathically overindulged by his mother and, owing to the sudden departure of his father when the patient was 5, had experienced an oedipal victory of sorts. During one of his sessions, he said, with some aplomb (!) "You know, I have discovered that I am a five foot ten inch penis walking around this world. I need constant stroking and when I don't get it, I just shrivel up." He then paused, as if for me to applaud this insight. Here the intermingling of narcissistic needs and phallic-exhibitionistic wishes is quite transparent. Also present, perhaps, are hidden unconscious fantasies of being stroked or not stroked (for instance, by whom?).

The need to be mirrored and affirmed can also be condensed with the need for optimal emotional availability of a love object (discussed below). While it can be argued that the two almost always coexist, their concurrence is most clear in certain patients' seeking of post-termination contacts. Note, for instance, Shengold's (1989) remarks about one of his patients: "Consciously he was coming back for advice about family problems. But there was a deeper *need* to show me what the analysis had done for him and to try to consolidate it" (p. 177, italics mine).

The Need for Interpersonal and Intrapsychic Boundaries

Patients need their interpersonal boundaries to be respected (Gabbard and Lester 1995). They "need a sense of space which protects them from the experience of being impinged upon by . . . the analyst" (Casement 1991, p. 277). At times, however, unconscious fantasies drive them to seek a transgression of their own boundaries by the analyst. In such circumstances, they need to be frustrated. Here the patient's wishes and needs seem to be in opposition. This underscores the fact that the analyst's paying attention to the patient's needs is not tantamount to acts of kindness and aggression-free indulgence. Indeed, meeting a patient's need, as in the instance of a "malignant erotic transference" (Akhtar 1994b), and the accompanying wish to have sex with the analyst, might require considerable counteraggression from the analyst.

The issue of boundaries, however, extends beyond the interpersonal realm. Patients also have a "need for control over the intrapsychic boundaries between (their) conscious and unconscious processes" (Settlage 1994, p. 46). Unempathically timed, deep interpretations only serve to shock the patient, no matter how erudite or correct these might be.

Case 3

A narcissistic lawyer spent the first two years of her analysis with me in a "cocoon transference" (Modell 1976). She came regularly but seemed completely unrelated to me. Nothing I did or said seemed to affect her. I plodded along, waited. In the third year of her analysis, I had to take a few days off on short notice. She took the news in her characteristically nonchalant fashion. However, she began the next session by saying that a client had canceled an appointment that morning and she had some free time on hand. She started going through her desk and came across a home insurance policy she had bought a few months ago. She was disappointed to discover that it was full of loopholes. Excited about the thinly disguised allusion to my going away, I intervened by saying, "Perhaps, it is easier for you to talk about an insurance policy with loopholes than an analysis with sudden interruptions." After a pause, the patient responded in a pained voice, "I can see how you arrived at what you said but it hurt my feelings because I was really worried about the policy and it seems that you were not paying attention to my concern about it."

While my interpretation might have been correct, its timing certainly was not. In quickly unmasking what lay behind a derivative of her feelings about our separation, I had overlooked the patient's need for such disguise. I had disregarded her need to control the boundaries between her conscious and unconscious psychic life and to yield such control at her own pace. The proper analytic recognition of this need requires a sustained regard for issues of "optimal distance" (Akhtar 1992a, Bouvet 1958, Escoll 1992) and tact (Poland 1975).

The Need for Causality

In the clinical situation, the analyst's interventions (especially resistance analysis) are aimed at encouraging the analysand's "need to know" (Steinberg 1993) the intrapsychic reasons behind his or her interpersonal experiences. The analyst thus helps strengthen the patient's "need for causality" (Nunberg 1931). When externalized, this need gives rise to questions about the analyst and his manner of working within the clinical situation. Frustration of this defensive and projected need for causality is, to a large extent, essential if the world of inner objects is to be called forth in a lively, affective fashion into the transference context. However, when the analyst shows a striking departure from his or her usual manner of functioning, the patient's credulity is taxed and the resulting associative material is colored by iatrogenesis and false compliance. Under such circumstances—a sudden, long absence, a serious or terminal illness (Schwartz 1987)—some explanation, geared to the patient's ego level of affective tolerance, has to be offered. Only thus is the patient's ordinary need for causality met (the fantasies resulting from the answer itself can then be handled in a traditional analytic manner).

Emphasis on such extraordinary situations should not, however, make one overlook that an occasional offering of causal explanations of one's intervention to the patient during early phases of an ordinarily progressing analysis is also an important part of the analyst's technical armamentarium.

Case 4

At the end of a session in the third month of her analysis, an otherwise psychologically sophisticated young woman offered me a bag full of apples. She said that she had gone apple-picking over the weekend and wanted me to have some. I was taken aback. Neither her characteristic way of being nor the material in the session had prepared me for this. I responded, "I appreciate your bringing me this gift but I am afraid that I cannot accept it. See, our task here is to understand, enlighten ourselves to your mental functioning and, thus, come to grips with your difficulties. We cannot, therefore, move into actions, especially ones whose meanings are unknown to us. Now, I regret if my stance hurts your feelings, but I do not apologize because my intent is not to hurt you." She listened carefully and nodded in agreement. I then spontaneously added, "For instance, apples. What comes to mind about apples?" She answered "Adam's apple! . . . Adam and Eve . . . forbidden fruit." She smiled, blushed and left shaking her head, saying, "I understand, I understand."

The important point here is my giving her an explanation of the refusal to accept the gift. An intervention of this sort meets the patient's need for causality and enhances therapeutic alliance. To have refused the gift without an explanation, (especially this early in analysis) would have left her baffled, rendered the analytic method unduly mysterious to her, robbed her of a sense of collaboration, and weakened the therapeutic alliance (see also Loewald 1977 in this connection).

Meeting the patient's need for causality, however, has one important caveat: if a patient insists upon seeing *everything* (e.g., random accidents, actual physical ailments) as psychologically caused, the analyst should be prepared to question this too. Inability to believe in random occurrences is usually a sign of poor psychological-mindedness (Werman 1979), though it can also reflect a false compliance with the analytic method as well as a thinly disguised mocking of it.

The Need for Optimal Emotional Availability

Drawing upon Rapaport's (1960b) reminder that the psychic structure needs "stimulus nutriment" for its stability, and upon the
developmental observations regarding optimal distance (Akhtar
1992a, Escoll 1992, Mahler et al. 1975) and the infantile appeal-
cycle (Settlage et al. 1991), the analyst must remain emotionally
available to the patient on an ongoing basis. The psychoanalytic
situation has many built-in deprivations for the patient and an exaggerated austerity of interaction is not helpful. For instance, if a
patient says a few words about the inclement weather upon entering the office, there is no reason not to respond briefly to it. A
verbal response might render the analyst less intrusive than a forced
silence. The idea is to create a smoothly flowing ambience within
which the hidden meanings of the patient's communications are
to be deciphered. Thus the weather comment of the patient will
be both responded to and kept on the mental index cards of the
analyst as the session unfolds.

> To provide this sort of object or environment is certainly an impor-
> tant part of the therapeutic task. Clearly, it is only a part, not the
> whole of the task. Apart from being a "need-recognizing" and per-
> haps even a "need-satisfying" object, the analyst must also be a "need-
> understanding" object who in addition, must be able to communi-
> cate this understanding to his patient. [Balint 1968, pp. 180–181]

The issue of optimal emotional availability applies to other situations in analysis as well. Separations between the patient and the
analyst especially bring out this matter forcefully.[60] While an interpretive handling is always the preferred intervention, this mode

---

[60]Two Hollywood movies involving psychiatrists depict the matter under consideration well, though admittedly in their characteristically exaggerated fashion. The first, *Ordinary People* (1980), shows the psychiatrist agreeing to see his
adolescent patient, who is undergoing a major crisis, for a session well past mid-
night in his office. He certainly meets his patient's need in this regard. The second, a hilarious affair called *What About Bob?* (1991), centers upon a psychia-

might have to be postponed if the patient is too regressed and is in too much distress. Under such circumstances, the analyst might offer some form of interim contact, for example, a phone call or a postcard (Gunderson 1996, Settlage 1994) to keep the patient stabilized until a return to customary interpretive work is possible. "Such availability emulates appropriate parental availability as observed in the appeal cycle. It provides auxiliary regulation pending improvements in the patient's self-regulatory capacity" (Settlage 1994, p. 48).

The Need for Resilient Responsiveness
Under Special Circumstances

On the way to developing self-regulation, a growing child needs a predictable pattern of responses by his parents to his physical and psychological requirements. However, the parental attitudes of control and permissiveness must oscillate in conjunction with varying levels of the child's drive excitation and shifts in external reality. Flexibly responsive parents adapt the "house rules" to fit special circumstances. For instance, they might allow a child to stay up later than his usual bedtime when his cousins from out of town are visiting. A similar resilience on the part of the analyst is required, though certainly not at the cost of inattention to the effects of such flexibility on the analytic process. These special circumstances might arise from within the patient or from the external reality.

Another Vignette from My Own Analysis

Once during my analysis, the city was hit by a snowstorm that set a new record for a century. More than two feet of snow was ex-

---

trist who is blind to the need element in his patient following him to his vacation home and simply refusing to go back. Insistent upon interpreting the wish elements and then behaviorally controlling the patient, the psychiatrist becomes a caricature of an analyst who would do nothing but interpret. The emotional availability here is surely less than optimal!

pected to be on the ground by late afternoon when I had my appointment. Sensing trouble, I called my analyst at about 10 A.M. asking him if we would meet that day and, if so, could we meet earlier than the scheduled time. He said that he was glad that I called as he, too, was worried about the road conditions and, since he had some cancellations, could I come at noon? The session that followed was not altered in any way or form, to the best of my recollection.

Besides such external circumstances, special considerations might also arise from the patient's inner world of affects and ego attributes (either on a state or trait level). A poignant emotional upsurge toward the end of a session might correctly prompt the analyst to extend the session by a few minutes (Pulver, 1985); this will be accommodating the patient's need for flexible responsiveness. On the other hand, if such extended sessions become frequent, skepticism has to be called forth both vis-à-vis the patient's dynamics and the issues of countertransference.

More difficult dilemmas are presented when patients seem to need special arrangements on a sustained basis in order to effectively participate in analysis. For instance, analysands who have to travel long distances for their appointments might need more than one daily appointment. Then there are patients who are better able to collaborate in the analytic process at the end of the day. In their midday sessions, they cannot relax enough to do meaningful analytic work. Regardless of its reasons, such ego rigidity can pose a major technical problem. If the usual analytic handling of this resistance fails, should the analyst regard it as a special sort of situation (rather like a parent dealing with a child of an unusual temperament) and arrange to see the patient only at the end of the day? In a provocative paper, Kurtz (1988) elucidates the theoretical support for such a technical maneuver. Whether this constitutes a meeting of the patient's need for well-attuned responsiveness or a temporary giving in to a wish à la "legitimate transference gratification" (Stone 1961) might turn out to be a matter of theoretical predilection in the setting of a clinical "common ground" (Wallerstein 1990).

Summary

Loewald (1960) conceptualized the analytic situation as a developmental one and was supported in this notion by many others
(Fleming 1975, Robbins, in Escoll 1977). To be sure, the technical interventions vis-à-vis needs outlined here are evident in the
writings of many other analysts (Abrams 1978, Escoll 1991, Kramer
1987, Settlage 1989, 1993, 1994, Stone 1961, Tahka 1993). Most
practicing analysts, it seems, intuitively make these interventions
though without thinking in terms of needs and wishes. Even those
who dispute the legitimacy or necessity of such a distinction en-
dorse the suppleness that the interventions outlined above impart
to the analytic technique. Theodore Jacobs, for one, states,

> While, theoretically, the unconscious fantasies that lie behind a neu-
> rotic patient's wish/need for more responsiveness from the analyst,
> for a measure of support, for him to shed some of his anonymity,
> or to offer a word of encouragement, or of guidance, can be under-
> stood and altered through interpretation, this is not always true. For
> some patients these wishes and needs are so deeply entrenched, so
> powerfully felt, and so emotionally important to the patient that
> interpretation alone can do little to change them.
>
> The reasons for this are diverse . . . and in many cases they can
> be effectively analyzed at some point in treatment; initially they may
> not be approachable by interpretation alone. The patient experi-
> ences our efforts to interpret very differently than we mean them.
> They are often experienced as failures to understand, as withhold-
> ing, as hostility, as repetitions of past deprivations, or unwillingness
> to meet legitimate needs, etc. While again these reactions must be
> analyzed in certain cases, no headway can be made until the patient
> expresses (sic) a measure of gratification from us. [Personal com-
> munication, September 1991]

The guideline for providing such gratifications emanates from
the analyst's understanding the following: (1) ego support and
id gratification are different, even if not easily separable; (2) transference is affected by gratification as well as deprivation; (3)
countertransference can manifest itself through both excessive

resilience and inordinate rigidity; (4) gratification of one need might thwart a competing need and gratify a problematic wish at the same time; (5) the intervention chosen should match the patient's ego strength and serve the "technical" (Bibring 1954) function of preserving the treatment alliance; and (6) the effects of one's intervention should be looked for and subsequently handled in an interpretive manner.

A THEORETICAL POSTSCRIPT

While civilized human behavior cannot be equated with the natural behavior of lower species, unless we deny the theory of evolution we must assume similarities between the inborn needs and drives of man and beast. Lower animals crave companionship even if they are physically self-sufficient. Is man's object need secondary to the need satisfaction for food, warmth, and equilibrium? Or, is there a primary object need, an inborn instinct in man also? [Rollman-Branch 1960, p. 699]

I believe that man's destructiveness as a psychological phenomenon is secondary, that it arises originally as a result of the failure of the self-object environment to meet the child's need for optimal—not maximal, it should be stressed—empathic responses. [Kohut 1977, p. 116]

At the end, I come back to the beginning, to the early Freudian notion of ego instincts. These, as noted above (1) were aimed at self-preservation and self-seeking, (2) fulfilled nonsexual aims, (3) operated under the reality principle, and (4) carried an energy of their own that was not libido but "interest" (Freud 1905c, 1910b, 1915b). All these are also the features of the psychological needs that have been delineated by the British independent analysts, the developmentalists of various persuasions, and the self psychologists. What then is the problem? Why is there a necessity for discussions like this one to remind us of the need concept?

The answer for the repeated discovery of the concept of psychological needs lies in the history of the psychoanalytic instinct theory. In moving from his first dual-instinct theory (Freud 1905c, 1915d) of sexual and ego instincts to his second dual-instinct theory (Freud 1920a) of life and death instincts, Freud relegated ego instincts to the domain of life instinct. Regrettably, this move led to a gradual loss of conceptual zeal about ego instincts. Motivations, psychopathology, and transferences were now infrequently traced back to thwarted self-preservative tendencies. The wishes generated by sexual and aggressive drives took center stage and the needs emanating from ego instincts were confined to the heuristic and clinical green room. Indeed, the entire concept of ego instincts became repressed. Yet, like the repressed, which exerts a "continuous pressure in the direction of the conscious" (Freud 1915d, p. 151), it kept seeking readmission into the main corpus of the psychoanalytic thought. Winnicott (1960b) spoke of "ego needs." Modell (1975) argued for "quieter" instincts, not associated with id function and accounting for the development of attachment and object relations. Casement (1991) reformulated the concept as "growth needs," distinguishing them from "libidinal demands." The thinking behind these diverse but overlapping concepts[61] also found a counterpart in the broadened view of psychoanalytic process outlined above.

This particular conundrum of having to rediscover ego instinct-like concepts ("psychic needs," "developmental needs," "ego needs," "growth needs," "self-object needs," etc.) over and over again might have been avoided had Freud gone from his first dual-instinct theory not to his second dual-instinct theory but to a triple-instinct theory (sexual, aggressive, and ego instincts). Tongue-in-cheek though it may sound, this idea is not entirely devoid of seriousness.

---

[61]Among the varying revivals of the concept of ego instincts, self psychology occupies a prominent, albeit curious, place. On the one hand, its distance from classical metapsychology precludes the acknowledgment of its having resurrected ego instincts. On the other hand, it might be the most methodical and far-reaching, though single-minded, elaboration of the heuristic and technical value of the ego instinct concept.

Freud once compared the repressed to a heckler who upon being removed from an auditorium keeps banging on its doors. The ego instinct concept has been such a heckler. Perhaps it is time that we let the heckler back in and listen to him. At the same time, his readmission should not diminish our regard for those already present in the audience: intrapsychic conflict, overdetermination, unconscious fantasy, the Oedipus complex, and, in the very front row, the two instinctual drives of sex and aggression.

Part IV

FANTASIES

7

"SOMEDAY . . ." AND "IF ONLY . . ." FANTASIES

The "widening scope of indications for psychoanalysis" (Stone 1954, p. 593) has led, over the last three decades, to an enormous growth in the psychoanalytic literature on severe character pathology. This literature, far from being uniform, contains many controversies of both a theoretical and technical nature. In the realm of theory, the most prominent controversies involve (1) the sufficiency of structural theory (Abend et al. 1983, Arlow and Brenner 1964, Willick 1983) versus the need of new approaches (Balint 1968, Kernberg 1975b, 1984, 1992, Kohut 1971, 1977, Searles 1986) to understand severe psychopathology; (2) the applicability of the conflict model to such conditions (Abend et al. 1983, Kernberg 1975b, 1992) versus the necessity to conceptualize them in terms of deficit (Adler 1985, Kohut 1977, Winnicott 1965); and (3) the application of the developmental perspective provided by separation-individuation theory (Kramer 1980b, Mahler, 1968, 1971, 1972b, Mahler et al. 1975, Parens 1991, Settlage 1977, 1991, 1993) versus self-psychology (Kohut 1977, Kohut and Wolf 1978, Wolf 1994) in shedding light on the ontogenesis of severe personality disorders. In the realm of technique, the most prominent controversies involve (1) the differential emphasis upon searching and skeptical (Abend et al. 1983, Kernberg 1975b, 1984) versus a credulous and affirming (Balint 1968, Kohut 1977) listening attitude; and (2) relative roles of interpretive interventions (Kernberg 1975b, 1984, 1992, Volkan 1976, 1987a, Yeomans et al. 1992) versus the "holding," containing, and empathic functions of the analyst (Balint 1968, Casement 1991, Khan 1974, 1983, Kohut 1984, Lewin and Schulz 1992, Winnicott 1965) in the treatment of these conditions.

Caught on the horns of these dilemmas are attempts to elucidate the affective experiences of individuals with these disorders. Their envy, rage, and hatred have received multiple, often contradictory, explanations. More important to the purposes of this chapter, the focus of psychoanalytic literature has largely remained on these patients' bitterness, pessimism, and vulnerability to despair. Less attention has been paid to their "blind optimism" (Kernberg 1967, p. 676), "unshakable determination to get on" (Balint 1968, p. 19), and tenacious, though often covert, attitude of waiting. The descriptions of "primitive idealization" (Kernberg 1967) and "idealizing transference" (Kohut 1971) did address this area of their inner experience. However, subsequent elaborations of these views became trapped in the polemic of such idealization being either a residual developmental need (Kohut 1977, Kohut and Wolf 1978, Wolf 1994) or an instinctualized defense against deepseated rage (Kernberg 1975b, 1992, Volkan 1976, 1987a). This polarization, with the inevitable pressure to amass evidence for one or the other position, has caused inattention to other aspects of such idealization, including the existence of unconscious fantasies related to it. This chapter seeks to fill this lacuna in the psychoanalytic literature.

In this chapter, I describe two fantasies, namely "someday . . ." and "if only . . . ," which seem not only to be important vehicles of idealization but also related to each other in intricate ways. I highlight their phenomenological characteristics, especially their relationship to optimism and nostalgia, and their deleterious effects upon the temporal continuity of the self-experience. I then elucidate their metapsychological substrate and trace their origin through various phases of psychic development. Having described the clinical, metapsychological, and developmental aspects of the two fantasies, I conclude with the implications of the foregoing to the technique of psychoanalysis and psychoanalytic psychotherapy. It seems advisable, however, to delineate the potential pitfalls in such conceptualization at the very outset.

SOME CAVEATS

> Caveat: (L. *caveat*, let him beware, 3rd pers. sing. pres. subj. of *cavere*, to behave, take heed): a warning, admonition. [*Webster's New Universal Unabridged Dictionary*, second edition, 1983, p. 289]

> Books must be read as deliberately and reservedly as they are written. [Thoreau, 1854, p. 92]

First and foremost, the fantasies I am about to describe should not be taken as literally representing the ideational events of the early infantile life. While feelings and wordless thoughts of infancy do form the building blocks of these fantasies, their specific content, requiring greater cognitive maturity, seems derived from later childhood. In a fashion analogous to writing a song on a preexisting tune, the experiences and images of later childhood give form to the nebulous residues of the preverbal period (Burland 1975, Frank 1969, Isakower 1936, Spitz 1965). Freud's (1918) designation of notions involving intrauterine life as "retrospective phantasying" (p. 103) is an apt reminder here. Second, the manner in which these fantasies are communicated (by the patient) and deciphered (by the analyst) precludes certainty about them. Patients fail to satisfactorily put them into words[62] and often resort to metaphors, while the analyst finds himself relying on his own affective experience to a greater than usual extent (Burland 1975). The ground is murky and the risks attendant upon excessive reliance on empathy (Akhtar 1989b, Rubovits-Seitz 1988, Wallerstein

---

[62]The meagerness of free-associative data has resulted in my resorting to a composite sketch of such individuals rather than specific case illustrations.

1983), including countertransference intrusions, loom large in such interpretive undertaking. Third, it should not be overlooked that the origin of these fantasies is often multilayered and their intrapsychic purposes complex. Longings implicit in them usually arise as a result of unresolved separation-individuation but such desires may also be mobilized by the developmentally later conflicts of the phallic-oedipal phase. Fourth, caution should be exercised in assigning diagnostic significance to such fantasies. In subtle and subterranean forms, these fantasies are ubiquitous. It is only when they are tenacious, serve major defensive and discharge functions, and encroach upon the executive functions of the ego, that they become pathological. Finally, it should be remembered that these fantasies may have an idiosyncratic relevance for a given patient. For instance, the "someday" fantasy of a patient might be based on an identification with a parent who had such a fantasy. Another patient's excessive optimism might be carrying out, in an ironic fashion, the parental demand to think only good thoughts, be cheerful, and not complain. Keeping such diverse determinants in mind would facilitate discovery and enrich reconstructions in this area.

THE "SOMEDAY" FANTASY

Some people are dominated by the belief that there will always be some kind person—a representative of the mother, of course—to care for them and to give them everything they need. This optimistic belief condemns them to inactivity. [Abraham 1924b, p. 399]

Only by remaining a hope does hope persist. [Bion 1961, pp. 151–152]

When hope attains ascendency over desire, future time takes on a correspondingly magnified importance. If hope is to be maintained against the erosions of hopelessness and desire, time needs to be conserved and preserved—the more so since the

> pleasures attendant upon gratification of desire are
> not present to console or compensate for the loss of
> hope. [Boris 1976, p. 145]

Like Balint (1968), who was led to choose the term *basic fault* because that was "exactly the word used by many patients to describe it" (p. 21), I am guided by my patients in calling this fantasy "someday." This is precisely how these individuals refer to a certain kind of expectation from themselves, from their analyses, from life in general. They undertake treatment with gusto, religiously keep their appointments, arrive punctually, pay their bills promptly, and, from all appearances, seem good patients. Most of them talk copiously, offering well-thought-out formulations regarding their maladies. They earnestly express the hope of overcoming this or that inhibition, resolving this or that symptom, and achieving this or that life goal. They often stir up much redemptive enthusiasm in the analyst as well, especially during the opening phase of the analysis.

Gradually, however, a different picture that challenges the assumed industriousness on these patients' part begins to emerge. They seem to be taking on too much, putting things off, never finishing anything. Whenever they run into difficulties, roadblocks, or "too much hassle," they withdraw. This withdrawal gives a superficial appearance of their being flexible and realistic. Actually the case is just the opposite, since their withdrawal is not caused by accepting realistic difficulties and the resultant mourning but is intended to negate the impact of such limits on their vision. It is a behavioral counterpart of denial. After a brief lull in their optimistic pursuits, they begin all over again. They do not truly look for alternatives for anything since they never accept defeat in the first place. They overlook discordant realities, cut ethical corners, and perpetually "shelve things away." Their secret hope is that "someday" all problems will vanish or they will be strong enough to deal with them.

The unrealistic optimism of these patients caricatures the "confident expectation" (Benedek 1938) or "basic trust" (Erikson 1950) that results from a satisfactory infant–mother relationship. These normatively inclined concepts illustrate a long-held tendency in psychoanalysis to regard optimism, even when excessive, in relatively positive terms. This tendency was set into motion by Freud's (1917a) well-known correlation of "confidence in success" with being mother's "undisputed darling" (p. 156) and by Abraham's (1924b) linking "imperturbable optimism" (p. 399) with an overly gratifying oral phase. Glover (1925) repeated that profound oral gratification leads to an "excess of optimism which is not lessened by reality experience" (p. 136). Later contributions (French 1945, French and Wheeler 1963, Menninger, 1959) also remained focused on the positive aspects of hope and optimism.

In an exception to such thinking, Angel (1934) noted that excessive optimism is often a defensive development.[63] She described five patients with chronic, unrealistic hope of a magical event (*Wunderglauben*) to improve their lots. She traced the origin of three female patients' undue hopefulness to a denial of their lacking a penis and associated feelings of inferiority. Angel offered a different explanation for undue optimism in two male patients. They had been prematurely and painfully deprived of their infantile omnipotence and were seeking its restoration by a fantasied regressive oneness with their mothers. Their optimism contained the hope of such longings being realized.

Over the sixty years following Angel's (1934) significant paper, only a few contributions commented upon the defensive functions of excessive optimism. First, Searles (1977) noted that realistic hope needs to be distinguished from "unconscious-denial-based, unrealistic hopefulness" (p. 484). The former emanates from a successful integration of prior disappointments. The latter results from an "essentially manic repression of loss and despair" (p. 483). In contrast to healthy hopefulness, which is a source of support and gratification for oneself and others, excessive hope serves sadomasochistic aims. Searles outlined two connections between such inordinate hope and sadism:

---

[63]Nearly two hundred years before this, Voltaire (1759) had declared optimism to be "a mania for maintaining that all is well when things are going badly" (p. 54).

First, one of the more formidable ways of being sadistic toward the other person is to engender hope, followed by disappointment, in him over and over. Second, the presenting of a hopeful demeanor under some circumstances can constitute, in itself, a form of sadism toward the other person, for it can be expressing, implicitly and subtly, cruel demands upon him to fulfill the hopes written upon one's face. [p. 485]

Following Searles's contribution, Amati-Mehler and Argentieri (1989) described two cases in which "pathological hope" (p. 300) represented "the last and unique possible tie with the primary object, [which] giving up would mean the definite downfall of illusion and the admission that it is really, truly lost" (p. 302). Then, highlighting the effects of unresolved separation-individuation and impaired object constancy, I (Akhtar 1991a, 1994b) briefly outlined the "someday" and "if only" fantasies discussed here in detail. Finally, Potamianou (1992) asserted that excessive hope can serve as a character armor that keeps reality at a distance. In normal and neurotic conditions, hope sustains a link with the good object and makes waiting bearable. In borderline conditions, however, hope serves as an expression of the patient's narcissistic self-sufficiency; waiting is made bearable only by recourse to infantile omnipotence. For such individuals, the present has only secondary importance. They can tolerate almost any current suffering in the hope that future rewards will make it all worthwhile.[64] Potamianou emphasized that excessive hope, besides fueling (and being fueled by) narcissism, strengthens and prolongs the hidden masochistic suffering of these individuals.

Besides these descriptions of pathological optimism, there exists the view of the independent British analysts that hope, even when expressed through pathological behavior, is essentially healthy and adaptive. Winnicott (1956) declared that "the antisocial act is an

---

[64]Boris (1976) has proposed a "fundamental antagonism between hope and desire" (p. 141); possession of hope acts as a restraint upon desire and loss of hope is followed by a burgeoning of desire.

expression of hope" (p. 309) insofar as it seeks a redress to an early environmental deprivation. Khan (1966) extended Winnicott's ideas to certain narcissistic and schizoid individuals who seemed uncannily capable of creating special and exciting experiences for themselves, experiences from which they nonetheless withdrew[65] and which left them basically unchanged. It is as if they had hoped for something ("someday"?) but did not find it. More recently, Casement (1991) related "unconscious hope" to repetition compulsion through which unconscious conflicts continue to generate attempts at solutions which do not actually work. At the same time, patients do contribute in various ways, and "hopefully" (p. 301), to finding the clinical setting needed by them. In sum, the psychoanalytic literature on hope can be grouped into three broad categories emphasizing (1) its normative, healthy aspects; (2) its employment as a defense against early loss and defective object constancy as well as its covert narcissistic and masochistic aims; and (3) its adaptive role in seeking redress, including that through pathological behavior, of early environmental loss. The "someday" fantasy described here subsumes all these aspects of hope and optimism.

Returning from this detour into the literature, one notes that patients vary greatly in the extent to which they provide details of their hopes from "someday." Often they feel puzzled, uncomfortable, ashamed, and even angry upon being asked to elaborate on their "someday." This is especially so if they are asked what would happen *after* "someday." It is as if "someday," like God, is not to be questioned. Some patients use metaphors and/or visual images to convey the essence of "someday," while others remain silent about it. Frequently, the analyst has to fill in the blanks and surmise the nature of their expectations from "someday." In either case, it is the affective texture of "someday" that seems its most important feature. Basically, "someday" refers to a time when one would be

---

[65]Much earlier, Eissler (1950) had pointed out that the "addiction to novelty" (p. 133) among antisocial personalities actually consists of a monotonous repetition of essentially similar experiences. True novelty scares them and they vehemently avoid it.

completely peaceful and conflict-free. Everything would be available, or nothing would be needed. Motor activity would either be unnecessary or effortless. Even thinking would not be required. There would be no aggression from within or from outside.[66] Needless to say, such a universe is also oblivious to the inconvenient considerations of the incest taboo and the anxieties and compromises consequent upon the oedipal situation.

A complex set of psychodynamic mechanisms helps maintain the structural integrity of "someday": (1) denial and negation of sectors of reality that challenge it; (2) splitting-off of those self and object representations that mobilize conflict and aggression; (3) a defensively motivated feeling of inauthenticity (Gediman 1985, Loewald 1979) in those areas of personality where a healthier, more realistic, compromise formation level of mentality and functioning has been achieved[67]; and (4) a temporal displacement, from past to future, of a preverbal state of blissful unity with the "all good" mother of the symbiotic phase (Mahler 1972b, Mahler et al. 1975). The speculation that this fantasy, at its core, contains a longing for a luxurious (and retrospectively idealized) symbiotic phase gains strength from the inactivity, timelessness, wordlessness, thoughtlessness, unexcited bliss, and absence of needs implicit in "someday." This genetic backdrop is supported by my observation that individuals who tenaciously cling to "someday" had often been suddenly "dropped" from maternal attention during their second year of life (at times due to major external events, e.g., birth of a sibling, prolonged maternal hospitalization). However, other factors including early parent or sibling loss, intense castration anxiety, and problematic oedipal scenarios also play a role in the genesis of the "someday" fantasy. Boys who were excessively close to their mothers, especially if they also had weak or absent fathers, might continue to believe that "someday" their oedipal triumph

---

[66]Rumbles of the "oceanic feeling" (Freud 1930) of psychic infancy during which the self-absorbed infant experiences all of space and time as coextensive with his ego, are unmistakably present here.

[67]In an extension of Winnicott's (1960a) terminology, the situation here can be described as a "pseudo-false self" organization.

could actually be consummated; Chasseguet-Smirgel's (1984) delineation of "perverse character" is pertinent in this context. Girls who were "dropped" by their mothers and valiantly rescued by their fathers in childhood persist in the hope of "someday" finding an all good mother–father combination in adult life.

Only the focal and externalized derivatives of "someday" are usually conscious. The infantile fused self and object representations powerfully invested with "primitive idealization" (Kernberg 1967) emerge only after considerable analytic work has been accomplished. The adaptive functions of the "someday" fantasy involve its fostering optimism, perseverance, and "search for an environmental provision" (Winnicott 1956, p. 310). The idealized "someday" is a defensive structure against the affective turmoil, including rage, consequent upon less than "optimal emotional availability" (Mahler 1971, p. 176) of the mother especially during the rapprochement subphase of separation-individuation. However, it might also defend against anxieties consequent upon the realization of the anatomical differences between sexes (Freud 1925), and of oedipal boundaries and limits (e.g., "someday" I will have a penis; "someday" I will be the romantic partner of my mother/father).[68] The excessive hope implicit in "someday" fantasy serves both narcissistic and masochistic aims. In an attempt to establish a related sort of link between narcissistic and masochistic character types, Cooper (1989) emphasized that "pathological narcissistic tendencies are unconscious vehicles for obtaining masochistic disappointment; and masochistic injuries are an affirmation of distorted narcissistic fantasies" (p. 551).[69]

---

[68]Among the growing ego's attempts to hold on to illusions of omnipotence, Dorn (1967) includes the "when I grow up . . ." incantation of childhood. Such motivating idealizations are already an advance over the more magical, earlier state of infantile omnipotence.

[69]States of addiction and codependency also depict the masochistic dimension of excessive hope. The addict continues to be self-destructive while hoping that the drug will somehow magically solve intrapsychic problems, and the codependent individual remains relentlessly optimistic that a terrible relationship will somehow become all right. The connection between pathological hope and masochism becomes blatant when the longed-for "someday" involves death.

On the behavioral level, the manner in which patients strive to reach "someday" varies greatly (Akhtar 1992b). Those with an overtly narcissistic personality seek to bring "someday" to life by actively searching for social success and admiration; the "shy narcissists" (Akhtar 1998) also work extremely hard, but quietly wait for belated recognition. Those with an antisocial bent seek similar magic through swindling, gambling, and other get-rich-quick schemes. Paranoid individuals focus on the obstacles in their path to "someday." Borderline individuals frantically look for this "someday" through infatuations, perverse sexuality, and mind-altering drugs. Schizoid individuals adopt a passive stance and hope for a magical happening, a windfall, or a chance encounter with a charismatic guru. All individuals with a severe personality disorder—be it narcissistic, antisocial, paranoid, borderline, or schizoid—seem to be seeking a "fantasied reversal of a calamity that has occurred" (Renik 1990, p. 234), and a restitution of an inner homeostasis that was disturbed years ago. All are in chronic pursuit.[70]

This relentless pursuit of the "all good" mother of symbiosis at times gets condensed with positive oedipal strivings. Condensation of the "good" mother representation with that of the desired oedipal partner gives rise to intense longings experienced as

---

Patients with this configuration manifest a chronic attitude of waiting for death, with or without occasional suicidal acts. Such incorporation of self-destructiveness into the ego ideal usually speaks for a guarded prognosis (Kernberg 1975b).

[70]To borrow terms used by Settlage and colleagues (1991) in a different context, it seems that all patients with severe character pathology are stuck in the appeal phase of the infantile "appeal cycle" (adaption-distress-appeal-interaction), only the manner of their appeal varies. Perhaps these stylistic differences contain remote echoes of early infantile experiences. Spitz (1953) points out that an infant, when separated "first becomes weepy, demanding and clinging to everybody who approaches it; it looks as though attempts are made by these infants to regain the lost object with the help of their aggressive drive. Later on, visible manifestations of the aggressive drive decrease" (p. 133). Could the various phenotypic variations of severe character pathology (e.g., borderline, narcissistic, schizoid) at least partly be due to their different locations on this spectrum of affectomotor responses of a betrayed child?

unquestionable needs (Akhtar 1992b, 1994a). The parallel amalgamation of the "bad" mother representation with the oedipal rival creates vengeful hostility that is often split off, denied, displaced onto others, or enacted in a contradictory but unassimilated manner toward the analyst. During analytic treatment, such "malignant erotic transference" (Akhtar 1994b)[71] often turns out to be an upward defense against faulty self and object constancy. Four aspects of this transference are (1) predominance of hostility over love in the seemingly erotic overtures; (2) intense coercion of the analyst to indulge in actions; (3) inconsolability in the face of the analyst's depriving stance;[72] and (4) the absence of erotic counterresonance in the analyst who experiences the patient's demands as intrusive, controlling, and hostile. In such cases, "the preeminent oral insatiability, the vulnerability to disappointment and detachment, the underlying sadomasochism soon become apparent" (Blum 1973, p. 69). In the throes of such intense erotic transference (see also Eickhoff 1987, Joseph 1993, Wallerstein 1993), the patient can become convinced the analyst should (or will) "someday" actually consummate their relationship and marry her. Here the emergence of the "someday" fantasy shows a beginning loss of reality testing and is therefore a cause for alarm. Conversely, in patients who, in a near-psychotic version of such transference, are insistent that the analyst marry them right now, a movement toward "someday" implies the dawning capacity to tolerate postponement of desire. It might constitute the first evidence of a strengthened capacity to mourn and renunciate omnipotent claims on reality.

---

[71]The choice of the modifier *malignant* to describe such "erotized" (Blum 1973) transference is to highlight these aggressive and coercive features and to extend the context in which this prefix has been earlier used in psychoanalysis, for example, "malignant regression" (Balint 1968) and "malignant narcissism" (Kernberg 1984).

[72]Freud (1915a) referred to such patients as "children of nature who refuse to accept the psychical in place of the material" (p. 166). In his experience, most such patients were "women of elemental passionateness who tolerate no surrogates" (p. 166). The explanation for the greater frequency of malignant erotic transference in women is given in Chapter 3 (see especially footnote 6).

THE "IF ONLY" FANTASY

> The first two years of life, in which external "omnipo-
> tent" persons took care of us, protected and provided
> us with food, shelter, sexual satisfaction, and reparti-
> cipation in the lost omnipotence, gave us a feeling
> of being secure in a greater unit, while, at the same
> time losing our own individuality. This memory es-
> tablishes in every human being a capacity for nos-
> talgia for such a state whenever attempts at active
> mastery fail. [Fenichel 1945, p. 561]

> The reiterative declarations of uselessness, failure
> and lack of hope made by our patients are placed in
> a non-temporal dimension in which the idea of fail-
> ure is fictitious, since all energies are pathologically
> directed to a past that needs to be kept immobile and
> therefore incapable of becoming "history." [Amati-
> Mehler and Argentieri 1989, pp. 300–301]

Individuals with the "if only" fantasy lack interest in the future and constantly wring their hands over something that happened in the past. They insist that "if only" it had not taken place, every-thing would have turned out (or would have been) all right. Life before that event is glossed over or retrospectively idealized. When a childhood event, for example, parental divorce, gets involved in the "if only" fantasy, an elaborate "personal myth" (Kris 1956) tends to develop that, with its seductive logic, might even go unques-tioned during analytic treatment (e.g., my case of Mr. A. in Kramer and Akhtar 1988). The "screen" nature of such "if only" formula-tions, however, is clearer when the trauma, relentlessly harped on, is from the recent past. Individuals who remain tormented year after year by the memories of a failed romance from college days, a psychotherapist who moved out of town, or an extramarital lover who withdrew his or her affection (see the case of Ms. H. in Chap-ter 1) often give histories of having been painfully "dropped" from maternal attention during early childhood.

A concomitant of the "if only" fantasy is intense nostalgia. The wish to recapture an idealized past stirs up a poignant mixture of "mental pain" (Freud 1926, p. 171) and joy. Pain is evoked by the

awareness of separation from the now idealized object and joy
by a fantasied reunion with it through reminiscences. "It is the
subtlety, iridescence, and ambivalence of these feelings that gives
nostalgia its inimitable coloration" (Werman 1977, p. 393). While
often attributed to a loss during adult life, this characteristically
"bitter-sweet pleasure" (Kleiner 1970, p. 11) has its origin in the
incomplete mourning of a traumatic disruption of the early
mother–child relationship. Sterba (1940) was the first to correlate
homesickness with a longing for the maternal breast. Fenichel
(1945) also explained nostalgia as a wish to return to the preoedipal
mother. Fodor (1950) went so far as to correlate nostalgic yearn-
ings with a deep-seated longing for the undisturbed prenatal state.[73]
However, these references to prenatal bliss, maternal breast, and
preoedipal mother are better regarded as largely metaphorical.
Much takes place between a premature traumatic rupture of the
infantile bliss and its alleged counterpart in adulthood. Hartmann's
(1964) warning regarding the "genetic fallacy" must be heeded
here. Recall of such early events is questionable, fantasies involving them are retrospective creations, and the idealization is intended to keep aggressively tinged self and object representations
in abeyance.[74] It is, however, unmistakable that the nostalgic individual is looking for a completely untroubled state. Such a person
is looking not only for the lost object but for an idealized object
and, even more important, for the time before the object was lost.
This covert element of search in the nostalgic hand-wringing is a
clue to the psychodynamic kinship between the "if only" and "someday" fantasies.

The metapsychological structure of the "if only" fantasy is indeed
similar to that of the "someday" fantasy. It too involves splitting,
denial, and primitive idealization. It too serves defensive purposes

---

[73]Chasseguet-Smirgel's (1984) notion of the pervert's "nostalgia for primary
narcissism" (p. 29) seems related to this view.

[74]Awareness of the resulting "screen" functions of such nostalgia has led to
the distinction between "normal and pathological" (Werman 1977) and "true
and false" (Sohn 1983) types of nostalgia. The former is supposed to reflect a
continuation of mourning and the latter its idealized blockade.

and reflects incomplete mourning over preoedipal (premature loss of adequate maternal attention), oedipal (being excluded from the parents' mutually intimate life), and narcissistic (painful awareness of being vulnerable) traumas. Under normal circumstances, mourning such traumas goes hand in hand with the ego's renunciation of infantile omnipotence. "The experiencing of hopelessness is thus a part of normal development and is necessary for the attainment of a more reality-oriented sense of psychic self" (Schmale 1964, p. 300). Klein's (1940) "depressive position" and Mahler's (1968) "object constancy" are both contingent upon renunciation of omnipotence, development of the capacity for ambivalence, and a certain diminution in optimism about the self and others. The "if only" fantasy, in contrast, is, at its core, a product of incomplete mourning over the loss of the all-good mother of symbiosis. It expresses a position whereby the idealized primary object is neither given up through the work of grieving nor assimilated into the ego through identification. Instead, the object is retained in psychic limbo by a stubborn "nostalgic relationship" (Geahchan 1968), which is

> characteristically indeterminate in its representations, and by its imaginary nature the subject is able to maintain separateness from the object. This leads to an indefinite and indefinable quest—and if an object should appear that seems to correspond to the nostalgic desire, it is promptly rejected, it becomes demythologized; it is not what it promised to be: the subject's projection of what it should be. The subject can thus only enjoy the search and never the possession. [Werman 1977, p. 391]

At the same time, the displaced derivatives of this "loss" are harped on ad infinitum. Here splitting mechanisms also play a significant role since the aggressively tinged representations of the lost object are totally repudiated and/or displaced onto other objects.

Similarities between the "someday" and "if only" fantasies do not end with dynamics of insufficient mourning. Their form might differ but their message is essentially the same. Indeed, the two can together be labeled as "the fantasies of ideal times" (Juan-David

Nasio, personal communication). The "someday" fantasy says, "A day will come when I will recapture the lost mother of symbiosis and also overcome the oedipal barrier." The "if only" fantasy says, "I wish the day had not come when I was dropped from maternal attention or the day when I become aware of the oedipal limitations." Another similarity between the two fantasies involves their pronounced sadomasochistic aims. In the "someday" fantasy, these are evident in the destruction of all here-and-now satisfactions. This destruction may be either an angry denigration of the available satisfactions or a defense against superego accusations for not having done better. In the "if only" fantasy, much hateful blaming of self and others underlies the preoccupation with an "unfortunate" external event.

> Those with ferocious superegos and masochistic inclinations are involved in endless self-condemnation: "If only I had said this, if only I had done that," etc. These fantasies are a way of paying back one's conscience without really intending to do anything different in the future. They are mea culpas: "I have confessed to being guilty and now we can close the books of this episode." Then there are the "if only" fantasies that blame others: "If only so and so had chosen to behave decently towards me . . ." "If only people could see the real me and realize how wonderful I am . . . ," and so on. In other words whatever catastrophe has befallen me, it is not my fault. It would not have happened had others not denied me my due or maliciously gotten in my way. [Arnold Cooper, unpublished discussion of this chapter, June 1995]

Yet another element common to "someday" and "if only" fantasies is the quest for a lost object and, behind it, for a lost self-experience. Moreover, the psychic ointment of idealization is used by both "someday" and "if only" fantasies. It serves a self-soothing purpose and helps to deny aggression toward the unavailable, frustrating object held responsible for the narcissistic disequilibrium. These advantages of idealization are matched by its deleterious effect on the temporal dimension of self-experience. In the "someday" fantasy, the future is idealized, leading to excessive hope and a search for ideal conditions. In the "if only" fantasy, the past is idealized, leading to nostalgia and self-pity. Individuals with the former fantasy live in the future and those with the latter live in the past; both are alienated from the present.[75] In other words, both fantasies cause a "temporal discontinuity in the self experience" (Akhtar 1992b, p. 30). Frequently, the two fantasies coexist and form a tandem theme: "If only this had not happened, life would be all right, but someday this will be reversed and life will (again) become totally blissful." This tandem theme is all too frequently found in religious motifs, literary productions, and various cultural institutions and rituals.

SOCIOCULTURAL VICISSITUDES

> In our nostalgia for the major freedom of animal life we remember a Golden Age, a Garden, a time before sin. The sacred does not beckon to us from up ahead, urging us forward toward higher spiritual realms. The sacred lies behind us. It blocks the way back to the freedom of our pre-human past. The sacred and the forbidden are one. [Wheelis 1994, p. 35]

The Christian notion of original sin, a transgression that brought the idyllic existence of mankind's mythic forebears to an abrupt end, embodies a parricidal oedipal theme (Freud 1913a) as well as a separation and loss of omnipotence scenario. Together the two yield an "if only" fantasy of cosmic proportions. Counterposed to this fall from grace is the possibility of "someday" returning to it in the form of heaven. Judaism, while not subscribing to the original sin idea, does hold that a Messiah will arrive "someday" and bring eternal peace on earth. Islam, like Christianity, subscribes to the notion of heaven, and certain of its sects, for example Shiites, also contribute to the notion of the Messiah's (*Mahdi*) return. Hinduism holds that after numerous

---

[75]I have elsewhere (Akhtar 1995b) highlighted such temporal fracture of the psyche and the associated role of "someday" and "if only" fantasies in the lives of immigrants, a group of people especially vulnerable to such experiences.

reincarnations the soul will ultimately be relieved of the anguish of corporeal existence. Achieving *moksha* (freedom), the individual *atma* (soul) will become one with *paramatma* (the supreme soul, Brahma, the creator). Thus, in one form or the other, themes of being "dropped" and "expelled" from a blissful existence and of return to it exist in all the major religions of the world.

This human desire to return to an earlier ideal (idealized!) state of total freedom from conflict finds nonreligious expression as well. The deep love of nature in some persons and the yearning for a reunion with it seem to have roots in a nostalgia of the kind described above. Themes of pining for a lost paradise (often displaced to its derivatives, e.g., bygone youth, cities and countries left behind, past lovers) have created some of the most powerful literary pieces in history. Kleiner (1970) and Werman (1977), in their papers on nostalgia, give many evocative examples of this sort, including that of Marcel Proust, whom Werman aptly calls "the most famous *grand nostalgique*" (p. 394). Hamilton's (1969) essay on Keats is also in the same vein. Art, too, frequently capitalizes on nostalgia; examples of this extend from Giorgio de Chirico's preoccupation with Italian landscapes (Krystal 1966) to the more plebeian themes of Norman Rockwell's popular paintings. The recent attempt to resurrect the 1969 Woodstock music festival might also have betrayed a yearning to recapture the spirit and feeling of a past, now idealized, place and time. It is with such longing that individuals with "someday" and "if only" fantasies arrive at the psychoanalysts' doorsteps.

TECHNICAL IMPLICATIONS

> Nostalgic tendencies are seen as associated with an inability to mourn in early life, and later, an unwillingness to do so. Only after the search for unification with infantile objects is given up is the nostalgic able to accept meaningful substitutes. [Kleiner 1970, p. 29]

> To firmly undo the idealization, to confront the pa-
> tient again and again with the unrealistic aspects of
> his transference distortion, while still acknowledging
> the positive feelings that are also part of this ideali-
> zation, is a very difficult task because underneath that
> idealization are often paranoid fears and quite direct,
> primitive aggressive feelings toward the transference
> object. [Kernberg 1975b, pp. 97–98]

Having acknowledged the ubiquitousness of "someday" and "if only" fantasies in human mental life, I have, by implication, conceded that all individuals entering psychotherapy or psychoanalysis bring such attitudes with them. The hope and idealization implicit in these fantasies serves, in most patients, as a therapeutic incentive that sustains the interpretive enterprise and makes treatment possible. Their hope has a realistic quality that contributes to the development of therapeutic or working alliance (Friedman 1969, Gitelson 1962b, Greenson 1965). "Someday" and "if only" fantasies do not become an explicit focus of analytic inquiry in these patients. Themes of disillusionment and loss of omnipotence appear mostly during the termination phase of their treatment.

Other patients are different.[76] Their entire psychic lives are governed by "someday" and "if only" fantasies; in their case, these fantasies reflect not only an inner organizing element of central importance but also an outer relational paradigm. In the analytic situation, the "someday" fantasy of many such patients gives rise

---

[76]In an unpublished discussion of this chapter, Nasio distinguished the "someday" and "if only" fantasies of the neurotic and the borderline patients on two grounds: (1) the neurotic postpones castration anxiety by temporally displacing his wishes, while the borderline avoids self-disintegration by hiding behind the hope or "memory" of absolute bliss; and (2) the neurotic attributes to the analyst the power to fulfill his needs while the borderline excludes the analyst and awaits no promise. Nasio's first notion is more agreeable to me than the second. In my experience, the narcissist (seemingly) excludes the analyst and waits for nothing, the borderline attributes to the analyst the power to realize his hope, and the neurotic retains an awareness of the illusory nature of his excessive optimism.

to an attitude of perpetual waiting. This might be expressed nakedly through protracted silences, or cloaked by superficial compliance, even verbal excess. Other patients develop a "malignant erotic transference" and coerce the analyst to have sex with them or marry them. All patients with a "someday" fantasy hope that analysis (or the analyst) will somehow magically solve all their problems. However, excessive optimism impedes realistic hope and paves the way to hopelessness. Consequently, such patients oscillate between inordinate optimism and a bruised sense of futility.[77]

The "if only" fantasy manifests in the analytic situation as either an abysmal preoccupation with an adult-life loss to the exclusion of other associations, or as a slow emergence of a "personal myth" (Kris 1956) involving a childhood trauma. The individual with the "someday" fantasy waits or coerces and the one with the "if only" fantasy laments, seeks to convince, or pleads for validation of a particular viewpoint. Issues of narcissistic vulnerability, shaky object constancy, repudiated aggression, and inconsolability are prominent in both. Secretly or openly, both types of individuals are given to intense idealization that betrays unmet "growth needs" (Casement 1991) of childhood *and* a defense against aggression. It is to the treatment of such patients that the following technical suggestions apply.

Before proceeding further, however, a brief return to the developmental perspective on these issues is necessary. Both Winnicott (1951) and Mahler (1972b) trace a developmental line from illusion to disillusion during childhood. In Winnicott's terminology, initially "omnipotence is nearly a fact of life" (Winnicott 1951, p. 238). Later, the transitional object appears, when the mother is in transition from being "merged with the infant to that of being perceived rather than conceived of" (Winnicott 1971, p. 115). In Mahler's terminology, it is during the rapprochement subphase that the child realizes that his wishes and those of the mother do

---

[77]Killingmo (1989) has also noted such oscillation between "desperate hope and resignation" (p. 73). According to him, when this happens, the clinical material at hand is based primarily on a deficit-driven sector of personality and not by that governed by conflict.

not always coincide. Unable to sustain the magic of symbiosis, "the child can no longer maintain his delusion of parental omnipotence" and also "must gradually and painfully give up the delusion of his own grandeur" (Mahler et al. 1975, p. 79). Adding a significant nuance to Freud's (1911a) outlining of the gradual replacement of pleasure principle by reality principle, both Winnicott and Mahler regard this journey from illusion to disillusion as necessary for psychic growth.[78] And, it is this movement from illusion to disillusion that is the central task in the treatment of individuals with tenacious "someday" and "if only" fantasies. Being able to take this agonizing step is what transforms their pathological hope to realistic expectation and their idealization to a mature, postambivalent object investment. For them to make such an advance, however, the treatment must offer both illusion and disillusionment.[79]

First and foremost, therefore, the analyst must provide a psychological atmosphere of trust, emotional security, and acceptance, attributes akin to the early maternal care of the child. Modell (1976) has spelled out those elements in the analyst's technique that facilitate the development and maintenance of such a "holding environment" (Winnicott 1960a).

> The analyst is constant and reliable; he responds to the patients' affects; he accepts the patient, and his judgement is less critical and more benign; he is there primarily for the patient's needs and not for his own; he does not retaliate; and he does at times have a better grasp of the patient's inner reality than does the patient himself and therefore may clarify what is bewildering and confusing. [Modell 1976, p. 291]

---

[78]This similarity should not lead one to overlook that significant conceptual differences do exist in the theories of Winnicott and Mahler (see Wolman 1991).

[79]Technical approaches in this realm have leaned either toward providing and sustaining illusion (Adler 1985, Balint 1968, Kohut 1977, Lewin and Schulz 1992) or toward interpretive dissolution of such illusion (Abend et al. 1983, Kernberg 1975b, Volkan 1976, Yeomans et al. 1992). Elsewhere (Akhtar 1992b) I have attempted a broader synthesis of these two trends related to the "romantic" and "classic" visions of psychoanalysis (Strenger 1989).

To be sure, all this is important in the conduct of any analysis. However, in patients with "someday" and "if only" fantasies, these factors acquire a much greater significance insofar as they help mobilize, and temporarily sustain, the patient's illusion that hope can be fulfilled and lost objects found. However illusory such goals might be, the patient does need to be able to feel and think them valid before seeing them as fantasies, with regressive aims and defensive functions. Volkan's (1981) observation that attuned listening and containment of emotions often constitute the only interventions for quite some time before any interpretive work can be done with individuals suffering from pathological grief is pertinent here. Also important is Amati-Mehler and Argentieri's (1989) caution that, before the patient's excessive hope is frustrated either directly or by way of interpretation,

> the patient ought to experience for a sufficient length of time and at different levels the soundness of the therapeutic rapport, the security of being understood, the benefit of a careful and thorough working through of the transference, and a relational structure that enables him or her to contain the comprehension and the elaboration of the disruption of the transference play. [p. 303]

Second, the analyst must be comfortable with the use of "affirmative interventions" (Killingmo 1989). These are composed of an "objectifying element," which conveys the sense to the patient that the therapist can feel what it is to be in the former's shoes, a "justifying element," which introduces a cause-and-effect relationship, and "an accepting element," which imparts a historical context to the current distress by including the mention of similar experiences from the patient's childhood. Affirmative interventions often necessitate that the analyst deliberately restrict the scope of his interventions, yet such superficiality paradoxically prepares the ground for unmasking interpretive interventions. The issue at hand, however, extends beyond matters of "tact" (Poland 1975) and "optimal distance" (Akhtar 1992a, Escoll 1992) from the depths of the patient's psyche. Considerations of actual time are involved here. For instance, when a patient endlessly laments the loss of a loved one, it is better, for a long while, to "agree" with the patient and to demonstrate one's understanding of the nature and conscious sources of the patient's agony. Balint (1968) emphasizes that, under such circumstances, the analytic process "must not be hurried by interpretations, however correct, since they may be felt as undue interference, as an attempt at devaluing the justification of their complaint and thus, instead of speeding up, they will slow down the therapeutic processes" (p. 182). To point out discrepancies and contradictions in the patient's story, to bring up the defensive nature of this idealization, and to analyze the potentially masochistic aspects of such continued pain, are tasks that must be left for much later.

Third, the analyst must help the patient unmask what underlies his waiting attitude. This will pave the way for the two of them to squarely face the idealization inherent in "someday" and "if only" fantasies. For instance, to a patient who after four years of analytic work continued to complain bitterly about the ineffectiveness of psychoanalysis vis-à-vis his short stature (a disguised but closed version of his actual complaint), I once responded by saying, "You know, the pained disbelief in your voice and the intensity with which you berate me about this issue makes me wonder if you really believe that analysis could or should lead you to become taller. Do you?" The patient was taken aback but, after some hesitation, did acknowledge that all along he had believed that he might become taller as a result of our hard work.

Once such omnipotent expectations from analysis are brought to the surface, the analyst can attempt to interpret their defensive aims against aggression in transference and, behind that, toward the early objects (Kernberg 1975b). He might also help the patient bring forth the narcissistic and masochistic gratifications derived from these fantasies, which keep the patient's existence in a grand, suffering limbo. He might now point out to the patient the illusory nature of his "someday" fantasy and the "screen functions" of the nostalgia (Freedman 1956, Sohn 1983, Werman, 1977) inherent in his "if only" fantasy. However, even during this phase, the analyst must remain respectful of the patient's psychic "soft spots" and be affectively and conceptually prepared to oscillate between affirmative interventions, when thwarted growth needs and ego deficits seem to dictate the transference demands, and interpretive interventions, when more traditional conflict-based transference is in the forefront (Akhtar 1992b, 1994a,b, Killingmo 1989, Strenger 1989). Such "oscillations in strategy" (Killingmo 1989, p. 75) would necessitate a conceptual freedom on the analyst's part to view the patient's idealization as both a thwarted developmental need (Kohut 1977) and a pathological defense (Kernberg 1975b), that is, a psychic configuration requiring both empathic and interpretive handling.

Fourth, failing to engage the patient in such an interpretive undertaking, the analyst must be prepared to rupture the patient's inordinate hope. Clearly, many analysts would question the need ever to rupture the patient's excessive hope. They would suggest that simply understanding its origins and functions and letting the usual analytic approach take its course would lead to the transformation of such fantasies. This does happen in milder cases. However, in those stubbornly fixated on "someday" and "if only" fantasies, a more "ruthless"[80] intervention is indicated. Basically it comes down to "having to state that neither analysis nor analyst [is an] omnipotent rescuer, as the patients in their illusion needed to believe" (Amati-Mehler and Argentieri 1989, p. 301). In a case of "malignant erotic transference," such intervention would translate into the analyst's explicit declaration that he would never marry the patient. With those endlessly lamenting a long dead parent, the analyst might have to literally confirm the irreversibility of the situation. A less dramatic, but essentially similar, example is of the patient who "kept crying and saying, 'I can't help it', and the analyst [who] said: 'I am afraid I can't help it either'" (Amati-Mehler and Argentieri 1989, p. 296).

Such interventions can be subsumed under the broad rubric of "optimal disillusionment" (Gedo and Goldberg 1973), which requires that the analysand learn to give up magical thinking. They are neither conventional nor risk-free. They disrupt the transference dynamics and, therefore, are inevitably traumatic to the pa-

---

[80]I am using the word in its paradoxically benevolent sense outlined by Mayer (1994).

tient. Indeed, when their "dosage" or timing is inappropriate—and this may not be entirely predictable—the resulting despair and psychic pain might lead the patient to become seriously suicidal. This puts the analysis to a most severe test. Temporary departures from neutrality might now become unavoidable and adjunct, stabilizing measures might have to be employed. On the other hand, interventions of this sort might constitute a turning point of the analytic process in less complicated circumstances, provided, of course, the analyst's "holding functions" are in place, and the effects of such an intervention can be analyzed. Rupture of pathological hope is a necessary precondition for mourning that is otherwise blocked in these patients.[81] At the same time, the analyst

> must convey to the patient not only the direction he wants the patient to move in, but also confidence that the movement is inherent in the patient, which means that what the uncured patient wants is indeed a representation, however distorted of what the cured patient will get. [Friedman 1969, p. 150]

In other words, the analyst must make sure (to the extent possible) that the consequence of his intervention is not a transition from pathological hope to hopelessness but one from pathological hope to realistic hope. This movement is facilitated if the analyst has faith in the patient's capacity in this regard, a proposition reflecting Loewald's (1960) outlining of the childhood need to identify with one's growth potential as seen in the eyes of one's parents.

---

[81]Beginning with Freud's injunction for phobics to face their feared objects (quoted in Alexander and French 1946) and his (1918) setting an end point to the Wolf Man's analysis, psychoanalytic literature is replete with "unconventional" measures in the service of facilitating analytic work. Kolansky and Eisner (1974), for instance, speak of the "spoiling" of preoedipal developmental arrest in impulse disorders and addictions in order to stir up a relatively more analyzable intrapsychic conflict, a notion extended to the treatment of sexual perversions by Socarides (1991). In Eissler's (1953) terminology, these are "parameters." However, since the publication of his paper, it has become increasingly evident that analytic technique includes not only interpretation but preparation for interpretation as well.

Fifth, the analyst, at this stage, must cautiously undertake actual reconstructions. The word *actual* here is not to denote their historical accuracy but to distinguish them from the historical dimension of the affirmative interventions made earlier during the course of analysis; the latter largely exert the psychotherapeutic effect of inexact interpretations (Glover 1931). It is only after the defensive and drive-related nature of idealization has been brought under analysis—an event that sometimes does not happen until the patient's hope has been actively ruptured—that meaningful reconstructions are possible. Since the core problems involved in tenacious "someday" and "if only" fantasies usually date back to early preverbal levels, such reconstructive attempts are fraught with pitfalls. Blum's (1981) astute observations regarding preoedipal reconstruction (see Chapter 1) must be kept in mind here.

Finally, throughout this work, the analyst must be highly vigilant toward his own emotional experience. The informative potential of countertransference in such cases is considerable. Since the idealization inherent in "someday" and "if only" fantasies is not easily verbalized by the patient, often the analyst has to decipher it through his own feelings. Within transference, the analyst is invested by these patients with the task of preserving an illusion. This puts pressure on the analyst. On the one hand, there is the temptation to actively rescue the patient. On the other hand, there is the allure of quickly showing the patient that his expectations are unrealistic and serve defensive aims. Cloaked in the guise of therapeutic zeal, hasty attempts of this sort often emanate from the analyst's own unresolved narcissism and infantile omnipotence. "The determinedly optimistic therapist coerces . . . his patients into experiencing the depression which he is too threatened to feel within himself" (Searles 1977, p. 483). Clearly, both extremes (rescue and rejection) are to be avoided. In this context, the issue of the analyst's own hope is pertinent (see also Mitchell 1993). While he does envision an ego more free of conflicts in the patient's future (Loewald 1960), his hope must not become unrealistic, whereby he keeps waiting for a day ("someday"!) when a patient who is appearing increasingly unanalyzable will suddenly become analyzable. An analyst–analysand collusion around such waiting is a certain recipe for an interminable analysis. Winnicott (1971) states that in such cases

> the psychoanalyst may collude for years with the patient's need to be psychoneurotic (as opposed to mad) and to be treated as psychoneurotic. The analysis goes well, and everyone is pleased. The only drawback is that the analysis never ends. It can be terminated, and the patient may even mobilize a psychoneurotic false self for the purpose of finishing and expressing gratitude. But, in fact, the patient knows that there has been no change in the underlying (psychotic) state and the analyst and the patient have succeeded in colluding to bring about a failure. [p. 102]

Yet another aspect of the countertransference important in such cases is the analyst's becoming restlessly aware of the passage of time while the patient seems oblivious to the months and years that have gone by with relatively little change in his situation. The analyst's dawning awareness of time suggests approaching termination (Akhtar 1992a) in most other analyses. In the case of patients with "someday" and "if only" fantasies, however, the situation is just the opposite. The analyst's awareness of passing time is reflective of the fact that termination is nowhere in sight and the analysis has bogged down. Indeed, in cases where "someday" and "if only" fantasies are deep and subtle, this countertransference experience might be the first clue of their existence. Interestingly, such entry of "the fatal limits of real time" (Boris 1976, p. 145) in the analytic situation might itself yield a technical intervention. The analyst might announce that much time has passed and the patient seems totally oblivious to it. This might be a catalyzing intervention for the analysis and, under fortunate circumstances, might be the only comment needed to rupture the patient's illusory stance.

In sum, the six tasks outlined above seem of considerable importance in working with individuals with "someday" and "if only" fantasies. Keeping these guidelines in mind, without turning them into a rigid strategy, and maintaining a firm allegiance to the "principle of multiple function" (Waelder 1936) would help the analyst develop a clinically responsive technique and avoid the conceptual dichotomies mentioned at the start of this chapter. An "informed eclecticism" (Akhtar 1992c, p. 44; see also Pulver 1993) of this sort seems the best approach to ameliorate the troubled and troubling existence associated with "someday" and "if only" fantasies.

SUMMARY

> Hope in the paranoid-schizoid position . . . is easy, a longing for a magical, omnipotently controlled, easily exchangeable object. Hope in the depressive position requires great courage, a longing for an all-too-human, irreplaceable object, outside of one's control. [Mitchell 1993, p. 212]

Fantasies whose core is constituted by the notions of "someday" and "if only" are ubiquitous in the human psyche. In severe character pathology, however, these fantasies have a particularly tenacious, defensive, and ego-depleting quality. The "someday" fantasy idealizes future and fosters optimism, and the "if only" fantasy idealizes the past and lays the groundwork for nostalgia. The two fantasies originate in the narcissistic disequilibrium consequent upon the early mother–child separation experiences, though the oedipal conflict also contributes to them. Both can be employed as defenses against defective self and object constancy as well as later narcissistic and oedipal traumas. This chapter highlighted the metapsychology and behavioral consequences of these fantasies as well as their unfolding in the treatment situation. It suggests six tasks as especially important for analytic work with such patients: (1) providing and sustaining a meaningful "holding environment"; (2) employing "affirmative interventions"; (3) helping the patient unmask these fantasies, and interpreting their defensive, narcissistic, and sadomasochistic aspects; (4) rupturing the patient's excessive hope, analyzing the effects of such rupture, and facilitating the resultant mourning; (5) reconstructing the early scenarios underlying the need for excessive hope; and (6) paying careful attention to countertransference feelings throughout such work.

8

TETHERS, ORBITS, AND INVISIBLE FENCES

"Anatomy is destiny" (Freud 1924b, p. 178) and "the ego is the first and foremost a bodily ego" (Freud 1923, p. 26) are two statements that epitomize Freud's lifelong stance on humanity's corporeal existence. This stance was characterized by a deep and sustained regard for the somatic underpinnings of the intrapsychic, the interpersonal, and the cultural. Indeed psychoanalysis, the most profound method to study the human mind, was born in the course of Freud's investigating the puzzling somatic phenomenon of hysteria.

From then on, evidence of this intricate psychosomatic partnership in all other emotional disorders became undeniable. We became aware that the catatonics with their volitional disturbances, the paranoics with their somatic delusions, the hypochondriacs with their tenacious self-absorption, and the perverts and the addicts with their pleasurable corruption of the body's purposes are all calling our attention to this matter. We began noticing the milder signals from those not so obviously disturbed. Such clues from the day-to-day life include William Shakespeare's "lean and hungry look," "bungled actions" (Freud 1905d), postural oddities (F. Deutsch 1952), "neurotic bathing habits (Fenichel 1945, p. 70), the peculiar "temperature and boundary sensitivity" of some individuals (Bach 1985, p. 21), those recurrent moments of unexplained nausea (Rossner 1983), and that "furtive pain around the mouth" (Wheelis 1966, p. 148) discernible in the prosperous crowd at a wine tasting or a private art exhibit. It is from these subtle reminders of psychosomatic unity that I have selected my topic: optimal distance.

In this chapter, I describe clinical manifestations of disturbed optimal distance, discuss the development of optimal distance and its pathology, and briefly comment on the sociocultural vicissitudes of these phenomena. In addition, I provide some clinical material to highlight certain fantasies related to anxieties regarding distance and discuss the technical implications of the concept of distance. However, it seems best to begin by defining our terms.

DEFINITIONS

Optimal: most desirable or satisfactory. [*Webster's Ninth New Collegiate Dictionary* 1987, p. 829]

Distance: an extent or advance of a or along from a point considered primary or original. [*Webster's Ninth New Collegiate Dictionary* 1987, p. 367]

The terms *distance* and *optimal distance* do not appear in the index to the *Standard Edition* of Freud's works,[82] nor are they listed in the index to Fenichel's (1945) encyclopedic compilation of early psychoanalytic literature. Psychiatric (*A Psychiatric Glossary* 1975, Hinsie and Campbell 1975) and psychoanalytic (Laplanche and

---

[82]Freud used the word *distance* ninety-two times in his writings (Guttman et al. 1980). He spoke of tracing a train of thought for some "distance through consciousness" (1895, p. 300), the "distance between the object and the ego" (1915b, p. 137), something "at a distance from consciousness" (1915c, p. 203), the "distance between this ego ideal and the real ego" (1921, p. 110), and of an individual's putting "distance between himself and what is threatening him" (1926, p. 146). Though these usages do occur in topographic, dynamic, structural, and adaptive contexts, the word *distance* is used colloquially and not as a scientific term itself.

Pontalis 1973, Moore and Fine 1968, 1990, Rycroft 1968) glossaries also do not include these terms. This leaves one no option but to extrapolate the standard-use definitions of them (see above) to psychoanalytic theory. This, however, is not easy matter. For instance, the question immediately arises: Where is there an interval or space? Between two psychic structures? Between drives and defenses? Between self and object? Between self representation and object representation? Between two self representations? Between the analyst and the analysand? And so on. Soon, the concept of distance begins to appear far from simple, and surely one cannot define "optimal distance" unless one decides what is meant by "distance."

In search of clarity one turns to earlier literature but finds that only two authors offer explicit definitions of the concept involved: Maurice Bouvet and Margaret Mahler. Bouvet (1958), in a pioneering paper entitled "Technical Variation and the Concept of Distance," defined "distance" as

> the gap [that] separates the way in which a subject expresses his instinctual drives from how he would express them if the process of "handling" or "managing" (in French: *amenagement*) these expressions did not intervene. [p. 211]

Bouvet goes on to explain that in his thinking this "managing"

> represents one aspect of the ego defenses, and this term seems to me useful since it draws attention to the *exterior aspect* of the ego's activity while "defense" characterizes more particularly its internal aspect. [p. 211, emphasis added]

A peculiar tension seems to exist in this definition. On the one hand, by regarding the gap between two manners of drive discharge as its cardinal characteristic, Bouvet posits an intrapsychic definition of the word *distance*. On the other hand, by focusing on "managing" or the "exterior" aspect rather than on "defense" or the "internal" aspect of the ego's activity, Bouvet leans toward an interpersonal definition of distance. This is more apparent in the following passage from the same paper.

The distance [that] a patient will take from his analyst varies constantly during the analysis, but in general it tends to diminish as the analysis progresses, until it disappears. It is this point which I call the *rapprocher* (which signifies in French drawing close, but progressively). Once attained, this partial *rapprocher* can be jeopardized by other conflicts, but appears to be more easily reestablished, and to lead finally to a more general *rapprocher*. [pp. 211–212, author's emphasis]

Such two-sidedness of definition is also evident in the writings of Margaret Mahler. Interestingly, she begins her view of "distance" as being within the largely interpersonal mother–child matrix but ends up with an internalized capacity for establishing optimal distance, in other words, with an ego-attribute. "Optimal distance" for her is "a position *between mother and child* that best allows the infant to develop those faculties which he needs in order to grow, that is, to individuate" (Mahler et al. 1975, p. 291, emphasis added).

This definition is an obviously interpersonal one. In other writings, however, Mahler (1971, 1975) takes a more intrapsychic perspective referring to the distance "between the self and the object world" (1975, p. 193). That she means *internalized* objects here is confirmed by the very next sentence, which refers to the

oscillation between longing to merge with the good object representation, with the erstwhile (in one's fantasy at least) blissful union with the symbiotic mother and the defense against reengulfment by her (which causes loss of autonomous self identity). [1975, p. 193]

To my mind, both Bouvet and Mahler imply that distance is a Janus-faced concept with both intrapsychic and interpersonal referents.[83] One way out of this paradox is to define the concept only in one particular context at a time. In the developmental and therapeutic contexts the concept appears best defined intrapsychically. Another way is to follow Sandler's (1987) lead in defining projec-

---

[83]This perhaps accounts for its lack of acceptance in psychoanalytic parlance. Moreover, to regard a distance as optimal involves a quantitative decision. This involves the much disputed economic principle of metapsychology and renders the concept theoretically even more cumbersome.

tion not as the attribution of an unacceptable impulse to an outside agency but as its shifting from a self representation to an object representation. Accordingly, one could define distance as the space not between the self and the object but between the self representation and the object representation. Both these solutions resolve some conceptual difficulties and add others. A third solution is to not simplify things, but to accept the paradox, and to regard the dialectical tension between two perspectives as being inherent to the phenomena involved. This is my preference, and a review of the factors contributing to the development of optimal distance tends to support my view.

DEVELOPMENTAL PERSPECTIVE

> Despite the children's apparent obliviousness to their mother during the early practicing period, most of them seemed to go through a brief period of increased separation anxiety. The fact that they were able to move away independently, yet remain connected with their mother—not physically, but by way of their seeing and hearing her—made the successful use of these distance modalities extra-ordinarily important. [Mahler 1974, pp. 157–158]

> The role of the father is also of great importance in establishing optimal distance, and this should not be overlooked as it too often is. It is the father who can aid and facilitate appropriate distancing from the mother in the symbiotic and separation-individuation phases. [Escoll 1992, p. 63]

In 1959, Balint proposed two fundamental attitudes about distance from objects. These he termed the "ocnophilic" (hesitant, clinging) and the "philobatic" (thrill-loving) attitudes. Balint described the ocnophilic world as consisting of objects separated by horrid empty spaces and the philobatic world of friendly expanses dotted with unpredictable objects. The ocnophil lives from object to object, cutting short his travels through empty spaces. The

philobat lives in friendly expanses, avoiding contact with potentially dangerous objects. The ocnophil feels safe as long as he is
in touch with his objects, while the philobat lives in the illusion
that he needs no objects. The ocnophil must please others. The
philobat has no such need since he feels able to conquer the world
without relying on potentially untrustworthy objects. The ocnophil likes to stay home; the philobat loves to travel. The two tendencies, however, never exist in isolation and their admixture is
the rule.

In tracing their infantile origins, Balint (1959) at first regarded
the ocnophilic tendency to be the earlier and the more primitive
one. He felt that the philobatic attitude involves more skills and
implies a greater acceptance of one's separate existence. However,
a deeper look suggested the opposite to him. The ocnophil, in
having to cling to others, betrays awareness of the gap between him
and his objects, while the philobat seems to be living in a struc-
tureless, primitive state where there are few unimportant, unpredictable objects, a world that consists only of kindly substances,
constituting the friendly expanses. His world is "a kind of loving
mother holding her child safely in her arms" (pp. 84–85).

While I follow Balint's second formulation, that is, that the
philobatic attitude is earlier than the ocnophilic one, I find his
first formulations (which suggests the reverse) theoretically more
sound. His own statement supports this. Balint (1959) finds that
whereas "the ocnophilic world is structured by physical proximity
and touch, the philobatic world is structured by safe distance and
sight" (p. 34). In other words, the ocnophilic attitude implies lesser
separation from primary objects, especially the mother, than does
the philobatic attitude. This makes the former seem the developmentally earlier one. Such thinking is supported by the observation that the shift from the tactile to the visual modality for contact with mother originates in experiences of separation.[84] Spitz
(1965) observes that

---

[84]Greenacre (1953) may have been the first to note this connection in describing the "uncanny reaching out with the eyes" (p. 90) of children not suffi-
ciently held and cuddled by their mothers.

when the infant loses the nipple and recovers it, contact with the need-gratifying percept is lost and recovered, and lost and recovered, again and again. During the interval between loss and recovery of *contact* the other element of the total perceptual unit, *distance perception* of the face, remains unchanged. In the course of these repetitive experiences visual perception comes to be relied upon, for it is not lost; it proves to be the more constant and therefore the more rewarding of the two. [p. 65, author's emphasis]

Thus philobatism, which relies heavily on vision, seems an attitude more accepting of separation than ocnophilia, which demands physical contact. The close correspondence between Balint's ocnophilic and philobatic attitudes and Mahler's symbiotic and practicing phases (Mahler 1965, 1971, 1972c, Mahler et al. 1975) respectively upholds this view. Balint's acknowledgment of the ubiquitous coexistence of these attitudes echoes in Mahler's recognition of "man's eternal struggle against both fusion and isolation" (Mahler, 1972c, p. 130). Balint's describing the occasionally painful tension between ocnophilic and philobatic attitudes within an individual parallels Mahler's (1971, 1974) conceptualization of "rapprochement crisis" and its reverberations in certain character constellations.

Let me take a few steps back, however, and point out that Mahler posits that at the beginning of life and for the first four to five months (the symbiotic stage) the mother and infant constitute a dual unity. There is no outside world for the infant. Gradually, however, there develops "the space between mother and child" (A. Bergman 1980, p. 201).[85] This is partly created by the mother's comings and goings and partly by a decrease in the baby's bodily dependence on the mother, permitting him to look "beyond the symbiotic orbit" (Mahler 1974, p. 155). During this, the differentiation subphase of separation-individuation (from 4 to 10 months),

---

[85]Winnicott (1971) is also interested in this space. However, his focus is not on the child's ambivalent efforts to minimize it but on its persistence and varying psychic uses throughout life.

the infant attempts to break away, in a bodily sense, from the hitherto passive lap-babyhood.

> All infants like to venture and stay just a bit of a distance away from
> the enveloping arms of the mother; and, as soon as they are
> motorically able to, they like to slide down from the mother's
> lap. But they tend to remain or crawl back as near as possible, to
> play at the mother's feet. [Mahler 1974, p. 155]

It is during the practicing subphase (from 10 to 18 months),
however, that the child shows greater ability to move away from
the mother, at first by crawling and later by upright locomotion.
The child makes pleasurable forays in the external world, is en-
amored by his burgeoning ego capacities, and seems oblivious to
the mother's presence.[86] Yet, revealing his continued need for a
"home base," he periodically returns to the mother.

Gradually, the cognitive strides made by the child make him all
too aware of his smallness, of his separateness, and of the fact that
he cannot coerce his mother to gratify his every need. His previously enjoyed fantasies of shared omnipotence collapse. The
child is now in the rapprochement subphase (from 18 to 24
months). Ambivalence and ambitendency prevail. Much intrapsychic conflict is produced by the coexisting progressive desires
for self-assertion, separation, and autonomy on the one hand, and
regressive wishes for closeness, even symbiotic merger with his
mother, on the other hand. There develops a tendency toward
mood swings. No distance from mother appears satisfactory. Closeness soothes narcissistic wounds but stirs up the dread of fusion.
Being apart enhances pride but leaves one lonely. Contradictory
demands are made on the mother. If the mother remains emotionally available despite such oscillations on the part of the child,
then there occurs a gradual mending of contradictory object (the

---

[86]Gender differences exist in the extent of this distance. Little girls have a
"lesser degree of motor-mindedness" (Mahler et al. 1975, p. 214) and do not
venture as far from their mothers as do boys of similar age. Moreover, the distance that mothers comfortably permit their children to move away is almost
always shorter than that allowed by fathers (Pruett 1990).

mother of symbiosis and the mother of separation) and self (the "lap baby" of symbiosis and the "conqueror" of practicing) representations. Capacity for object and self constancy develops, along with a capacity for maintaining optimal distance. However, if the mother is not optimally available during the rapprochement subphase, these developmental achievements do not result (see also Chapter 1). The contradictory self and object representations remain split, infantile omnipotence is not renunciated, and capacity for optimal distance fails to develop. This leads to a lifelong tendency toward oscillation between passionate intimacy and hateful withdrawal from objects.

In light of this, optimal distance is best viewed as a psychic position that permits intimacy without loss of autonomy and separateness without painful aloneness.[87] This definition, though not clearly spelled out by Mahler in the context of adult character organization, is, I believe, the essence of her position on this matter. Having thus enriched the definition of optimal distance from a developmental perspective, we are now prepared to discuss its disturbances.

PSYCHOPATHOLOGY OF OPTIMAL DISTANCE

> A number of porcupines huddled together for
> warmth on a cold day in winter; but, as they began
> to prick one another with their quills, they were
> obliged to disperse. However, the cold drove them

---

[87]In a discussion that appeared alongside the original publication of this chapter, Escoll (1992) further elaborated the concept of optimal distance, giving examples from fiction, poetry, art, and the animal kingdom. More important, he elucidated (1) the somatic foundations of the concept; (2) gender differences in optimal distance, noting that while I opted for the term *optimal distance,* Edward and her colleagues (1981) employ the term *optimal closeness* for the same concept; (3) the role of father in the development of optimal distance during both the separation-individuation process and the Oedipus complex; and (4) the manner in which sexual and aggressive drive derivatives are often encoded in conflicts that superficially involve closeness and distance.

together again, when just the same thing happened.
At last, after many turns of huddling and dispers-
ing, they discovered that they would be best off by
remaining at a little distance from one another.
[Schopenhauer 1981, p. 226]

A whole host of defensive maneuvers can be called
into service to defend against the threat of a closeness that might snuff the self out. Many borderline
patients have elevated interpersonal distance regulation to the level of an art form. [Lewin and Schulz
1992, p. 30]

Many psychopathological syndromes are characterized by behaviors suggestive of difficulty in maintaining optimal distance. A
prominent example is agoraphobia, which typically involves a "fearful aversion to leaving familiar surroundings" (Roth 1959) unless
accompanied by a reassuring companion. While this is often the
end product of the repressed prostitution fantasy identified by
Freud (1892–1899) other dynamic factors also play a role in its
causation. In an early paper on "locomotor anxiety," Abraham
(1913b) noted that neurotic inhibitions of motility emanate not
only from defenses against constitutionally strong pleasure in
movement and unconscious sexual concerns but also from difficulty in separating from love objects. Some years later, Helene
Deutsch (1929) declared the involvement of a partner to be the
crucial determinant of the agoraphobic's malady. However, she felt
that hostile and controlling fantasies were frequently hidden underneath the consciously experienced need for libidinal attachment.
Following this, Mittleman (1957) observed the confinement of
the agoraphobic to a "limited circumference" (p. 289), and Weiss
(1964) noted that such patients grow more anxious the farther they
go from their homes. This led him to define "agoraphobia" as an
anxiety reaction to abandoning a fixed point of support. More
recently, Kohut (1980) concluded that the agoraphobic's consciously felt need for a reassuring companion is the key to what
lies in his psychic depths, namely, the continued search for a maternal self-object. Clearly, all these authors regard agoraphobia as

a malady of distance. How far can one go away from one's objects without endangering the integrity of one's self?

Contributing to claustrophobia is the opposite question. How close can one get to another person without risking one's autonomy? An alternate activation of these concerns is evident in certain chronic marital difficulties. Like Schopenhauer's (1981) porcupines, the two partners fluctuate between intimacy and distance, trust and mistrust, betrayal and confession, and separation and reunion. They cannot live peacefully together, nor can they do without each other. They lack the capacity to establish complementarity of roles and are unable to follow Gibran's (1923) counsel for marital partners[88] to

> stand together yet not too near together:
> For the pillars of the temple stand apart, and the oak tree and the cypress grow not in each other's shadow. [p. 16]

Although the proximity afforded by marriage does play a triggering role, such hopeless failure in negotiating an optimal distance almost invariably betrays separate character pathology in the two partners. Actually, severe personality disorders constitute the cardinal example of psychopathology involving optimal distance. Included here are narcissistic, borderline, schizoid, paranoid, hypomanic (Akhtar 1988a), infantile or histrionic, as-if (Deutsch 1942), and antisocial personality disorders. For such individuals, involvement with others stirs up a characteristic "need-fear dilemma" (Burnham et al. 1969): to be intimate is to risk engulfment, and to be apart is to court aloneness. This leads to a variety of compromises. The borderline continues to go back and forth (Akhtar 1990a, Gunderson 1985, Melges and Swartz 1989). The narcissist can sustain allegiances longer and therefore shows such oscillations less often (Adler 1981, Akhtar 1989a, Kernberg 1970b). The para-

---

[88]My own poem on love, quoted in its entirety in Chapter 3, similarly underscores the dialectics between opposing tensions characterizing the state of being in love.

noid individual bristles at any change in distance initiated by others (Akhtar 1990b), preferring the "reliability" of his fear of being betrayed (Blum 1981). The schizoid individual opts for withdrawal on the surface while maintaining an intense imaginative tie to his objects (Akhtar 1987, Fairbairn 1952b, Guntrip 1969). Antisocial and hypomanic individuals, though internally uncommitted, develop rapid intimacy with others. This tendency to be highly attuned to others, even magically identifying with them, is most evident in the "as-if" personalities (Deutsch 1942) and underlies the fraudulent tendency in these and other individuals (Gediman 1985).

I would like to emphasize, however, that agoraphobia, marital difficulties, and severe personality disorders display the most overt difficulties of optimal distance. More subtle anxieties in this realm become discernible only during psychoanalytic work. Here the ebb and flow of the associative material and evolving transferences frequently reveal anxieties pertaining to distance and closeness, as well as fantasies defending against these anxieties.

THE TETHER FANTASY AND ITS VARIANTS

> The child had a wooden reel with a piece of string tied round it. It never occurred to him to pull it along the floor behind him, for instance, and play at its being a carriage. What he did was to hold the reel by the string and very skillfully throw it over the edge of his curtained cot, so that it disappeared into it, at the same time uttering his expressive "o-o-o-o." He then pulled the reel out of the cot again by the string and hailed its reappearance with a joyful "da" ("there"). This, then, was the complete game—disappearance and return. . . . It was related to the child's great cultural achievement—the instinctual renunciation (that is, the renunciation of instinctual satisfaction) which he had made in allowing his mother to go away without protesting. He compensated himself for this, as it were, by himself staging the disappearance and return of the objects within his reach. [Freud 1920a, p. 15]

One such fantasy is that of a tether, that is, a rope or chain that keeps one within certain bounds. While only one analysand referred to it literally as such, three other patients reported essentially similar fantasies. In all four instances, the fantasy defended against anxiety regarding distance and seemed to have links with the rapprochement subphase of separation-individuation (Mahler 1971, 1975, Mahler et al. 1975). However, there are a few caveats. First, these fantasies should not be taken as representing the actual ideational events of the latter half of the second year of life. While "the unrememberable and the unforgettable" (Frank 1969, p. 50) affects and wordless thoughts of that period do form the building blocks of these fantasies, their specific content requires greater cognitive maturity and appears derived from later childhood. Second, the manner in which these fantasies are communicated (by the patient) and deciphered (by the analyst) makes certainty about them difficult. Pertaining largely to the preverbal period, these are hardly ever well put into words. Patients resort to allusions and metaphors, while the analysts find themselves relying to a greater than usual extent on their own affective experience (Akhtar 1991a, Burland 1975). The ground is murky and clarity is in short supply. Third, while the tether fantasy and its variants seem related to rapprochement-subphase issues, in accordance with the principle of multiple function (Waelder 1936), they also contain drive-defense-type conflicts from various psychosexual levels, including the phallic-oedipal phase. Escoll (1992) stated,

Issues of optimal distance are also an important factor in clinical problems related to sexuality and aggression. Here the internal bodily representations and self and object are of tremendous significance. Men may fear engulfment by women: some male patients describe the vagina as a vast cavern, a cave, and have a fearful fantasy of being permanently lost or imprisoned in it. To defend against this, emotional and/or physical distance is established. In turn, women frequently complain that there is too much distance on the male's part and insufficient cuddling or hugging, particularly as related to sexuality. There are related forces at work regarding aggression. Distance may be stretched, for example, to avoid the dangerous expression of one's own aggressive impulses or to avoid retaliation. Distancing may also be used to express contempt and anger. This may be done by physically distancing oneself and becoming emotionally remote through inattentiveness, detachment, and silence. On the other hand, closeness may express aggression with such reactions as a crushing embrace or a fracturing handshake. [pp. 65–66]

The issue of distance is also paramount during the oedipal phase,[89] and these fantasies often have parallel meanings derived from that context. Finally, the fantasies' potentially idiosyncratic relevance for a given patient should also be considered. With these caveats, let me proceed to the tether fantasy.

Case 1

This fantasy was first brought to my attention by Mr. B., a successful, twice-divorced businessman in his mid-forties. Mr. B. had sought analysis because he was again considering marriage and was afraid about its outcome. Initial interviews suggested that Mr. B. often fell in love with needy women who had a "faint breath of scandal" (Freud 1910a, p. 166) about them and lost interest in them after his rescue of them. This oedipal dynamic seemed to have a solid footing in his account of a reasonably peaceful early childhood; an excessively conscientious latency; and a family constellation of a rebellious older brother, an admired but distant father, and a very involved, somewhat anxious mother. However, there were also hints of anxiety in Mr. B. about separation and fusion.

---

[89]The establishment of the incest barrier is an apt illustration of the relevance of distance during the oedipal phase. However, "the task of mastering the oedipal complex is not simply to renounce primary oedipal objects, but to do so in a way that simultaneously permits individual autonomy together with maintenance of valued traditional continuity" (Poland 1977, p. 410). Moreover, the prohibition of sexual transgression resulting from this phase need not eliminate aim-inhibited, subtle affirmation of attractiveness between parents and children. Indeed, there might exist an "oedipally optimal" optimal distance, that is, a distance between two generations that is neither incestuously intrusive nor oblivious of each other's attractiveness.

On the one hand, he had broken off his marriages because of feeling "suffocated"; on the other hand, he was not able to give up anything.

Mr. B. began analysis with the fervor of the dedicated student he always had been. He worked hard at it, talked incessantly, and was quick to identify with my analyzing style. His concerns about separation showed in many ways. He expressed a fear of never being able to leave analysis, do nothing but analysis, become an "analytic monk." At the end of each session, he would get up, look at me— as if taking me in for safekeeping—and announce our next appointment with a subtle questioning tone at the end. (This often extracted a nod from me but was not brought into analysis for quite a while.)

The tether fantasy appeared in the third month of his analysis. One day he announced that he was going away to a sales meeting on the West Coast, adding in the same breath that his attendance there was not mandatory. I pointed out his ambivalence and commented on the anxiety he seemed to be experiencing with his wish to be temporarily away and thus be separated from me. He agreed and said that he wanted somehow to be at both places simultaneously. Further associations during this and later sessions revealed that he frequently had difficulty leaving places, people, even ideas and options. He was never fully at one place and often carried something of where he had formerly been with him. As the day of his departure drew closer, Mr. B. became more anxious. He started fearing being so far away from my office and from me. He had disturbing thoughts about feeling hungry late at night while staying in the hotel on the West Coast, not being able to find food in the lobby, going hungry, and dying of starvation.

It was around this time that Mr. B. first reported the fantasy of a tether, a long rope by which he was tied to my office while being on the West Coast. With this he could be there safely and feel much less anxiety. As he was talking about this, he visualized a little boy learning to walk. As is often typical of visual images during analytic sessions (Warren 1961), this picture was at first affectless and experienced as having little or no connection with the patient's own self. Gradually, however, Mr. B. was able to acknowledge more directly both the anxiety and the pleasure in his wish to walk away from me. The imagined tether clearly served a defensive purpose insofar as it minimized the anxiety of separation while permitting him autonomous functioning.

During later periods of Mr. B.'s analysis, the fantasied tether reappeared off and on around separations. While in the beginning only its reassuring aspects were evident, ambivalence gradually became attached to it. At times, it felt like an enslaving chain from which he wanted to escape. Were he not tied to me, he could go have more fun, have sex with more women! Such associations gradually propelled Mr. B.'s analysis to more familiar oedipal themes. The tether disappeared from his associations, and became irrelevant. During termination Mr. B. did recall the tether, however. This was associated with jocular disbelief, which at times seemed to hide a wistful longing for continued attachment to me. At other times, his humor displayed pleasure in his increased psychic freedom both within himself and in relation to me.

Less graphic but similar themes were reported by three other patients, as described in the next three cases.

Case 2

Ms. D. felt that an "invisible fence" precluded too much movement on her part. It prevented her from taking up a better job at a location about four miles farther from her current place of employment and from my office. Significant assertiveness of any sort, especially vis-à-vis her domineering and controlling mother (and later toward me), led her to feel a jolting "electric shock." She said that she felt like a dog in a yard with an invisible electric fence. "I can only go this far, but if I try to hit the street I get the shock." The idea of "hitting the street" led her to think of leaving home, as well as to "street walking" and loss of control of sexual impulses. Further analysis revealed a childhood of intense engulfment by an exhibitionistic, hypochondriacal, and controlling mother, and marked inattention from a self-engrossed, heavily drinking father.

Case 3

Mr. E., a young college student who, as far back as he could remember, had felt "completely forgotten" by his mother, reported many social and motoric inhibitions. One among these was his anxiety about jogging. While he enjoyed jogging, he constantly worried that he would end up too far away from his home, get hopelessly lost, and be unable to find his way back. As a result, he jogged only around the block, never permitting himself to go "too far away" from his apartment building.

Case 4

Ms. F. felt a similar inhibition in mental activities. A politically conscious attorney who at the age of 18 months had been separated from her mother for about six to eight weeks, Ms. F. had never felt close to her mother. While growing up she felt her mother to be an "all duty and no love" type of person who pushed Ms. F. toward premature independence. As a child she feared acquiring skills, since it led to greater autonomy and loss of attention from her mother. Further exploration revealed that she found reading fiction especially difficult, since rapt absorption took her "away" from her surroundings. In the midst of reading a "fat novel" (an unmistakable reference to the oral-visual incorporative axis), for instance, she would suddenly become aware of her absorption and start to worry lest she get "lost" in reading at the expense of other chores. It was as if she had stretched her mental tether to the limit and had to return to the secure base of reality for refueling.

Common to these patients was their concern about distance from an anchoring person or environment. They felt confined to an orbit. Upon reaching the outer limit of this orbit, they felt anxious and retreated to a comfortable distance within it. They felt reassured by a central point of reference and feared getting lost if they broke the tether by going "too far." At times, however, they experienced a hypomanic-like excitement at the thought of this eventuality. Mr. E., for instance, imagined that if he allowed himself to jog freely, he might go on for 100 or 200 miles, perhaps even farther. Ms. F. felt that if she allowed herself to read with concentration, she might keep reading, miss her work, and disregard her analytic appointments. In such moments, real or imagined, these patients were flooded with elation and grandiosity, covered over during the analytic sessions by slightly apologetic giggling and shyness.

Their concerns were strongly reminiscent of those experienced by children in the practicing and rapprochement subphase of separation-individuation. The main issue here is that of distance versus safety. Although distancing from mother begins in the differentiation subphase, it is not until the practicing and rapprochement subphases that the "symbiotic orbit" (Mahler et al. 1975, p. 293) actually begins to be mapped out and the strength of the "invisible bond" (p. 25) between mother and child is truly tested. Mr. B., in feeling reassured that a tether connected him to me while he traveled, was like a toddler in the practicing subphase. During this time, despite pleasurable forays into the external world, the "mother continues to be needed as a stable point, a 'home base' to fulfill the need for refueling" (Mahler et al. 1975, p. 69). Mr. E.'s and Ms. F.'s hypomanic excitement while at the furthest extremes of their tethers also resembled practicing-phase children's elation upon freely exercising their ego apparatuses and escaping from fusion with the mother. These patients also showed the characteristic ambitendency of rapprochement-subphase children. They wanted to assert themselves and experiment with a wider segment of the world but feared losing touch with the "home base." At the same time, they feared moving too close to the center of their orbit (note Mr. B.'s fear of becoming an "analytic monk"). Fearing both progression and regression, they existed in a "satellite state" (Volkan and Corney 1968), that is, as captive bodies orbiting within the gravitational field of an intense, though ambivalent, dependency. Their distancing attempts (e.g., travels, jogging, assertiveness) reassured them against the dread of fusion while their imaginary tethers provided them "distance contact" (Mahler et al. 1975, p. 67) with the analyst, who remained available despite their comings and goings. It gave them time to work out both their separation anxiety and their dread of merger and to negotiate an optimal distance from early maternal object representations and their transferential re-creations during analysis.

To the best of my knowledge, the tether fantasy described here is not mentioned in the psychoanalytic literature. However, there do exist three accounts of children with similar undertones. Freud's (1920a) description of his grandson's playing with a wooden reel, which serves as the epigraph of this section of the chapter, seems to refer to an enactment of the tether fantasy. Following Freud, Winnicott (1960b) reported the case of a 7-year-old boy who was preoccupied with strings and was constantly tying up various household objects to each other. In view of the child's many traumatic separations from his mother beginning around the age of 3, Winnicott felt that the boy was "attempting to deny separation by his use of string, as one would deny separation from a friend by using the telephone" (p. 154). More recently, Fischer (1991) noted the preoccupation with a "transatlantic cable" in an 8-year-old boy facing separation from his analyst and worrying about the latter's whereabouts during their summer break.

Besides being particularly apt as a metaphor in this regard, the fantasy of a tether may also have contributions from childhood realities.[90] The joining functions of strings and ropes are routinely witnessed by children. They may see pets on leashes and farm animals on tethers. They play with yo-yos and other string-manipulated toys. Toddlers in stores are sometimes restrained by "leashes" held by harried parents. Kindergarten children on school-sponsored field trips often hold on to a rope whose end is held by their teacher. Thus there are ample opportunities for ropes, leashes, tethers, and strings to be incorporated in inner

---

[90]Issues from other levels may also contribute to the tether fantasy. Two such examples are, at the deepest, "prehistoric" level, the somatic schemata involving the umbilical cord and, at the highest, most elaborate level, the imagoes of maternal phallus.

concerns about maintaining contact with someone while being physically apart.[91]

Colloquial wisdom seems aware of the kinship between metaphor and reality in this regard. This is evident in such expressions as "He's tied to his mother's apron strings," "He has her on a leash," "He hasn't been able to cut the cord yet," and "She's at the end of her rope." Such linguistic clues bring us to other significant reverberations of distance and closeness in the sociocultural realm.

SOCIOCULTURAL VICISSITUDES

> And when the shadow fades and is no more, the light that lingers becomes a shadow to another light.
> And thus your freedom when it loses its fetters becomes itself the fetter of a greater freedom. [Gibran, 1923, p. 49]

> A particular obsession with boundaries usually characterizes groups that perceive themselves as minorities in constant danger of extinction. They regard their boundaries as critical to their survival and feel that, unless they seal them off so as to preserve their distinctiveness, they will inevitably be assimilated into their surroundings and cease to exist as a distinct entity. [Zerubavel 1991, p. 51]

Conflicts regarding distance can also be discerned in three sociocultural realms: (1) childhood games and amusement park rides, (2) travel and vacations, and (3) migration and exile. A closer look

---

[91]Ropes, strings, and chains have been used throughout history as symbols for binding and connection (Cirlot 1971). The sacred thread (*Janaiyu*) worn across their chests by all high-caste Hindus is the external symbol of things in existence. The Egyptian hieroglyphic of a vertical chain of three links with the bottom link left open holds dual symbolism. On the one hand, it signifies the evolution and involution of the heaven and earth, and on the other hand, the matrimony between man and woman. Perhaps all sashes, bows, braids, and stripes worn by soldiers and officials are, besides being obvious phallic symbols, emblems of cohesion.

at each of these realms reveals the common intrapsychic denominator of distance, although with varying magnitude and different results.

Childhood Games and Amusement Park Rides

Prominent among the multiple determinants of childhood games (Balint 1959, Erikson 1950, Freud 1920a, Glenn 1991, Kleeman 1967, Phillips 1960, Waelder 1933, Winnicott 1971) is the attempt to master anxiety about separation and loss. Peekaboo, the universal childhood game initiated by the mother during the differentiation subphase and resumed vigorously by the child during rapprochement (Kleeman 1967, Mahler 1971, 1972c, Mahler et al. 1975), is mostly aimed at fostering tolerance of separation from the mother. The child's pleasure in it comes from his rediscovering the mother after a brief, tense moment of losing her. This theme of losing and regaining safety also underlies later, more formal games of latency, though clearly these also have prominent phallic-oedipal undercurrents (Glenn 1991). All these games involve leaving a zone of safety, courting danger more or less voluntarily, and returning to the secure zone (almost always called "home"). Attempts at mastering separation anxiety are clearly evident here. At the same time, these games permit the player, rather like the rapprochement-phase toddler, the vicarious enjoyment of both merger and separateness from the "home base," that is, mother.

A similar "mixture of fear, pleasure, and confident hope in face of an external danger is what constitutes the fundamental nature of all *thrills*" (Balint 1959, p. 23). This is nowhere more evident than at amusement parks. The rides offered there involve high speeds, exposed situations, tunnels, darkness, giddiness and vertigo, and unfamiliar angles. By exposing the thrill seeker to physical danger and then returning him unhurt, such rides serve as counterphobic reassurances against castration anxiety. However, by removing an individual from familiar and safe ground (home, mother) and then returning him to it, these rides also capitalize on libidinization of separation-related fears.

Travel and Vacations

Travel powerfully activates distance-related anxieties (Chmiel et al. 1979). Some people travel easily, while others are homebound (Balint 1959). Some enjoy traveling a shade too much, raising suspicions of counterphobic mechanisms at work. Still others are literally vagabonds and hoboes, hopelessly unable to stay put. All these individuals betray conflicts over distance from their love objects.

In the midst of such conflicted attitudes is the social institution of vacations. In a thoughtful exposition of the dynamic, economic, structural, and adoptive correlates of a "good" vacation, Grinstein (1955) somehow omits the issue of distance from home. This is important in two ways here. First, the distance to which one can go for a vacation unaccompanied by one's loved ones is much shorter (in time and space) than the one traveled in their company. Second, there seems to be an optimal distance from home needed to have a good time. We cannot have a relaxing vacation in a hotel five miles from home, nor can we go too far away (using the rationalization that such places lack adequate resources to sustain us). We need to go away yet remain within a certain boundary.[92]

Migration and Exile

The issue of distance is of extreme relevance to the situation of the immigrant. Leaving one's country involves profound losses. Often one has to give up familiar foods, native music, even one's language ("mother tongue"). The new country offers strange-tasting foods, new songs, different political concerns, unfamiliar

---

[92]Such extension of the boundary of one's home, as it were, is also discernible in certain religious concessions. For instance, the Hebrew laws of *eruv* are meant to facilitate locomotor freedom and enhance carrying privileges on the Sabbath (Kaplan 1971). These laws involve the symbolic creation of new "home bases" along the way, thus extending the boundary of one's original dwelling. I am thankful to Jeanne Meisler, M.D., for bringing this to my attention.

language, awkward attires, pale festivals, unknown heroes, un-
earned history, and visually unfamiliar landscapes. The immigrant
finds himself at too much distance from the land of those constituting his multilayered internal objects, that is, his ancestors ("My
lands are where my dead lie buried," proclaimed Crazy Horse;
quoted in Dewall 1984, p. 26). He lacks the "refueling" privilege
of college students who return to parental homes with an unspo-
ken regularity (typically around occasions that offer sumptuous
meals). Immigration experience seems to constitute a "third individuation," although deeper attention to an individual immigrant's
dynamics may indeed reveal it to be simultaneously a continuation
of the "second individuation of adolescence" (Blos 1967).

The "psychic pain" (Freud 1926, p. 169) caused by the distance
between the immigrant's first and second homes leads to fluctuations between intense nostalgia for the lost land and anxious setting of roots in the new culture. Homesickness in this connection
contains at its kernel a longing for the mother's breast (Sterba
1940). Fantasies of "someday" (Akhtar 1991a) returning to one's
earlier home (mother) sustain the immigrant through mourning
(Grinberg and Grinberg 1989, Pollock 1989) warranted by separation from it. A frequent stopgap measure is actual travel back to
the country of origin for refueling purposes. Carrying back gifts
to the relatives left behind, and bringing artifacts, childhood me-
mentos, and old photographs upon return to the new home, the
immigrant reminds one of a growing child crisscrossing the space
between himself and his mother. The following observations of
A. Bergman (1980), though made in connection with the young
child, seem equally applicable to the immigrant:

> As . . . he is able to move away farther, his world begins to widen,
> there is more to see, more to hear, more to touch, and each time
> he returns to mother he brings with him some of the new experi-
> ence. In other words, each time he returns he is ever so slightly
> changed. The mother is the center of his universe to whom he re-
> turns as the circles of his exploration widen. [p. 203]

The distance between two lands (two mothers, i.e., the "mother
of symbiosis" and the "mother of separation") is also bridged by

developing homoethnic ties in the new country, and by making use of the radio or cassette player to listen to one's own music. These serve as "transitional objects" (Winnicott 1953) and facilitate a progressive move in the mourning process consequent upon migration. Clearly, this mourning is not only for important love objects but also for "lost parts of the self" (Grinberg and Grinberg 1984, p. 13).

At the same time, migration provides an opportunity for psychic expansion, growth, and alteration. New channels of self-expression become available. There are new identification models, different superego prohibitions, different ideals. Ethnocentric clinging to fellow immigrants or a chameleonlike identity change are two problematic outcomes (Teja and Akhtar 1981) of the failure to negotiate the distance between the old and the emerging self representations.[93] An optimal distance facilitates synthesis, leading to the emergence of a new hybrid identity. Such identity might lack deep anchoring in either historical or identification systems but may possess a greater than usual breadth of experience, knowledge, and, at times, wisdom.

The situation is, of course, much more complex with involuntary migration. Individuals who had to flee from the Nazis, from Latin America, from Haiti, from Cuba, and more recently from Cambodia, Laos, and Vietnam often can never return to their lands of origins. This blocks access to refueling. The child within is orphaned and must reclaim inch by inch (with the aid of old photographs, music, books, relics, news, and above all new transferences, introspection, and creativity) the psychic territory lost. Such a mourning process may, however, last a lifetime and even then be incomplete.

All in all it seems that (1) childhood games and amusement park rides involve relatively safer journeys to and from love objects; (2) travel and vacations stretch the tether and map out the outer limits of the symbiotic orbit; there is a lot of fun to be had, but one has to return; and (3) migration involves a loss of "home base," a

---

[93]Elsewhere, I have discussed the vicissitudes of identity transformation following immigration in much greater detail (Akhtar 1995b).

mourning over it, and a creation of a new home and a hybrid self; exile is a "malignant" form of migration where refueling is not possible, practicing is aborted, and mourning is incomplete. This digression into the sociocultural realm, however, must not take us away from the fact that the issue of distance is basically an intrapsychic one. It has ontogenetic roots, pathological presentations, and, above all, implications for the technique of psychoanalysis and intensive psychotherapy.

TECHNICAL IMPLICATIONS

> Tact derives from separation experiences. Here the model is literally that of the mother's soothing touch. It extends, of course, beyond touch to all modalities available for the infant's experience of the mothering one in that early phase. In particular, we think of the quality of the analyst's warmth, not the excessive warmth of denied hostility, but the basic readiness of the analyst to be available to understand the patient. The tact of the analyst is a highly refined technical correlate of the physician's well-known art of "laying on the hands." [Poland 1975, p. 157]

> Unempathically timed confrontative and interpretative intrusions on . . . boundaries [between self and other, and between conscious and unconscious processes] tend to unduly disrupt the patient's emotional equilibrium. Empathically ensured safety from such intrusion helps enable the patient to open these boundaries to developmental and therapeutic interaction. [Settlage 1994, p. 46]

The concept of distance has many technical implications. These implications affect our work from its beginning until its end, perhaps even afterward. For instance, during an initial consultation in which the recommendation of an analysis is going to be made, it is of utmost importance that the consultant avoid any premature closeness with the patient. Most concretely, this applies to not answering factually those questions of the patient that pertain to

the analyst's personality around which transference would develop. Another early situation that warrants exploration instead of
a quick reality decision is when a patient declares that he will be
leaving town in two, three, or even four years. Such realities often
involve anxiety about closeness. This needs to be gently brought
up for discussion and not permitted to compromise the open-
ended nature of commitment for psychoanalysis.

A more subtle issue during the initial consultation, however,
involves making sure that a recommendation of analysis is not
confused by the patient with a recommendation of analysis with
the consultant (Klauber 1971). This confusion is the basis of much
narcissistic injury to the patient when a referral to a colleague is
made and may even cause difficulties in subsequent treatment.
Confusion is more likely to occur during initial evaluations with
famous analysts (with whom an idealizing patient brings himself
too close too quickly) or with charismatic analysts (who for stylistic and characterological reasons may bring the patient too close
to themselves too quickly). It is possible that an early supervisor of
mine had such distance issues in mind when he suggested an alternate way of asking the same question. The patient, a man in his
mid-twenties, was talking in his second or third consultation session with me about his ambivalent feelings toward recent Asian
immigrants. After listening for a while, I asked him how he felt
about being in any kind of treatment with me (an Asian immigrant). My supervisor remarked that rather than saying, "How
might you feel being in treatment with me?" I could have said, "How
might you feel being in treatment with someone you might recognize as an immigrant?" The latter question is less personal and
therefore allows the patient greater freedom of expression. To have
made no comment on the patient's associations would have created too much distance (i.e., leaving him no choice but to drop
the subject), but to comment as I did left the patient too little distance (forcing him to address its unacceptable transference significance). My supervisor's stance facilitated optimal distance.

Another early situation that brings up the issue of distance is
when a patient gives up sitting and begins to lie down on the couch.
The ensuing loss of visual contact increases the distance from the

analyst. The analyst then has to be mindful of the effects of this upon the patient's feeling states and ego capacities, as well as of the defensive strategies mobilized by the patient to compensate for this increased distance. Talking rapidly and incessantly to seek contact with the analyst, curling up in a frightened ball to hold on to oneself, asking provocative questions and mumbling inaudibly to evoke activity from the analyst, and focusing on the details of the office as a derivative of the wish to maintain visual contact with the analyst, are all manifestations that betray anxiety over this increased distance and should be interpreted as such. Unusual manifestations of anxieties pertaining to this sudden increase in distance should also be kept in mind.

> Ms. D., for instance, began to lie on the couch so that a significant portion of her face was visible to me, and I found myself repeatedly looking at her. The interpretation of this situation appeared multidetermined and included her childhood overstimulation by parental nudity. However, this reversal of anxious scopophilia into teasing exhibitionism was also linked to her distress at losing visual contact with me.

Many questions arise here. Do patients who have sat up for long periods before using the couch react more or less intensely, similarly, or differently to lying down? Are there patients who should not be kept sitting up for long because the distance might become socially too close or, conversely, fixated in a more than optimal apartness from their deepest, inner lives? Should some patients be seen at first sitting up, even four or five sessions a week, for a long period of time so that they can establish a "reality base" (Volkan 1987a, p. 85) about the analyst's personality necessary for them to avoid dangerous transference regressions? Finally, can the analyst undertake active measures, besides the usual empathic remarks and clarifications, to minimize the patient's distress on beginning to use the couch? Some analysts do report an early "noisy phase" (Boyer 1967, Volkan 1987a) when they grunt more than usual to assure their sicker patients of their continued involvement. What do we think of this? Or of Winnicott's remark at the end of the first session of Guntrip's analysis with him? Winnicott remained totally silent throughout the session and said at the end, "I've nothing particular to say yet, but if I don't say something, you may begin to feel I'm not here" (Guntrip 1975, p. 152).

The significance of the issue of distance is not restricted to the initial evaluation and the beginning phase. It appears again and again in the course of our work. Indeed, with some patients this happens so often that we might conclude that when the issue is not overtly present it is being adequately addressed. For instance, if we move a bit closer to the couch and lean forward to make a point, we may encroach painfully upon these patients.[94] The optimal distance that was until that moment taken for granted is suddenly ruptured, and an "impingement" (Winnicott 1960c) results. This often detours the course of analytic work. Conversely, not acting on a patient's behalf at times painfully increases the distance. Here I am reminded of the analytic patient described in an earlier chapter who, because of a coughing fit, was having much difficulty talking and asked me where she could get a glass of water. I helped her obtain a glass of water (we had just moved into a new office building and water fountains had not yet been turned on). I wondered about the effects of my doing this but felt that not doing so would have highlighted my abstinent stance too much, increased the distance between us, and rendered me realistically intrusive and transferentially unusable.

Similar considerations apply to the analyst's vacations and to accidental meetings between the analyst and the analysand outside the office. Both alter the distance between the two parties. Vacations tend to put the analyst too far and accidental encounters too close. Both the analyst and the patient are put to some

---

[94]The issue of actual physical distance between the analyst and the patient is perhaps even more important in working with children. "A fixed ('sessile' in James Anthony's terms) sitting position, even while working with very young children, facilitates the development of an invisible therapeutic tether in the office setting. This is highly useful in monitoring the child's adaptive and resistive motivations which are often manifested through vacillations of closeness and distance from the analyst" (Purnima Mehta, personal communication, September 1997).

test under such circumstances. While clearly the optimal distance in such circumstances varies with various analyst–patient dyads, and perhaps also from early to middle to final phases of analysis, it remains the analyst's responsibility to safeguard this optimal distance.

Even outside such unusual situations, the concept of optimal distance is of utmost importance to analytic technique. For instance, a proper mixture of experiencing and observing on the part of our patients facilitates the analytic work. In other words a patient's ego takes an equidistant position from affects and intellect, known and unknown, past and present, and transference distortion and therapeutic alliance. Similarly, for maintaining his neutrality, the analyst is advised to be "equidistant" (A. Freud 1936, p. 38) from the patient's id, reality, and superego concerns. The concept of distance is equally applicable to interpretation, especially the "mutative interpretations" (Strachey 1934) that lead to an enlightenment through experience

> or a coming together which establishes the identity between a present emotional experience and its prototype in the past, and requires the coming together of the unconscious of the analyst and patient, thus making possible a revelation which affirms the *rapprocher*. . . . The tone and the form in which it is expressed are dictated by the necessity of not breaking this *rapprocher*, still in a potential state, but on the contrary of reinforcing it. Of equal importance, as already noted in other terms by Loewenstein, referring to Hartmann, is the avoidance of comprising [sic] by an interpretation, even though accurate, the gradual development of the analysis as a whole. The need for preserving the *rapprocher* in general, is more important than partial interpretation. . . . Thus at a certain moment a simple affirmative will suffice to underline the importance of a destructive phantasy, while its interpretation in the transference would not be well tolerated. [Bouvet 1958, pp. 215–216]

Here we see the conceptual overlap between optimal distance and the use of "tact" (Loewenstein 1951, Poland 1975) in the analytic situation—that intuitive and subtle understanding of every moment of drift of the analysis, and the response that is called for.

Finally, the concept of distance deepens our understanding of certain instances of negative therapeutic reaction.[95] As is well known, Freud (1923) originally considered it a response to "a sense of guilt, which is finding its satisfaction in the illness and refuses to give up the punishment of suffering" (p. 49). The following year, he modified the concept to "a need for punishment" (1924a, p. 166) and traced this need to the fantasized oedipal crimes of incest and parricide. Later observers, however, began to discern that more pernicious negative therapeutic reactions are often based on unresolved preoedipal issues including (1) a feeling of guilt in having a separate existence or "separation guilt" (Modell 1965) and (2) a characterological defense against the dread of symbiotic fusion (Asch 1976). A narcissistically needy mother who cannot let go of her child renders him vulnerable to unconsciously equating separation with causing injury to her, even killing her. Asch notes that certain "specific accusations by mother ('Your birth was so difficult, I almost died; I was so torn up inside')

---

[95]An important area of the psychoanalytic enterprise, affected by the concept of optimal distance and overlooked by me, has been recently addressed by Haesler (1993). This pertains to the "optimal distance between the two parties to the supervising process" (p. 547). Haesler points out that, during the supervisory hour, the supervisor functions both as a teacher and as an analyst. In the former role he teaches not only the accumulated psychoanalytic knowledge but also how the analytic skill is to be acquired, "comparable to a teacher who teaches a musical instrument, or even better, one who teaches how to use one's voice in specific ways to become a competent singer" (p. 550). In the latter role, the supervisor listens to the patient's material in his usual analytic manner, discerns the specific nature of the unfolding analytic encounter between the patient and the candidate analyst, and observes the candidate's blind spots in dealing with the patient's material, especially if these blind spots show up repeatedly. Haesler emphasizes that while it is necessary for such blind spots to be pointed out, in doing so the supervisor should not deal with them as a personality trait of the candidate but rather as "a specific response to the patient or resonance phenomenon within the candidate, and the specific dynamic interaction between himself and the patient" (p. 552). Maintaining this perspective, Haesler believes, helps the supervisor "to keep an optimal distance both as *unobtrusive analyst* and as *unobtrusive teacher.*' He will thus find, when necessary, the optimal balance between the two positions: maintaining the position of an *unobtrusive supervisor*'" (p. 553, italics in the original).

often add fixating elements of historical 'reality'" (p. 392) to such fears. Subsequent separations, as heralded by any increase in distance (at first from the primary objects and after from their transferential re-creations), provoke guilt and are dreaded. Besides Modell and Asch, Gruenert (1979) has noted negative therapeutic reactions based on guilt and anxiety of separation. I too have briefly commented elsewhere (Akhtar 1991a) on a patient who, with each progressive movement in her analysis, would develop a fear of abandonment by me and, motivated by this fear, a regressive loss of her newly acquired insights.[96]

The second dynamic mentioned above derives from the negativism of oral and anal conflicts that is used to guard against oral fusion or anal submission fantasies. Here compliance with the analyst, especially that based on a recognition of the validity of his stance, stirs up the dread of symbiotic fusion and a threat to the integrity of the self (Asch 1976). While I have some reservation in labeling this second phenomenon negative therapeutic reaction, I cannot but note that the issue in both these dynamics is one of distance. In separation guilt the anxiety is about too much distance, and in the defense against fusion dynamic the anxiety is about too little. The analyst's awareness of these concerns would enhance his empathy, modulate his technique, and minimize such reversals of hard-won battles against other resistances.

SUMMARY

One would like to think of an ideal person who, while not abandoning his wish to achieve the oneness and harmony of his early experience, can still accept objects as friendly and yet independent, who need not deny them their freedom either by clinging or by degrading them to the rank of "equipment." [Balint 1959, p. 41]

---

[96]Miller (1965) suggests that the exacerbation of symptoms during the terminal phase of analysis might also reflect a defense against separation anxiety.

In this chapter I discussed the concept of "optimal distance," noting that a dialectical tension between the interpersonal and intrapsychic perspectives is essential to its proper definition. I described the gross psychopathology of optimal distance, including various types of severe character pathology, neurotic formations such as agoraphobia, and certain fluctuating marital difficulties. Following this, I highlighted the more subtle anxieties in this realm and described the tether fantasy and its variants involving orbits and invisible fences. I then reviewed the development of optimal distance and its disturbances. I also attempted to show the reverberations of these phenomena in the sociocultural realm of childhood games, thrill seeking, travel, vacations, migration, and exile. Finally, I discussed the varied and profound implications of these concepts to the technique of psychoanalysis and intensive psychotherapy.

Two disclaimers seem warranted before I conclude. First, although I have emphasized the preoedipal basis for the development of optimal distance and its pathology, this should not be taken to mean that I do not recognize the oedipal contributions to these matters. Indeed, I have mentioned them briefly in this chapter. Second, with the exception of my description of the tether fantasy and its variants, I do not claim any significant originality for the ideas presented here. My work has largely been one of synthesis and exposition. Through this, I have attempted to extend the work of many outstanding analysts, especially Maurice Bouvet, Michael Balint, and Margaret Mahler.

Let me conclude with a poem and a question. The poem was written by the noted psychoanalyst Jill Scharff after she had attended a meeting where I presented my views on optimal distance and the tether fantasy.

> Whether the tether be short
> Or whether the tether be not
> Whatever the tether
> We'll not ever sever
> The tether, and never abort

> Whether the tether be fought
> Or whether the tether be sought
> We'll weather the tether
> And learn hell-for-leather
> Whenever the tether be taut

Clearly, Dr. Scharff developed a playfully creative tether with me just as I have established a conceptual tether here with Mahler, Balint, and Bouvet. What remains to be seen is how far my phenomenological and technical notions will travel. They might find no resonance in others or they might become anchoring points for those struggling with similar clinical issues. Need I say that my hope is that my ideas meet the latter fate?

REFERENCES

Abend, S. M., Porder, N. S., and Willick, M. S. (1983). *Borderline Patients: Psychoanalytic Perspectives.* New York: International Universities Press.

Abraham, K. (1913a). On neurotic exogamy: a contribution to the similarities in the psychic life of neurotics and of primitive man. In *Clinical Papers and Essays on PsychoAnalysis*, pp. 48–56. New York: Brunner/Mazel, 1955.

———— (1913b). A constitutional basis of locomotor anxiety. In *Selected Papers of Karl Abraham, M.D.*, pp. 235–244. London: Hogarth, 1927.

———— (1924a). A short study of the development of the libido. In *Selected Papers of Karl Abraham, M.D.*, pp. 418–501. New York: Basic Books, 1953.

———— (1924b). The influence of oral erotism on character formation. In *Selected Papers of Karl Abraham, M.D.*, pp. 393–406. New York: Brunner/Mazel.

Abrams, S. (1978). The teaching and learning of psychoanalytic developmental psychology. *Journal of the American Psychoanalytic Association* 26:387–406.

Adler, G. (1981). The borderline-narcissistic personality disorders continuum. *American Journal of Psychiatry* 138:46–50.

———— (1985). *Borderline Psychopathology and Its Treatment.* New York: Jason Aronson.

Adorno, J., and Frenkel-Brunswick, E. (1950). *The Authoritarian Personality.* New York: Norton.

Akhtar, S. (1984a). The syndrome of identity diffusion. *American Journal of Psychiatry* 141:1381–1385.

————— (1984b). Self psychology vs. mainstream psychoanalysis. *Contemporary Psychiatry* 3:113–117.

————— (1985). The other woman: phenomenological, psychodynamic and therapeutic considerations. In *Contemporary Marriage*, ed. D. Goldberg, pp. 215–240. Homeswood, IL: Dow Jones-Irwin.

————— (1987). Schizoid personality disorder. *American Journal of Psychotherapy* 41:499–518.

————— (1988a). Hypomanic personality disorder. *Integrative Psychiatry* 6:37–52.

————— (1988b). Some reflections on the theory of psychopathology, and personality development in Kohut's self psychology. In *New Concepts in Psychoanalytic Psychotherapy*, ed. J. M. Ross and W. Myers, pp. 226–252. Washington, DC: American Psychiatric Press.

————— (1989a). Narcissistic personality disorder. *Psychiatric Clinics of North America* 12:505–529.

————— (1989b). Kohut and Kernberg: a critical comparison. In *Self Psychology: Comparisons and Contrasts*, ed. D. W. Detrick and D. P. Detrick, pp. 329–362. Hillsdale, NJ: Analytic Press.

————— (1990a). Concept of interpersonal distance in borderline personality disorder (letter to editor). *American Journal of Psychiatry* 147:2.

————— (1990b). Paranoid personality disorder. *American Journal of Psychotherapy* 44:5–25.

————— (1991a). Three fantasies related to unresolved separation-individuation: a less recognized aspect of severe character pathology. In *Beyond the Symbiotic Orbit: Advances in Separation-Individuation Theory—Essays in Honor of Selma Kramer, M.D.*, ed. S. Akhtar and H. Parens, pp. 261–284. Hillsdale, NJ: Analytic Press.

————— (1991b). Panel report: sadomasochism in perversions. *Journal of the American Psychoanalytic Association* 39:741–755.

————— (1992a). Tethers, orbits, and invisible fences: clinical, developmental, sociocultural, and technical aspects of optimal distance. In *When the Body Speaks: Psychological Meanings in Kinetic Clues*, ed. S. Kramer and S. Akhtar, pp. 21–57. Northvale, NJ: Jason Aronson.

————— (1992b). *Broken Structures: Severe Personality Disorders and Their Treatment*. Northvale, NJ: Jason Aronson.

————— (1992c). Review of *Between Freud and Klein: The Psychoanalytic Quest of Knowledge and Truth*, by Adam Limentani. *Psychoanalytic Books* 3: 43–49.

————— (1994a). Needs, disruptions, and the return of ego instincts. In *Mahler and Kohut: Perspectives on Development, Psychopathology, and Tech-*

nique, ed. S. Kramer and S. Akhtar, pp. 97–115. Northvale, NJ: Jason Aronson.

―――― (1994b). Object constancy and adult psychopathology. *International Journal of Psycho-Analysis* 75:441–455.

―――― (1995a). *Quest for Answers: A Primer for Understanding and Treating Severe Personality Disorders.* Northvale, NJ: Jason Aronson.

―――― (1995b). A third individuation: immigration, identity, and the psychoanalytic process. *Journal of the American Psychoanalytic Association* 43:1051–1084.

―――― (1995c). Some reflections on the nature of hatred and its emergence in the treatment process. In *The Birth of Hatred: Developmental, Clinical, and Technical Aspects of Intense Aggression,* ed. S. Akhtar, S. Kramer, and H. Parens, pp. 83–102. Northvale, NJ: Jason Aronson.

―――― (1995d). Review of *Treating the Borderline Patient* by F. Yeomans, M. Selzer, and J. Clarkin. *Journal of the American Psychoanalytic Association* 43:270–275.

―――― (1995e). Review of *Losing and Fusing: Borderline Transitional Object and Self Relations* by R. Lewin and C. Schulz. *Psychoanalytic Quarterly* 64:583–588.

―――― (1998). From simplicity through contradiction to paradox: the evolving psychic reality of the borderline patient in treatment. *International Journal of Psycho-Analysis* 79:241–252.

―――― (1999). The shy narcissist. *American Journal of Psychiatry* (in press).

Akhtar, S., and Byrne, J. P. (1983). The concept of splitting and its clinical relevance. *American Journal of Psychiatry* 140:1013–1016.

Akhtar, S., and Samuel, S. (1996). The concept of identity: developmental origins, phenomenology, clinical relevance, and measurement. *Harvard Review of Psychiatry* 3:254–267.

Akhtar, S., and Thomson, J. A. (1982). Overview: narcissistic personality disorder. *American Journal of Psychiatry* 139:12–20.

Alexander, F. (1929). The need for punishment and the death-instinct. *International Journal of Psycho-Analysis* 10:256–269.

Alexander, F., and French, T. M. (1946). *Psychoanalytic Therapy.* New York: Ronald Press.

Altman, L. L. (1977). Some vicissitudes of love. *Journal of the American Psychoanalytic Association* 25:35–52.

Altshuler, K. Z. (1979). Panel report: the interrelationship between academic psychiatry and psychoanalysis. *Journal of the American Psychoanalytic Association* 27:157–168.

Amati-Mehler, J., and Argentieri, S. (1989). Hope and hopelessness: A technical problem? *International Journal of Psycho-Analysis* 70:295–304.

American Psychiatric Association. (1980). *Diagnostic and Statistical Manual of Mental Disorders (DSM-III)*. Washington, DC: American Psychiatric Press.

Angel, A. (1934). Einige bemerkungen uber den optimismus. *International Journal of Psycho-Analysis* 20:191–199.

Arlow, J. A. (1973). Perspectives on aggression in human adaptation. *Psychoanalytic Quarterly* 42:178–184.

Arlow, J. A., and Brenner, C. (1964). *Psychoanalytic Concepts and the Structural Theory*. New York: International Universities Press.

Arlow, J. A., Freud, A., Lampl-de Groot, J. and Beres, D. (1968). Panel discussion. *International Journal of Psychoanalysis* 49:506–512.

Arnold, M. B. (1970). Brain function in emotion: a phenomenological analysis. In *Physiological Correlates of Emotion*, ed. P. Black, pp. 261–285. New York: Academic Press.

Asch, S. (1976). Varieties of negative therapeutic reactions and problems of technique. *Journal of the American Psychoanalytic Association* 24:383–407.

Atkin, S. (1975). Ego synthesis and cognition in a borderline case. *Psychoanalytic Quarterly* 46:29–61.

Bacal, H. A. (1987). British object-relations theorists and self-psychology: some critical reflections. *International Journal of Psycho-Analysis* 68:87–98.

Bacal, H. A., and Newman, K. M. (1990). *Theories of Object Relations: Bridges to Self Psychology*. New York: Columbia University Press.

Bach, S. (1977). On the narcissistic state of consciousness. *International Journal of Psycho-Analysis* 58:209–233.

―――― (1985). *Narcissistic States and the Therapeutic Process*. New York: Jason Aronson.

Baker, H. S., and Baker, M. N. (1987). Heinz Kohut's self psychology: an overview. *American Journal of Psychiatry* 144:1–9.

Balint, M. (1935). Critical notes on the pregenital organization of the libido. In *Primary Love and Psychoanalytic Technique*, pp. 37–58. London: Tavistock, 1965.

―――― (1937). Early developmental stages of the ego: primary object-love. In *Primary Love and Psychoanalytic Technique*, pp. 90–108. London: Hogarth, 1952.

―――― (1948). On genital love. In *Primary Love and Psychoanalytic Technique*, pp. 109–120. London: Tavistock, 1959.

——— (1952). On love and hate. *International Journal of Psycho-Analysis* 33:355–362.

——— (1959). *Thrills and Regression*. London: Hogarth.

——— (1968). *The Basic Fault: Therapeutic Aspects of Regression*. London: Tavistock.

Bartlett, J. (1980). *Familiar Quotations*, 15th ed. Boston: Little, Brown.

Begley, L. (1993). *The Man Who Was Late*. New York: Knopf.

Benedek, T. (1938). Adaptation to reality in early infancy. *Psychoanalytic Quarterly* 7:200–214.

——— (1977). Ambivalence, passion, and love. *Journal of the American Psychoanalytic Association* 25:53–79.

Bergman, A. (1980). Ours, yours, mine. In *Rapprochement: The Critical Subphase of Separation-Individuation*, ed. R. Lax, S. Bach, and J. A. Burland, pp. 199–216. New York: Jason Aronson.

——— (1996). Identifications on the way to constancy. In *The Internal Mother: Conceptual and Technical Aspects of Object Constancy*, ed. S. Akhtar, S. Kramer, and H. Parens, pp. 67–76. Northvale, NJ: Jason Aronson.

Bergman, P., and Escalona, S. K. (1949). Unusual sensitivities in very young children. *Psychoanalytic Study of the Child* 4:333–352. New York: International Universities Press.

Bergmann, M. S. (1971). Psychoanalytic observations on the capacity to love. In *Separation-Individuation: Essays in Honor of Margaret S. Mahler*, ed. J. McDevitt and C. Settlage, pp. 15–40. New York: International Universities Press.

——— (1980). On the intrapsychic function of falling in love. *Psychoanalytic Quarterly* 49:56–77.

——— (1982). Platonic love, transference, and love in real life. *Journal of the American Psychoanalytic Association* 30:87–111.

Berliner, B. (1958). The role of object relations in moral masochism. *Psychoanalytic Quarterly* 27:38–56.

Bibring, E. (1954). Psychoanalysis and the dynamic psychotherapies. *Journal of the American Psychoanalytic Association* 2:745–770.

Bion, W. (1956). Development of schizophrenic thought. *International Journal of Psycho-Analysis* 37:344–346.

——— (1957). On arrogance. In *Second Thoughts: Selected Papers on Psychoanalysis*, pp. 86–92. New York: Basic Books, 1968.

——— (1959). Attacks on linking. *International Journal of Psycho-Analysis* 40:308–315.

——— (1961). *Experience in Groups*. New York: Basic Books.

——— (1967). *Second Thoughts*. New York: Jason Aronson.

Blashfield, R. K., and McElroy, R. A. (1987). The 1985 journal literature on personality disorders. *Comprehensive Psychiatry* 28:536–546.

Blos, P. (1967). The second individuation process of adolescence. *Psychoanalytic Study of the Child* 22:162–186. New York: International Universities Press.

Blum, H. P. (1971). Transference and structure. In *The Unconscious Today*, ed. M. Kanzer, pp. 177–195. New York: International Universities Press.

———— (1973). The concept of erotized transference. *Journal of the American Psychoanalytic Association* 21:61–76.

———— (1977). The prototype of preoedipal reconstruction. *Journal of the American Psychoanalytic Association* 25:757–786.

———— (1981). Object inconstancy and paranoid conspiracy. *Journal of the American Psychoanalytic Association* 29:789–813.

———— (1995). Sanctified aggression, hate, and the alteration of standards and values. *The Birth of Hatred: Developmental, Clinical, and Technical Aspects of Intense Aggression*, ed. S. Akhtar, S. Kramer, and H. Parens, pp. 15–38. Northvale, NJ: Jason Aronson.

———— (1997). Clinical and developmental dimensions of hate. *Journal of the American Psychoanalytic Association* 45:359–375.

Bollas, C. (1979). The transformational object. *International Journal of Psycho-Analysis* 60:97–107.

———— (1992). *Being a Character*. New York: Hill and Wang.

Boris, H. N. (1976). On hope: its nature and psychotherapy. *International Review of Psycho-Analysis* 3:139–150.

Bouvet, M. (1958). Technical variation and the concept of distance. *International Journal of Psycho-Analysis* 39:211–221.

Bowlby, J. (1969). *Attachment and Loss: Vol. 1. Attachment.* New York: Basic Books.

———— (1973). *Attachment and Loss: Vol. 2. Separation: Anxiety and Anger.* New York: Basic Books.

———— (1980). *Attachment and Loss: Vol. 3. Loss: Sadness and Depression.* New York: Basic Books.

Boyer, L. B. (1967). Office treatment of schizophrenic patients: the use of psychoanalytic therapy with few parameters. In *Psychoanalytic Treatment of Characterological and Schizophrenic Disorders*, ed. L. B. Boyer and P. L. Giovacchini, pp. 143–188. New York: Science House.

Braunschweig, D., and Fain, M. (1971). *Eros et Anteros.* Paris: Petit Bibliotheque Payot.

Brenman, E. (1985). Cruelty and narrowmindedness. *International Journal of Psycho-Analysis* 66:273–281.

Brenner, C. (1971). The psychoanalytic concept of aggression. *International Journal of Psycho-Analysis* 52:137–144.

—— (1976a). *Psychotherapy and Social Sciences Review* 10:13.

—— (1976b). *Psychoanalytic Technique and Psychic Conflict.* New York: International Universities Press.

—— (1982). *The Mind in Conflict.* New York: International Universities Press.

Britton, R. (1995). Psychic reality and unconscious belief. *International Journal of Psycho-Analysis* 76:19–23.

Brome, V. (1982). *Ernest Jones: Freud's Alter Ego.* London: Norton.

Burland, J. A. (1975). Separation-individuation and reconstruction in psychoanalysis. *International Journal of Psychoanalytic Psychotherapy* 4:303–335.

—— (1986). Illusion, reality, and fantasy. In *Self and Object Constancy,* ed. R. F. Lax, S. Bach, and J. A. Burland, pp. 291–303. New York: Guilford.

Burnham, D. L., Gladstone, A. E., and Gibson, R. W. (1969). *Schizophrenia and the Need-Fear Dilemma.* New York: International Universities Press.

Bychowski, G. (1963). Frigidity and object relationship. *International Journal of Psycho-Analysis* 44:57–62.

Calef, V., and Weinshel, E. (1979). The new psychoanalysis and psychoanalytic revisionism. *Psychoanalytic Quarterly* 48:470–491.

Casement, P. (1991). *Learning from the Patient.* New York: Guilford.

Chasseguet-Smirgel, J. (1984). *Creativity and Perversion.* New York: Norton.

—— (1985). *The Ego Ideal: A Psychoanalytic Essay on the Malady of the Ideal.* New York: Norton.

Chmiel, A. J., Akhtar, S., and Morris, J. (1979). The long-distance psychiatric patient in the emergency room: insights regarding travel and mental illness. *International Journal of Social Psychiatry* 25:38–46.

Cirlot, J. E. (1971). *A Dictionary of Symbols,* trans. J. Sage. New York: Philosophical Library.

Coen, S. J. (1988). Sadomasochistic excitement: character disorder and perversion. In *Masochism: Current Psychoanalytic Perspectives,* ed. R. A. Glick and D. I. Meyers, pp. 43–59. Hillsdale, NJ: Analytic Press.

Colarusso, C. (1990). The third individuation: the effect of biological parenthood on separation-individuation processes in adulthood. *Psychoanalytic Study of the Child* 45:179–194. New Haven, CT: Yale University Press.

Cooper, A. M. (1983). The place of self psychology in the history of depth psychology. In *The Future of Psychoanalysis,* ed. A. Goldberg, pp. 3–17. New York: International Universities Press.

———— (1988). Review of *How Does Analysis Cure?* by H. Kohut. *Journal of the American Psychoanalytic Association* 36:175–179.

———— (1989). Narcissism and masochism: the narcissistic-masochistic character. *Psychiatric Clinics of North America* 12:541–552.

Curtis, H. C. (1983). Book review: *The Search for the Self: Selected Writings of Heinz Kohut*, ed. P. H. Ornstein. *Journal of the American Psychoanalytic Association* 31:272–285.

De Clerambault, C. G. (1942). *Oeuvre Psychiatrique.* Paris: Presses Universitaires.

Deutsch, F. (1952). Analytic posturology. *Psychoanalytic Quarterly* 21:196–214.

Deutsch, H. (1929). The genesis of agoraphobia. *International Journal of Psycho-Analysis* 10:51–69.

———— (1942). Some forms of emotional disturbance and their relationship to schizophrenia. *Psychoanalytic Quarterly* 11:301–321.

Dewall, R. (1984). *Korczak: Storyteller in Stone.* Crazy Horse, SD: Korczak's Heritage.

Dorn, R. N. (1967). Crying and weddings (and) "When I Grow Up." *International Journal of Psycho-Analysis* 48:298–307.

Dorpat, T. (1976). Structural conflict and object relations conflict. *Journal of the American Psychoanalytic Association* 25:855–874.

Downey, T. W. (1984). Within the pleasure principle: child analytic perspectives on aggression. *Psychoanalytic Study of the Child* 39:101–136. New Haven, CT: Yale University Press.

Edgcumbe, R., and Burgner, M. (1972). Some problems in the conceptualization of early object relationships. *Psychoanalytic Study of the Child* 27:283–314. New Haven, CT: Yale University Press.

Edward, J., Ruskin, N., and Turrini, P. (1981). *Separation-Individuation Theory and Application.* New York: Gardener.

Ehrlich, H. (1993). Reality, fantasy, and adolescence. *Psychoanalytic Study of the Child* 48:209–224. New Haven, CT: Yale University Press.

Eickhoff, F. W. (1987). A short annotation to Sigmund Freud's "Observations on Transference-Love." *International Review of Psycho-Analysis* 14:103–109.

———— (1993). A rereading of Freud's "Observations on Transference-Love." In *On Freud's "Observations on Transference-Love,"* ed. E. S. Person, A. Hagelin, and P. Fonagy, pp. 33–56. New Haven, CT: Yale University Press.

Eidelberg, L. (1968). *Encyclopedia of Psychoanalysis*, pp. 21–22. New York: The Free Press.

Eissler, K. R. (1950). Ego psychological implications of the psychoanalytic treatment of delinquents. *Psychoanalytic Study of the Child* 6:97–121. New York: International Universities Press.

———— (1953). The effects of the structure of the ego on psychoanalytic technique. *Journal of the American Psychoanalytic Association* 1:104–143.

———— (1971). Death drive, ambivalence, and narcissism. *Psychoanalytic Study of the Child* 26:25–78. New Haven, CT: Yale University Press.

Ekstein, R., and Friedman, S. (1967). Object constancy and psychotic reconstruction. *Psychoanalytic Study of the Child* 22:357–374. New York: International Universities Press.

Emch, M. (1944). On "the need to know" as related to identification and acting out. *International Journal of Psycho-Analysis* 25:13–19.

Emde, R. (1987). *Constitutional aspects of the drives.* Presented at the meetings of the International Psychoanalytic Association, Montreal, July.

Emde, R., Graensbauer, T., and Harmon, R. (1976). *Emotional Expression in Infancy.* New York: International Universities Press.

English, H. B., and English, A. C. (1976). *A Comprehensive Dictionary of Psychological and Psychoanalytic Terms: A Guide to Usage,* p. 19. New York: David McKay.

Erikson, E. H. (1950). *Childhood and Society.* New York: Norton.

———— (1959). *Identity and the Life Cycle.* New York: International Universities Press.

———— (1982). *The Life Cycle Completed.* New York: Norton.

Escoll, P. (1977). Panel report: the contribution of psychoanalytic developmental concepts to adult analysis. *Journal of the American Psychoanalytic Association* 25:219–234.

———— (1991). Treatment implications of separation-individuation theory in the analysis of young adults. In *Beyond the Symbiotic Orbit: Advances in Separation-Individuation Theory—Essays in Honor of Selma Kramer, M.D.,* ed. S. Akhtar and H. Parens, pp. 369–387. Hillsdale, NJ: Analytic Press.

———— (1992). Vicissitudes of optimal distance through the life cycle. In *When the Body Speaks: Psychological Meanings in Kinetic Clues,* ed. S. Kramer and S. Akhtar, pp. 59–87. Northvale, NJ: Jason Aronson.

Fairbairn, W. R. D. (1940). Schizoid factors in the personality. In *An Object Relations Theory of Personality,* pp. 3–27. New York: Basic Books, 1952.

———— (1943). The repression and the return of bad objects. In *Psychoanalytic Studies of the Personality,* pp. 59–81. London: Routledge & Kegan Paul, 1952.

———— (1944). Endopsychic structure considered in terms of object-relationships. In *Psychoanalytic Studies of the Personality*, pp. 82–137. London: Routledge & Kegan Paul.

———— (1952a). *Psychoanalytic Studies of the Personality*. London: Tavistock.

———— (1952b). *An Object-Relations Theory of the Personality*. New York: Basic Books.

Fenichel, O. (1928). The clinical aspect of the need for punishment. *International Journal of Psycho-Analysis* 9:47–70.

———— (1945). *The Psychoanalytic Theory of Neurosis*. New York: Norton.

———— (1954). The ego and the affects. In *The Collected Papers*, Second Series, pp. 215–227. New York: Norton.

Ferenczi, S. (1926). The problem of acceptance of unpleasant ideas: advances in knowledge of the sense of reality. In *Further Contributions to the Theory and Technique of Psycho-Analysis*, pp. 366–379. New York: Boni and Liveright, 1927.

———— (1929). The unwelcome child and his death instinct. In *Final Contributions to the Problems and Methods of Psychoanalysis*, pp. 102–107. London: Maresfield Library, 1980.

Fischer, N. (1991). *The psychoanalytic experience and psychic change*. Paper presented at the 27th biannual meeting of the International Psycho-analytical Association, Buenos Aires, Argentina, August.

Fleming, J. (1972). Early object deprivation and transference phenomena: the working alliance. *Psychoanalytic Quarterly* 21:23–49.

———— (1975). Some observations on object constancy in the psychoanalysis of adults. *Journal of the American Psychoanalytic Association* 23:743–759.

Fodor, N. (1950). Varieties of nostalgia. *Psychoanalytic Review* 37:25–38.

Frank, A. (1969). The unrememberable and the unforgettable: passive primal repression. *Psychoanalytic Study of the Child* 24:48–77. New York: International Universities Press.

———— (1992). A problem with the couch: incapacities and conflicts. In *When the Body Speaks: Psychological Meanings in Kinetic Clues*, ed. S. Kramer and S. Akhtar, pp. 89–112. Northvale, NJ: Jason Aronson.

Freedman, A. (1956). The feeling of nostalgia and its relationship to phobia. *Bulletin of the Philadelphia Association for Psychoanalysis* 6:84–92.

Freedman, A. M., Kaplan, H. I., and Sadock, B. J. (1975). *Comprehensive Textbook of Psychiatry/II*. Baltimore, MD: Williams & Wilkins.

French, T. M. (1945). The integration of social behavior. *Psychoanalytic Quarterly* 14:149–161.

French, T. M., and Wheeler, D. R. (1963). Hope and repudiation of hope in psycho-analytic therapy. *International Journal of Psycho-Analysis* 44:304–316.

Freud, A. (1936). *The Ego and the Mechanisms of Defense.* New York: International Universities Press.

———— (1963). The concept of developmental lines. *Psychoanalytic Study of the Child* 18:245–265. New York: International Universities Press.

———— (1965). Normality and pathology in childhood. In *The Writings of Anna Freud,* vol. 6. New York: International Universities Press.

———— (1966). Some thoughts about the place of psychoanalytic theory in the training of psychiatrists. In *The Writings of Anna Freud,* vol. 7. New York: International Universities Press.

———— (1972). Comments on aggression. *International Journal of Psycho-Analysis* 53:163–171.

Freud, S. (1892–1899). Extracts from the Fliess papers. *Standard Edition* 1:173–280.

———— (1895). Studies on hysteria (with J. Breuer). *Standard Edition* 2:1–323.

———— (1896). Specific aetiology of hysteria. *Standard Edition* 3:163–168.

———— (1900). The interpretation of dreams. *Standard Edition* 4/5:1–626.

———— (1905a). The purpose of jokes. *Standard Edition* 8:90–116.

———— (1905b). Fragment of an analysis of a case of hysteria. *Standard Edition* 7:3–122.

———— (1905c). Three essays on the theory of sexuality. *Standard Edition* 7:135–243.

———— (1905d). The psychopathology of everyday life. *Standard Edition* 6:1–310.

———— (1908). On the sexual theories of children. *Standard Edition* 9:209–226.

———— (1909a). A phobia in a five-year-old boy. *Standard Edition* 10:5–149.

———— (1909b). Notes upon a case of obsessional neurosis. *Standard Edition* 10:155–318.

———— (1909c). Five lectures on psycho-analysis. *Standard Edition* 11:9–55.

———— (1910a). A special type of object choice made by men. *Standard Edition* 11:163–175.

———— (1910b). The psychoanalytic view of psychogenic disturbances of vision. *Standard Edition* 11:209–218.

———— (1911a). Formulations on the two principles of mental functioning. *Standard Edition* 12:213–226.

———— (1911b). Psychoanalytic notes on an autobiographical account of a case of paranoia. *Standard Edition* 12:9–88.

———— (1912a). On the universal tendency to debasement in the sphere of love. *Standard Edition* 11:178–190.

———— (1912b). The dynamics of transference. *Standard Edition* 12:97–108.

———— (1912c). Recommendations to physicians practicing psychoanalysis. *Standard Edition* 12:111–120.

———— (1913a). Totem and taboo. *Standard Edition* 13:1–161.

———— (1913b). The dispositions to obsessional neurosis. *Standard Edition* 12:311–326.

———— (1914). On narcissism. *Standard Edition* 14:69–102.

———— (1915a). Observations on transference love. *Standard Edition* 12:159–171.

———— (1915b). Instincts and their vicissitudes. *Standard Edition* 14:117–140.

———— (1915c). The unconscious. *Standard Edition* 14:159–216.

———— (1915d). Regression. *Standard Edition* 14:141–158.

———— (1915e). Our attitude towards death. *Standard Edition* 14:289–300.

———— (1917a). A childhood recollection from Dichtung und Wahrheit. *Standard Edition* 17:145–157.

———— (1917b). The taboo of virginity. *Standard Edition* 11:191–208.

———— (1918). From the history of an infantile neurosis. *Standard Edition* 17:1–122.

———— (1919). On the teaching of psychoanalysis in universities. *Standard Edition* 17:169–173.

———— (1920a). Beyond the pleasure principle. *Standard Edition* 18:7–64.

———— (1920b). The psychogenesis of a case of homosexuality in a woman. *Standard Edition* 18:145–172.

———— (1921). Group psychology and the analysis of the ego. *Standard Edition* 18:67–144.

———— (1923). The ego and the id. *Standard Edition* 17:3–68.

———— (1924a). The economic problem of masochism. *Standard Edition* 19:157–170.

———— (1924b). The dissolution of the oedipus complex. *Standard Edition* 19:173–182.

———— (1925). Some psychical consequences of the anatomical distinction between the sexes. *Standard Edition* 19:241–258.

———— (1926). Inhibitions, symptoms and anxiety. *Standard Edition* 20:77–174.

———— (1927). Dostoevsky and parricide. *Standard Edition* 21:175–194.

———— (1930). Civilization and its discontents. *Standard Edition* 21:59–145.

———— (1931a). Female Sexuality *Standard Edition* 21: 223–243.

—— (1931b). Libidinal types. *Standard Edition* 21:215–220.

—— (1933). New introductory lectures on psychoanalysis. *Standard Edition* 22:3–182.

—— (1937a). Constructions in analysis. *Standard Edition* 23:255–270.

—— (1937b). Analysis terminable and interminable. *Standard Edition* 23:211–253.

—— (1940). An outline of psycho-analysis. *Standard Edition* 23:139–207.

Friedman, L. (1969). The therapeutic alliance. *International Journal of Psycho-Analysis* 50:139–153.

Fromm, E. (1950). *Psychoanalysis and Religion.* New Haven, CT: Yale University Press.

Frosch, J. (1966). A note on reality constancy. In *Psychoanalysis—A General Psychology*, ed. R. M. Loewenstein, L. M. Newman, M. Schur, and A. J. Solnit, pp. 349–376. New York: International Universities Press.

Furman, E. (1987). *Helping Young Children Grow.* Madison, CT: International Universities Press.

Gabbard, G. O., and Lester, E. P. (1995). *Boundaries and Boundary Violations in Psychoanalysis.* New York: Basic Books.

Gaddini, E. (1972). Aggression and the pleasure principle: towards a psychoanalytic theory of aggression. *International Journal of Psycho-Analysis* 53:191–197.

Galbraith, J. K. (1971). *Economics, Peace and Laughter.* Boston, MA: Houghton Mifflin.

Galdston, R. (1987). The longest pleasure: a psychoanalytic study of hatred. *International Journal of Psycho-Analysis* 68:371–378.

Gandhi, M. K. (1940). *An Autobiography: The Story of My Experiments with Truth*, trans. M. Desai. Boston, MA: Beacon Press, 1957.

Gaoni, B. (1985). Love as fierce as death. *Israel Journal of Psychiatry and Related Science* 22:89–93.

Gay, P. (1988). *Freud: A Life for Our Time.* New York: Norton.

Geahchan, D. (1968). Deuil et nostalgie. *Revue françoise de Psychoanalyse* 32:39–65.

Gediman, H. K. (1985). Imposture, inauthenticity, and feeling fraudulent. *Journal of the American Psychoanalytic Association* 33:911–936.

Gedo, J. E., and Goldberg, A. (1973). *Models of the Mind.* Chicago: University of Chicago Press.

Gibran, K. (1923). *The Prophet.* New York: Knopf.

Gillespie, W. H. (1952). Notes on the analysis of sexual perversions. In *Life, Sex and Death: Selected Writings of William H. Gillespie*, ed. M. Sinason, pp. 70–80. London: Routledge.

—— (1956). The general theory of sexual perversion. In *Life, Sex and Death: Selected Writings of William H. Gillespie*, ed. M. Sinason, pp. 81–92. London: Routledge.

—— (1971). Aggression and instinct theory. *International Journal of Psycho-Analysis* 52:155–167.

Gitelson, M. (1962a). The place of psychoanalysis in psychiatric training. *Bulletin of the Menninger Clinic* 26:57–72.

—— (1962b). The curative factors in psychoanalysis. *International Journal of Psycho-Analysis* 43:194–205.

Glenn, J. (1991). Transformations in normal and pathological latency. In *Beyond the Symbiotic Orbit: Advances in Separation-Individuation Theory— Essays in Honor of Selma Kramer, M.D.*, ed. S. Akhtar and H. Parens, pp. 171–187. Hillsdale, NJ: Analytic Press.

Glover, E. (1925). Notes on oral character formation. *International Journal of Psycho-Analysis* 6:131–153.

—— (1931). The therapeutic effect of inexact interpretation. *International Journal of Psycho-Analysis* 12:397–418.

Greenacre, P. (1953). Certain relationships between fetishism and the faulty development of the body image. *Psychoanalytic Study of the Child* 8:79–97. New York: International Universities Press.

—— (1975). On reconstruction. *Journal of the American Psychoanalytic Association* 23:693–712.

Greenberg, J. R., and Mitchell, S. A. (1983). *Object Relations in Psychoanalytic Theory*. Cambridge, MA: Harvard University Press.

Greenson, R. R. (1965). The working alliance and the transference neurosis. *Psychoanalytic Quarterly* 34:155–181.

Greenspan, S. I. (1977). The oedipal-preoedipal dilemma: a reformulation in the light of object relations theory. *International Review of Psycho-Analysis* 4:381–391.

Grinberg, L. R., and Grinberg, R. (1984). A psychoanalytic study of migration: its normal and pathological aspects. *Journal of the American Psychoanalytic Association* 32:13–38.

—— (1989). *Psychoanalytic Perspectives on Migration and Exile*. New Haven, CT: Yale University Press.

Grinspoon, L., ed. (1982). *American Psychiatric Association's 1982 Annual Review*. Washington, DC: American Psychiatric Press.

Grinstein, A. (1955). Vacations: a psycho-analytic study. *International Journal of Psycho-Analysis* 36:177–186.

Grotstein, J. S. (1981). *Splitting and Projective Identification.* New York: Jason Aronson.

Group for the Advancement of Psychiatry. [GAP] (1978). *Self Involvement in the Middle East Conflict.* GAP report 103. New York: GAP.

Grunberger, B. (1975). *Narcissism.* New York: International Universities Press.

Gruenert, U. (1979). The negative therapeutic reaction as a reactivation of a disturbed process of separation in the transference. *Bulletin of the European Psychoanalytical Federation* 65:5–19.

Gunderson, J. G. (1985). *Borderline Personality Disorder.* Washington, DC: American Psychiatric Press.

——— (1996). The borderline patient's intolerance of aloneness: insecure attachments and therapist availability. *American Journal of Psychiatry* 153:752–758.

Gunther, M. (1980). Aggression, self-psychology, and the concept of health. In *Advances in Self-Psychology,* ed. A. Goldberg, pp. 167–192. New York: International Universities Press.

Guntrip, H. (1969). *Schizoid Phenomena, Object Relations and the Self.* New York: International Universities Press.

——— (1971). *Psychoanalytic Theory, Therapy, and the Self.* London: Hogarth.

——— (1975). My experience of analysis with Fairbairn and Winnicott. *International Review of Psycho-Analysis* 2:145–156.

Guttman, S. A., Jones R. L., and Parrish, S. M., eds. (1980). *The Concordance to the Standard Edition of the Complete Psychological Works of Sigmund Freud,* vol 2, p. 203. Boston: G. K. Hall.

Haesler, L. (1993). Adequate distance in the relationship between supervisor and supervisee. *International Journal of Psycho-Analysis* 74:547–555.

Hamburg, D. A. (1973). An evolutionary and developmental approach to human aggressiveness. *Psychoanalytic Quarterly* 42:185–196.

Hamilton, J. W. (1969). Object loss, dreaming, and creativity: the poetry of John Keats. *Psychoanalytic Study of the Child* 24:488–531. New York: International Universities Press.

Harnik, E. J. (1932). Pleasure in disguise, the need for decoration, and the sense of beauty. *Psychoanalytic Quarterly* 1:216–264.

Hart, J. (1991). *Damage.* New York: Knopf.

Hartmann, H. (1939). *Ego Psychology and the Problem of Adaptation,* trans. D. Rapaport. New York: International Universities Press, 1958.

———— (1950). Comments on the psychoanalytic theory of the ego. In *Essays on Ego Psychology*, pp. 113–141. New York: International Universities Press.

———— (1952a). Mutual influences in the development of the ego and the id. *Psychoanalytic Study of the Child* 7:9–30. New York: International Universities Press.

———— (1952b). The mutual influence on the development of ego and id. In *Essays on Ego Psychology*, pp. 151–181. New York: International Universities Press.

———— (1955). Notes on the theory of sublimation. In *Essays on Ego Psychology*, pp. 215–240. New York: International Universities Press.

———— (1958). Discussion of Anna Freud's *Child Observation and Prediction of Development. Psychoanalytic Study of the Child* 13:120–122. New York: International Universities Press.

———— (1964). *Essays on Ego Psychology*. New York: International Universities Press.

Hartmann, H., Kris, E., and Loewenstein, R. M. (1946). Comments on the formation of psychic structure. In *Papers on Psychoanalytic Psychology* [Psychological Issues, Monogr. 14], pp. 27–55. New York: International Universities Press, 1964.

———— (1949). Notes on the theory of aggression. *Psychoanalytic Study of the Child* 3/4:9–56. New York: International Universities Press.

Hayman, A. (1989). What do we mean by "phantasy?" *International Journal of Psycho-Analysis* 70:105–114.

Heimann, P. (1952). Preliminary notes on some defence mechanisms in paranoid states. *International Journal of Psycho-Analysis* 33:206–213.

Heimann, P., and Valenstein, A. F. (1972). The psychoanalytical concept of aggression: an integrated summary. *International Journal of Psycho-Analysis* 53:31–35.

Heller, A. (1976). *The Theory of Needs in Marx*. London: Allison and Busby.

Hendrick, I. (1942). Instinct and the ego during infancy. *Psychoanalytic Quarterly* 11:33–58.

Hill, L. B. (1938). The use of hostility as a defense. *Psychoanalytic Quarterly* 7:254–264.

Hinsie, L. E., and Campbell, R. J. (1975). *Psychiatric Dictionary*, 4th ed. New York: Oxford University Press.

Holzman, P. (1976). The future of psychoanalysis and its institutes. *Psychoanalytic Quarterly* 45:250–273.

Horney, K. (1928). The problem of monogamous ideal. *International Journal of Psycho-Analysis* 9:318–331.

Hurwitz, M. R. (1986). The analyst, his theory, and the psychoanalytic process. *Psychoanaltyic Study of the Child* 41:439–466. New Haven, CT: Yale University Press.

Isakower, O. (1936). A contribution to the pathopsychology of phenomena associated with falling asleep. *International Journal of Psycho-Analysis* 19:331–345.

Izard, C. (1978). On the ontogenesis of emotions and emotion-cognition relationships in infancy. In *The Development of Affect*, ed. M. Lewis and A. Rosenblum, pp. 389–413. New York: Plenum.

Jacobson, E. (1953). The affects and their pleasure–unpleasure qualities in relation to the psychic discharge process. In *Drives, Affects, Behavior*, ed. R. M. Loewenstein, pp. 38–66. New York: International Universities Press.

——— (1964). *The Self and the Object World.* New York: International Universities Press.

——— (1971). *Depression.* New York: International Universities Press.

Jones, E. (1928). Fear, guilt, and hate. In *Papers on Psychoanalysis.* Baltimore, MD: Williams & Wilkins, 1950.

——— (1953). *The Life and Work of Sigmund Freud,* vol. I. New York: Basic Books.

——— (1957). *The Life and Work of Sigmund Freud,* vol. III. New York: Basic Books.

Joseph, B. (1975). The patient who is difficult to reach. In *Tactics and Techniques in Psychoanalytic Therapy, vol. 2: Countertransference*, ed. P. L. Giovacchini, pp. 205–216. New York: Jason Aronson.

——— (1993). On transference love: some current observations. In *On Freud's "Observations on Transference-Love,"* ed. E. S. Person, A. Hagelin, and P. Fonagy, pp. 102–113. New Haven, CT: Yale University Press.

Joseph, E. D. (1973). Aggression redefined—its adaptational aspects. *Psychoanalytic Quarterly* 42:197–213.

Kafka, J. S. (1989). *Multiple Realities in Clinical Practice.* New Haven, CT: Yale University Press.

Kaplan, L. (1977). *Oneness and Separateness: From Infant to Individual.* New York: Simon & Schuster.

Kaplan, Z. (1971). Eruv. In *Encyclopedia Judaica*, vol. 6., p. 849. Jerusalem: Keter.

Kernberg, O. F. (1967). Borderline personality organization. *Journal of the American Psychoanalytic Association* 15:641–685.

——— (1970a). Psychoanalytic classification of character pathology. *Journal of the American Psychoanalytic Association* 18:800–822.

——— (1970b). Factors in the psychoanalytic treatment of narcissistic personalities. *Journal of the American Psychoanalytic Association* 18:51–85.

——— (1974a). Barriers to falling and remaining in love. In *Object Relations Theory and Clinical Psycho-Analysis*, pp. 185–213. New York: Jason Aronson.

——— (1974b). Mature love: prerequisites and characteristics. In *Object Relations Theory and Clinical Psycho-Analysis*, pp. 215–139. New York: Jason Aronson.

——— (1974c). Further contributions to the treatment of the narcissistic personality. *International Journal of Psycho-Analysis* 55:215–240.

——— (1975a). Melanie Klein. In *Comprehensive Textbook of Psychiatry—II, vol. 1*, ed. A. M. Freedman, H. I. Kaplan, and B. J. Sadock, pp. 641–650. Baltimore, MD: Williams & Wilkins.

——— (1975b). *Borderline Conditions and Pathological Narcissism.* New York: Jason Aronson.

——— (1976). *Object Relations Theory and Clinical Psychoanalysis.* New York: International Universities Press.

——— (1977a). Normal psychology of the aging process revisited—II. *Journal of Geriatric Psychiatry* 10:27–45.

——— (1977b). Clinical observation regarding the diagnosis, prognosis and intensive treatment of chronic schizophrenics. In *Traitements An Long Courses Des Etats Psychotiques*, ed. C. Chiland and P. Bequart, pp. 332–360. New York: Human Sciences.

——— (1978a). Leadership and organizational functioning: organizational regression. *International Journal of Group Psychotherapy* 28:3–25.

——— (1978b). The diagnosis of borderline conditions in adolescence. *Adolescent Psychiatry* 16:298–319.

——— (1979). The contributions of Edith Jacobson: an overview. *Journal of the American Psychoanalytic Association* 27:793–819.

——— (1980). *Internal World and External Reality.* New York: Jason Aronson.

——— (1981). Structural interviewing. *Psychiatric Clinics of North America* 4:169–195.

——— (1982a). Self, ego, affects, and drives. *Journal of the American Psychoanalytic Association* 30:893–918.

——— (1982b). Supportive psychotherapy with borderline conditions. In *Critical Problems in Psychiatry*, ed. J. O. Cavenar and H. K. H. Brodie, pp. 180–202. Philadelphia: Lippincott.

——— (1984). *Severe Personality Disorders: Psychotherapeutic Strategies.* New Haven, CT: Yale University Press.

———— (1985). Hysterical and histrionic personality disorders. In *Psychiatry*, vol. 1, ed. J. O. Cavenar and R. Michels, pp. 1–11. Philadelphia: Lippincott.

———— (1988). Book review of *Borderline Psychopathology and Its Treatment* by G. Adler. *American Journal of Psychiatry* 145:264–265.

———— (1989). The narcissistic personality disorder and the differential diagnosis of antisocial behavior. *Psychiatric Clinics of North America* 12:533–570.

———— (1991a). Sadomasochism, sexual excitement and perversion. *Journal of the American Psychoanalytic Association* 39:333–362.

———— (1991b). The psychopathology of hatred. *Journal of the American Psychoanalytic Association* 39(suppl.):209–238.

———— (1991c). Some comments on early development. In *Beyond the Symbiotic Orbit: Advances in Separation-Individuation Theory—Essays in Honor of Selma Kramer, M.D.*, ed. S. Akhtar and H. Parens, pp. 103–120. Hillsdale, NJ: Analytic Press.

———— (1991d). Aggression and love in the relationship of the couple. *Journal of the American Psychoanalytic Association* 39:486–511.

———— (1992). *Aggression in Personality Disorders and Perversions.* New Haven, CT: Yale University Press.

———— (1993). The couple's constructive and destructive superego functions. *Journal of the American Psychoanalytic Association* 41:653–677.

———— (1995a). *Love Relations: Normality and Pathology.* New Haven, CT: Yale University Press.

———— (1995b). Hatred as a core affect of aggression. In *The Birth of Hatred: Developmental, Clinical, and Technical Aspects of Intense Aggression*, ed. S. Akhtar, S. Kramer, and H. Parens, pp. 53–82. Northvale, NJ: Jason Aronson.

Kernberg, O. F., Goldstein, E., Carr, A., et al. (1981). Diagnosing borderline personality organization. *Journal of Nervous and Mental Disease* 169:225–231.

Kernberg, O. F., Selzer, M. A., Koenigsberg, H. W., et al. (1989). *Psychodynamic Psychotherapy of Borderline Patients.* New York: Basic Books.

Khan, M. M. R. (1966). Role of phobic and counterphobic mechanisms and separation anxiety in schizoid character formation. In *The Privacy of the Self*, pp. 69–81. New York: International Universities Press, 1974.

———— (1972). Dread of surrender to resourceless dependence in the analytic situation. In *The Privacy of the Self*, pp. 270–279. New York: International Universities Press, 1974.

——— (1974). *The Privacy of the Self.* New York: International Universities Press.

——— (1983). *Hidden Selves.* New York: International Universities Press.

Kiell, N. (1988). *Freud Without Hindsight: Reviews of His Work 1893–1939.* New York: International Universities Press.

Killingmo, B. (1989). Conflict and deficit: implications for technique. *International Journal of Psycho-Analysis* 70:65–79.

Klauber, J. (1971). Personal attitudes to psychoanalytic consultation. In *Difficulties in the Analytic Encounter,* pp. 141–159. New York: Jason Aronson, 1981.

Kleeman, J. A. (1967). The peek-a-boo game: part I: its origins, meanings, and related phenomena in the first year. *Psychoanalytic Study of the Child* 22:239–273. New York: International Universities Press.

Klein, G. (1976). *Psychoanalytic Theory.* New York: International Universities Press.

Klein, M. (1932). *The Psycho-Analysis of Children.* New York: Norton.

——— (1933). The early development of conscience in the child. In *Love, Guilt and Reparation and Other Works 1921–1945,* pp. 248–257. New York: The Free Press, 1975.

——— (1935). A contribution to the psychogenesis of manic-depressive states. In *Love, Guilt and Reparation and Other Works 1921–1945,* pp. 262–289. New York: The Free Press, 1975.

——— (1940). Mourning and its relation to manic-depressive states. In *Love, Guilt and Reparation and Other Works 1921–1945,* pp. 344–369. New York: The Free Press.

——— (1946). Notes on some schizoid mechanisms. In *Envy and Gratitude and Other Works 1946–1963,* pp. 1–24. New York: The Free Press, 1975.

——— (1948). *Contributions to Psychoanalysis* (1921–1945). London: Hogarth.

——— (1952). The mutual influences in the development of ego and id. In *Envy and Gratitude and Other Works 1946–1963,* pp. 57–60. New York: The Free Press, 1975.

——— (1960). On mental health. In *Envy and Gratitude and Other Works 1946–1963,* pp. 268–274. New York: The Free Press, 1975.

Klein, M., and Tribich, D. (1981). Kernberg's object-relations theory: a critical evaluation. *International Journal of Psycho-Analysis* 62:27–43.

Kleiner, J. (1970). On nostalgia. *Bulletin of the Philadelphia Association for Psychoanalysis* 20:11–30.

Knapp, P. H. (1979). Core processes in the organization of emotions. In

Affect: Psychoanalytic Theory and Practice, ed. M. B. Cantor and M. L. Glucksman, pp. 51–70. New York: Wiley.

Koenigsberg, H. W., Kernberg, O. F., and Schomer, J. (1983). Diagnosing borderline conditions in an outpatient setting. *Archives of General Psychiatry* 40:49–53.

Kohon, G. (1986). *The British School of Psychoanalysis: The Independent Tradition.* New Haven: Yale University Press.

Kohut, H. (1957). Observation on the psychological functions of music. *Journal of the American Psychoanalytic Association* 5:389–407.

——— (1964). Some problems of a metapsychological formulation of fantasy. *International Journal of Psycho-Analysis* 45:199–202.

——— (1971). *The Analysis of the Self.* New York: International Universities Press.

——— (1972). Thoughts on narcissism and narcissistic rage. *Psychoanalytic Study of the Child* 27:360–400. New Haven, CT: Yale University Press.

——— (1976). Creativeness, charisma, group psychology: reflections on the self analysis of Freud. *Psychological Issues,* Monograph 9. New York: International Universities Press.

——— (1977). *Restoration of the Self.* New York: International Universities Press.

——— (1980). Summarizing reflections. In *Advances in Self Psychology,* ed. A. Goldberg, pp. 473–554. New York: International Universities Press.

——— (1982). Introspection, empathy, and the semi-circle of mental health. *International Journal of Psycho-Analysis* 63:395–407.

——— (1984). *How Does Analysis Cure?* Chicago: University of Chicago Press.

Kohut, H., and Levarie, S. (1950). On the enjoyment of listening to music. *Psychoanalytic Quarterly* 19:64–71.

Kohut, H., and Wolf, E. (1978). The disorders of the self and their treatment: an outline. *International Journal of Psycho-Analysis* 59:413–425.

Kolansky, H., and Eisner, H. (1974). *The psychoanalytic concept of preoedipal developmental arrest.* Paper presented at the Fall Meetings of the American Psychoanalytic Association, New York, December.

Kramer, S. (1980a). Residues of split-object and split-self dichotomies in adolescence. In *Rapprochement: The Critical Subphase of Separation-Individuation,* ed. R. Lax, S. Bach, and J. A. Burland, pp. 417–437. New York: Jason Aronson.

——— (1980b). The technical significance and application of Mahler's separation-individuation theory. In *Psychoanalytic Explorations of Tech-*

nique: Discourses on the Theory of Therapy, ed. H. Blum, pp. 240–262. New York: International Universities Press.

———— (1987). A contribution to the concept "the exception" as a developmental phenomenon. *Child Abuse and Neglect* 11:367–370.

———— (1991). The technical handling of incest-related material. In *The Trauma of Transgression: Psychotherapy of Incest Victims*, ed. S. Kramer and S. Akhtar, pp. 169–180. Northvale, NJ: Jason Aronson.

Kramer, S., and Akhtar, S. (1988). The developmental context of internalized preoedipal object relations: clinical applications of Mahler's theory of symbiosis and separation-individuation. *Psychoanalytic Quarterly* 57:547–576.

Kris, E. (1947). The nature of psychoanalytic propositions and their validation. In *Selected Papers of Ernst Kris*. New Haven, CT: Yale University Press, 1975.

———— (1950). Notes on the development and on some current problems of psychoanalytic child psychology. *Psychoanalytic Study of the Child* 5:24–46. New York: International Universities Press.

———— (1956). The personal myth: a problem in psychoanalytic technique. *Journal of the American Psychoanalytic Association* 4:653–681.

Krystal, H. (1966). Giorgio de Chirico: ego states and artistic production. *American Imago* 23:210–226.

Kundera, M. (1990). *Immortality*. New York: Grove Weidenfeld.

Kurtz, S. A. (1988). The psychoanalysis of time. *Journal of the American Psychoanalytic Association* 36:985–1094.

Lacan, J. (1958). The signification of the phallus. In *Ecrits: A Selection*, trans. A. Sheridan, pp. 281–291. London: Tavistock.

Lacayo, R. (1984). Meeting of two masters: Sir David Lean and Lord Snowdon take aim at *A Passage to India*. *Time*, August 27, pp. 54–55.

Lafarge, L. (1995). Transferences of deception. *Journal of the American Psychoanalytic Association* 43:765–792.

Lantos, B. (1958). The two genetic derivations of aggression with reference to sublimation and neutralization. *International Journal of Psycho-Analysis* 33:444–449.

Laplanche, J. and Pontalis, J.-B. (1973). *The Language of Psychoanalysis*, trans. D. Nicholson-Smith. New York: Norton.

Lax, R. (1986). Libidinal object and self constancy enhanced by the analytic process. In *Self and Object Constancy*, ed. R. Lax, S. Bach, and J. A. Burland, pp. 271–290. New York: Guilford.

Lerner, B., Raskin, R., and Davis, E. B. (1967). On the need to be pregnant. *International Journal of Psycho-Analysis* 48:288–297.

Levin, F. M. (1995). Psychoanalysis and the brain. In *Psychoanalysis: The Major Concepts*, ed. B. Moore and B. Fine, p. 539. New Haven, CT: Yale University Press.

Levy, S. T. (1987). Therapeutic strategy and psychoanalytic technique. *Journal of the American Psychoanalytic Association* 35:447–466.

Lewin, B. D. (1950). *The Psychoanalysis of Elation.* New York: Norton.

Lewin, R. A. and Schulz, C. (1992). *Losing and Fusing: Borderline Transitional Object and Self Relations.* Northvale, NJ: Jason Aronson.

Lichtenberg, J. D. (1989). *Psychoanalysis and Motivation.* Hillsdale, NJ: Analytic Press.

Lichtenberg, J. D., Fosshage, J., and Lachmann, F. (1992). *Self and Motivational Systems: Toward a Theory of Psychoanalytic Technique.* Hillsdale, NJ: Analytic Press.

Lichtenstein, H. (1961). Identity and sexuality: a study of their interrelationship in man. *Journal of the American Psychoanalytic Association* 9:179–260.

Little, M. (1957). "R"—the analyst's total response to his patient's needs. *International Journal of Psycho-Analysis* 47:240–254.

Loewald, H. W. (1960). On the therapeutic action of psychoanalysis. *International Journal of Psycho-Analysis* 41:16–33.

———— (1977). Instinct theory, object relations, and psychic structure formation. In *Papers on Psychoanalysis*, pp. 207–218. New Haven, CT: Yale University Press, 1980.

———— (1979). The waning of the oedipus complex. *Journal of the American Psychoanalytic Association* 27:751–755.

Loewenberg, P. (1995). *Fantasy and Reality in History.* New York: Oxford University Press.

Loewenstein, R. (1951). The problem of interpretation. *Psychoanalytic Quarterly* 20:1–23.

Lorenz, K. (1963). *On Aggression.* New York: Bantam.

Lussier, A. (1972). Panel Report on: Aggression. *International Journal of Psycho-Analysis* 53:13–19.

Lustman, S. L. (1956). Rudiments of the ego. *Psychoanalytic Study of the Child* 11:89–98. New York: International Universities Press.

Madow, L. (1982). *Love: How to Understand and Enjoy It.* New York: Charles Scribner's Sons.

Mahler, M. S. (1958a). Autism and symbiosis: two extreme disturbances of identity. *International Journal of Psycho-Analysis* 39:77–83.

———— (1958b). On two crucial phases of integration of the sense of identity. *Journal of the American Psychoanalytic Association* 6:136–139.

————— (1965). On the significance of the normal separation-individuation phase with reference to research in symbiotic childhood psychosis. In *The Selected Papers of Margaret S. Mahler, Vol. 2*, pp. 49–58. New York: Jason Aronson, 1979.

————— (1966). Notes on the development of basic moods: the depressive affect. In *The Selected Papers of Margaret S. Mahler, Vol. 2*, pp. 59–76. New York: Jason Aronson, 1979.

————— (1968). *On Human Symbiosis and the Vicissitudes of Individuation, vol I: Infantile Psychosis*. New York: International Universities Press.

————— (1971). A study of the separation-individuation process and its possible application to borderline phenomena in the psychoanalytic situation. In *The Selected Papers of Margaret S. Mahler, Vol. 2*, pp. 169–187. New York: Jason Aronson, 1979.

————— (1972a). A study of the separation and individuation process and its possible application to borderline phenomena in the psychoanalytic situation. *Psychoanalytic Study of the Child* 26:403–424. New Haven, CT: Yale University Press.

————— (1972b). Rapprochement subphase of the separation-individuation process. In *The Selected Papers of Margaret S. Mahler, Vol 2*, pp. 131–148. New York: Jason Aronson, 1979.

————— (1972c). On the first three subphases of the separation-individuation process. In *The Selected Papers of Margaret S. Mahler, Vol. 2*, pp. 119–130. New York: Jason Aronson, 1979.

————— (1974). Symbiosis and individuation: the psychological birth of the human infant. In *The Selected Papers of Margaret S. Mahler, Vol. 2*, pp. 149–165. New York: Jason Aronson, 1979.

————— (1975). On the current status of the infantile neurosis. In *The Selected Papers of Margaret S. Mahler, Vol. 2*, pp. 189–194. New York: Jason Aronson, 1979.

Mahler, M. S., and Furer, M. (1968). *On Human Symbiosis and the Vicissitudes of Individuation*. New York: International Universities Press.

Mahler, M. S., and Kaplan, L. (1977). Developmental aspects in the assessment of narcissistic and so-called borderline personalities. In *Borderline Personality Disorders*, ed. P. Hartocollis, pp. 71–86. New York: International Universities Press.

Mahler, M. S., and McDevitt, J. B. (1968). Observations on adaptation and defense in statu nascendi: developmental precursors in the first two years of life. *Psychoanalytic Quarterly* 37:1–21.

————— (1980). The separation-individuation process and identity formation. In *The Course of Life*, ed. S. I. Greenspan and G. H. Pollack, pp. 395–406. Bethesda, MD: NIMH.

Mahler, M. S., Pine, F., and Bergman, A. (1975). *The Psychological Birth of the Human Infant.* New York: Basic Books.

Maltsberger, J. T., and Buie, D. H. (1974). Countertransference hate in the treatment of suicidal patients. *Archives of General Psychiatry* 30:625–633.

Marcovitz, E. (1973). Aggression in human adaptation. *Psychoanalytic Quarterly* 42:226–233.

Marx, K. (1867). *Das Kapital.* Hamburg, Germany: Verlag Von Otto Meissner.

Maslow, A. (1968). *Toward a Psychology of Being*, 2nd ed. Princeton, NJ: Van Nostrand.

——— (1970). *Motivation and Personality*, 2nd ed. New York: Harper & Row.

Masson, J. M., ed. and trans. (1985). *The Complete Letters of Sigmund Freud to Wilhelm Fliess 1887–1904.* Cambridge, MA: Belknap Press of Harvard University Press.

Mayer, E. (1994). Some implications for psychoanalytic technique drawn from analysis of a dying patient. *Psychoanalytic Quarterly* 63:1–19.

McDevitt, J. (1975). Separation-individuation and object constancy. *Journal of the American Psychoanalytic Association* 23:713–743.

——— (1983). The emergence of hostile aggression and its defensive and adaptive modification during the separation-individuation process. *Journal of the American Psychoanalytic Association* 31 (suppl.):273–300.

——— (1991). Contributions of separation-individuation theory to the understanding of psychopathology during the prelatency years. In *Beyond the Symbiotic Orbit: Advances in Separation-Individuation Theory—Essays in Honor of Selma Kramer, M.D.*, ed. S. Akhtar and H. Parens, pp. 153–170. Hillsdale, NJ: Analytic Press.

McLaughlin, J. T. (1992). Nonverbal behaviors in the analytic situation: the search for meaning in nonverbal cues. In *When the Body Speaks: Psychological Meanings in Kinetic Clues*, ed. S. Kramer and S. Akhtar, pp. 131–162. Northvale, NJ: Jason Aronson.

Meissner, W. W. (1976). The relationship of psychoanalysis to current changes in medical and psychiatric education—historical perspective. *Journal of the American Psychoanalytic Association* 24:329–346.

Melges, F. T., and Swartz, M. S. (1989). Oscillations of attachment in borderline personality disorder. *American Journal of Psychiatry* 146:1115–1120.

Menninger, K. (1938). *Man Against Himself.* New York: Harcourt, Brace.
———— (1959). Hope. *American Journal of Psychiatry* 116:481–491.
Miller, J. (1965). On the return of symptoms in the terminal phase of psychoanalysis. *International Journal of Psycho-Analysis* 46:487–501.
Mitchell, S. A. (1993). *Hope and Dread in Psychoanalysis.* New York: Basic Books.
Mittleman, B. (1957). Motility in the therapy of children and adults. *Psychoanalytic Study of the Child* 12:284–319. New York: International Universities Press.
Modell, A. (1965). On aspects of the superego's development. *International Journal of Psycho-Analysis* 46:323–331.
———— (1975). The ego and the id. *International Journal of Psycho-Analysis* 56:57–68.
———— (1976). The holding environment and the therapeutic action of psychoanalysis. *Journal of the American Psychoanalytic Association* 24:285–307.
———— (1984). *Psychoanalysis in a New Context.* New York: International Universities Press.
Moore, B. E. (1964). Frigidity: a review of psychoanalytic literature. *Psychoanalytic Quarterly* 33:323–349.
Moore, B., and Fine, B. (1968). *A Glossary of Psychoanalytic Terms and Concepts,* pp. 18–19. New York: American Psychoanalytic Association.
———— (1990). *Psychoanalytic Terms and Concepts,* pp. 1–210. New York: American Psychoanalytic Association.
———— (1995). *Psychoanalysis: The Major Concepts.* New Haven, CT: Yale University Press.
Mullen, P. E. (1990). Morbid jealousy and the delusion of infidelity. In *Principles and Practice of Forensic Psychiatry,* ed. R. Bluglass and P. Bowden, pp. 823–834. London: Churchill Livingstone.
Nemiah, J. C. (1961). *Foundations of Psychopathology.* New York: Oxford University Press.
Neubauer, P. (1995). Hate and developmental sequences and group dynamics. In *The Birth of Hatred: Developmental, Clinical, and Technical Aspects of Intense Aggression,* ed. S. Akhtar, S. Kramer, and H. Parens, pp. 149–164. Northvale, NJ: Jason Aronson.
Nickman, S. L. (1985). Losses in adoption: the need for dialogue. *Psychoanalytic Study of the Child* 40:365–397. New Haven, CT: Yale University Press.
Nunberg, H. (1926). The sense of guilt and the need for punishment. *International Journal of Psycho-Analysis* 7:420–433.

————— (1931). The synthetic function of the ego. *International Journal of Psycho-Analysis* 12:123–140.

Olden, C. (1941). About the fascinating effect of the narcissistic personality. *American Imago* 2:347–355.

Ornstein, P. H. (1992). How to read *The Basic Fault:* An introduction to Michael Balint's seminal ideas on the psychoanalytic treatment process. In *The Basic Fault*, by M. Balint (new American edition), pp. vii–xxv. Evanston, IL: Northwestern University Press.

O'Shaughnessy, E. (1990). Can a liar be psychoanalyzed? *International Journal of Psycho-Analysis* 71:187–196.

Ostow, M., ed. (1974). *Sexual Deviation: Psychoanalytic Insights*. New York: Quadrangle.

Ovesey, L. (1969). *Homosexuality and Pseudohomosexuality*. New York: Science House.

Oxford English Dictionary. (1961). Oxford: Clarendon Press.

Oxford Latin Dictionary. (1982). Oxford: Clarendon Press.

Pao, P. N. (1965). The role of hatred in the ego. *Psychoanalytic Quarterly* 34:257–264.

Parens, H. (1973). Aggression: a reconsideration. *Journal of the American Psychoanalytic Association* 21:34–60.

————— (1979). *The Development of Aggression in Early Childhood*. New York: Jason Aronson.

————— (1980). An exploration of the relations of instinctual drives and the symbiosis-separation-individuation process. *Journal of the American Psychoanalytic Association* 28:89–114.

————— (1984). Toward a reformulation of the theory of aggression and its implications for primary prevention. In *Psychoanalysis: The Vital Issues*, vol. I, ed. J. Gedo and G. Pollock, pp. 87–114. New York: International Universities Press.

————— (1987). *Aggression in Our Children: Coping With It Constructively*. Northvale, NJ: Jason Aronson.

————— (1989a). Toward a reformulation of the psychoanalytic theory of aggression in early childhood. In *The Course of Life: vol. II. Early Childhood*, 2nd ed., ed. S. I. Greenspan and G. H. Pollock, pp. 83–127. New York: International Universities Press.

————— (1989b). Toward an epigenesis of aggression in early childhood. In *The Course of Life: vol. II. Early Childhood*, 2nd ed., ed. S. I. Greenspan and G. H. Pollock, pp. 129–161. New York: International Universities Press.

————— (1991). Separation-individuation theory and the psychosexual theory. In *Beyond the Symbiotic Orbit: Advances in Separation-Individuation Theory—Essays in Honor of Selma Kramer, M.D.*, ed. S. Akhtar and H. Parens, pp. 3–34. Hillsdale, NJ: Analytic Press.

———— (1995). Notes on perversions of the superego by hate. In *The Birth of Hatred: Developmental, Clinical, and Technical Aspects of Intense Aggression*, ed. S. Akhtar, S. Kramer, and H. Parens, pp. 39–52. Northvale, NJ: Jason Aronson.

Parens, H., Scattergood, E., Singletary, W., and Duff, A. (1987). *Aggression in Our Children: Coping with It Constructively*. Northvale, NJ: Jason Aronson.

Paris, J. (1994). *Sexual abuse and dissociative processes in the etiology of borderline personality disorder*. Plenary presentation at the Conference on Borderline Personality Disorder of the New York Hospital-Cornell Medical Center, Westchester Division, June 9.

Perry, J. C., and Herman, J. L. (1993). Trauma and defense in the etiology of borderline personality disorder. In *Borderline Personality Disorder*, ed. J. Paris, pp. 123–139. Washington, DC: American Psychiatric Press.

Person, E. (1988). *Dreams of Love and Fateful Encounters*. New York: Norton.

Pfeiffer, E. (1974). Borderline states. *Diseases of the Nervous System* 35:212–219.

Phillips, R. H. (1960). The nature and function of children's formal games. *Psychoanalytic Quarterly* 29:200–207.

Piaget, J. (1937). *The Construction of Reality in the Child*. New York: Basic Books, 1954.

Pine, F. (1985). *Developmental Theory and Clinical Process*. New Haven, CT: Yale University Press.

———— (1995). On the origin and the evolution of a species of hate: a clinical-literary excursion. In *The Birth of Hatred: Developmental, Clinical, and Technical Aspects of Intense Aggression*, ed. S. Akhtar, S. Kramer, and H. Parens, pp. 103–132. Northvale, NJ: Jason Aronson.

Pinter, H. (1975). *No Man's Land*. New York: Grove.

Poland, W. S. (1975). Tact as a psychoanalytic function. *International Journal of Psycho-Analysis* 56:155–161.

———— (1977). Pilgrimage: action and tradition in self analysis. *Journal of the American Psychoanalytic Association* 25:399–416.

Pollock, G. (1989). On migration—voluntary and coerced. *Annual of Psychoanalysis* 17:145–619.

Potamianou, A. (1992). *Un Bouclier dans L'Economie des Etats Limites L'Espoir*. Paris: Presses Universitaires de France.

Potter, H., and Klein, H. (1951). Toward unification of training in psychiatry and psychoanalysis. *American Journal of Psychiatry* 108:193–197.

Pruett, K. D. (1990). *The impact of involved fatherhood on child development: research and clinical perspectives.* Paper presented at the meeting of the Philadelphia Psychoanalytic Society, October.

A Psychiatric Glossary. (1975). Washington, DC: American Psychiatric Association.

Pulver, S. (1985). Psychoanalytic technique: some personal reflections. In *Analysts at Work*, ed. J. Reppen, pp. 165–186. Hillsdale, NJ: Analytic Press.

———— (1993). The eclectic analyst, or the many roads to insight and change. *Journal of the American Psychoanalytic Association* 41:339–357.

Rangell, L. (1972). Aggression, Oedipus and historical perspective. *International Journal of Psycho-Analysis* 53:3–11.

Rapaport, D. (1960a). On the psychoanalytic theory of motivation. In *The Collected Papers of David Rapaport*, ed. M. M. Gill, pp. 853–915. New York: Basic Books, 1967.

———— (1960b). The structure of psychoanalytic theory. *Psychological Issues* 6:39–72.

Reich, W. (1928). Discussion on the need for punishment and the neurotic process: a criticism of recent theories of the problem of neurosis. *International Journal of Psycho-Analysis* 9:227–246.

———— (1933). *Character Analysis*, trans. T. P. Wolfe. New York: Orgone Institute Press, 1945.

Renik, O. (1990). Comments on the clinical analysis of anxiety and depressive affect. *Psychoanalytic Quarterly* 59:226–248.

Richards, A. (1996). Freud's theory of motivation and others. *Psychoanalysis at the Political Border: Essays in Honor of Rafael Moses*, ed. L. Rangell and R. Moses-Hrushovski, pp. 69–83. Madison, CT: International Universities Press.

Riviere, J. (1937). *The Inner World and Joan Riviere: Collected Papers 1920–1958.* London: Karnac.

Robbins, M. (1980). Current controversy in object relations theory as outgrowth of a schism between Klein and Fairbairn. *International Journal of Psycho-Analysis* 61:477–492.

Rochlin, G. (1982). Aggression reconsidered: a critique of psychoanalysis. *Psychoanalytic Inquiry* 2:121–132.

Rollman-Branch, H. (1960). On the question of primary object need. *Journal of the American Psychoanalytic Association* 8:686–700.

Romm, M. (1955) The unconscious need to be an only child. *Psychoanalytic Quarterly* 24:331–342.

Rosenfeld, H. (1965). *Psychotic States: A Psychoanalytic Approach.* New York: International Universities Press.

———— (1971a). Theory of life and death instincts: aggressive aspects of narcissism. *International Journal of Psycho-Analysis* 45:332–337.

———— (1971b). A clinical approach to the psychoanalytic theory of the life and death instincts: an investigation into the aggressive aspects of narcissism. *International Journal of Psycho-Analysis* 52:169–178.

Ross, J. M. (1996). Male infidelity in long marriages: second adolescences and fourth individuations. In *Intimacy and Infidelity: Separation-Individuation Perspectives,* ed. S. Akhtar and S. Kramer, pp. 107–130. Northvale, NJ: Jason Aronson.

Rossner, J. (1983). *August.* Boston: Houghton Mifflin.

Roth, M. (1959). The phobic anxiety depersonalization syndrome. *Proceedings of the Royal Society of Medicine* 52:587–595.

Rothstein, A. (1978). Oedipal conflicts in narcissistic personality disorders. *International Journal of Psycho-Analysis* 60:189–199.

———— (1980). Toward a critique of the psychology of the self. *Psychoanalytic Quarterly* 49:423–455.

———— (1995). *Psychoanalytic Technique and the Creation of Analytic Patients.* Madison, CT: International Universities Press.

Rubovits-Seitz, P. (1988). Kohut's method of interpretation: a critique. *Journal of the American Psychoanalytic Association* 36:933–959.

Rudolph, S. H., and Rudolph, L. I. (1993). Modern hate. *The New Republic,* March 22, pp. 24–29.

Rushdie, S. (1989). *The Satanic Verses.* New York: Viking.

Rycroft, C. (1968). *A Critical Dictionary of Psychoanalysis.* London: Penguin, 1972.

Sacks, M. H. (1991). Panel report: sadism and masochism in character disorder and resistance. *Journal of the American Psychoanalytic Association* 39:215–226.

Sandford, B. (1952). An obsessional man's need to be "kept." *International Journal of Psycho-Analysis* 33:144–152.

Sandler, J. (1987). Internalization and externalization. In *Projection, Identification and Projective Identification,* ed. J. Sandler, pp. 1–12. Madison CT: International Universities Press.

Savitt, R. A. (1969). Transference, somatization, and symbiotic need. *Journal of the American Psychoanalytic Association* 17:1030–1054.

Schafer, R. (1993). Five readings of Freud's "Observations on Transference-Love." In *On Freud's "Observations on Transference-Love,"* ed. E. S. Person, A. Hagelin, and P. Fonagy, pp. 75–95. New Haven, CT: Yale University Press.

Schlessinger, N., and Robbins, F. P. (1983). *A Developmental View of the Psychoanalytic Process.* New York: International Universities Press.

Schmale, A. H. (1964). A genetic view of affects: helplessness and hopelessness. *Psychoanalytic Study of the Child* 19:289–300. New York: International Universities Press.

Schopenhauer, A. (1981). *The Pessimist's Handbook: A Collection of Popular Essays,* ed. H. E. Barnes, trans. T. B. Saunders. Omaha: University of Nebraska Press.

Schur, M. (1966). *The Id and the Regulatory Principles of Mental Functioning.* New York: International Universities Press.

Schwaber, E. (1983a). Psychoanalytic listening and psychic reality. *International Review of Psycho-Analysis* 10:379–390.

———— (1983b). Perspectives on analytic listening. *Psychoanalytic Study of the Child* 38:519–546. New Haven, CT: Yale University Press.

Schwartz, H. J. (1987). Illness in the doctor: implications for the psychoanalytic process. *Journal of the American Psychoanalytic Association* 35:657–692.

Searles, H. F. (1956). The psychodynamics of vengefulness. *Psychiatry* 19:31–39.

———— (1962). Scorn, disillusionment and adoration in the psychotherapy of schizophrenia. *Psychoanalytic Review* 49:39–60.

———— (1977). The development of mature hope in the patient–therapist relationship. In *Countertransference and Related Subjects: Selected Papers,* pp. 479–502. New York: International Universities Press, 1979.

———— (1986). *My Work with Borderline Patients.* Northvale, NJ: Jason Aronson.

Seeman, D. (1978). Delusional loving. *Archives of General Psychiatry* 35:1265–1267.

Segal, H. (1964). *Introduction to the Work of Melanie Klein,* 2nd ed. New York: Basis Books.

Segal, J. H. (1989). Erotomania revisited: from Kraepelin to *DSM-III-R. American Journal of Psychiatry* 146:1261–1266.

Segal, N. P. (1981). Book review of *Borderline Conditions and Pathological Narcissism* and *Object Relations Theory and Clinical Psychoanalysis. Journal of the American Psychoanalytic Association* 29:221–236.

Selzer, M. A., Koenigsberg, H. W., and Kernberg, O. F. (1987). Initial contract in treatment of borderline patients. *American Journal of Psychiatry* 144:927–930.

Settlage, C. F. (1977). The psychoanalytic understanding of narcissistic and borderline personality disorders: advances in developmental theory. *Journal of the American Psychoanalytic Association* 25:805–833.

—— (1989). The interplay of therapeutic and developmental processes in the treatment of children: an application of contemporary object relations theory. *Psychoanalytic Inquiry* 9:375–396.

—— (1991). On the treatment of preoedipal pathology. In *Beyond the Symbiotic Orbit: Advances in Separation-Individuation Theory—Essays in Honor of Selma Kramer, M.D.*, ed. S. Akhtar and H. Parens, pp. 351–367. Hillsdale, NJ: Analytic Press.

—— (1992). Psychoanalytic observations on adult development in life and in the therapeutic relationship. *Psychoanalysis and Contemporary Thought* 15:349–375.

—— (1993). Therapeutic process and developmental process in the restructuring of object and self constancy. *Journal of the American Psychoanalytic Association* 41:473–492.

—— (1994). On the contribution of separation-individuation theory to psychoanalysis: developmental process, pathogenesis, therapeutic process, and technique. In *Mahler and Kohut: Perspectives on Development Psychopathology, and Technique*, ed. S. Kramer and S. Akhtar, pp. 19–52. Northvale, NJ: Jason Aronson.

Settlage, C. F., Bemesderfer, S., Rosenthal, J., et al. (1991). The appeal cycle in early mother–child interaction: the nature and implications of a finding from developmental research. *Journal of the American Psychoanalytic Association* 39:987–1014.

Shapiro, D. (1965). *Neurotic Styles*. New York: Basic Books.

Shengold, L. (1989). *Soul Murder: The Effects of Childhood Abuse and Deprivation*. New Haven, CT: Yale University Press.

—— (1991). *Father, Don't You See I'm Burning?* New Haven, CT: Yale University Press.

Shevrin, H., and Povl, W. T. (1965). Vicissitudes of the need for tactile stimulation in instinctual development. *Psychoanalytic Study of the Child* 20:310–339. New York: International Universities Press.

Simon, B. (1993). In search of psychoanalytic technique: perspectives from on the couch and from behind the couch. *Journal of the American Psychoanalytic Association* 41:1051–1082.

Socarides, C. W. (1966). On vengeance: the desire to "get even." *Journal of the American Psychoanalytic Association* 14:356–375.

——— (1978). *Homosexuality*. New York: Jason Aronson.

——— (1991). The specific tasks in the psychoanalytic treatment of well-structured sexual deviations. In *The Homosexualities and the Therapeutic Process*, vol. 2, ed. C. W. Socarides and V. D. Volkan, pp. 277–291. New York: International Universities Press.

Sohn, L. (1983). Nostalgia. *International Journal of Psycho-Analysis* 64:203–211.

Solnit, A. J. (1966). Some adaptive functions of aggressive behavior. In *Psychoanalysis: A General Psychology*, ed. R. M. Loewenstein, L. M. Newmann, M. Schur, and A. J. Solnit, pp. 169–189. New York: International Universities Press.

——— (1972). Aggression: a view of theory building in psychoanalysis. *Journal of the American Psychoanalytic Association* 20:435–450.

Sperling, M. (1967). Transference neurosis in patients with psychosomatic disorders. *Psychoanalytic Quarterly* 36:342–355.

Spitz, R. (1946a). The smiling response: a contribution to the ontogenesis of social relations. *Genetic Psychology Monograph* 34:57–125.

——— (1946b). Anaclitic depression: an inquiry into the genesis of psychiatric conditions in early childhood. *Psychoanalytic Study of the Child* 2:313–342. New York: International Universities Press.

——— (1950). Anxiety in infancy: a study of its manifestations in the first year of life. *International Journal of Psycho-Analysis* 31:138–143.

——— (1953). Aggression. In *Drives, Affects, Behavior*, ed. R. M. Loewenstein, pp. 126–138. New York: International Universities Press.

——— (1965). *The First Year of Life*. New York: International Universities Press.

——— (1957). *No and Yes*. New York: International Universities Press.

Springborg, P. (1981). *The Problem of Human Needs and the Critique of Civilization*. London: Allen and Unwin.

Spruiell, V. (1975). Three strands of narcissism. *Psychoanalytic Quarterly* 44:577–583.

Stechler, G. (1987). Clinical applications of a psychoanalytic systems model of assertion and aggression. *Psychoanalytic Inquiry* 1:348–363.

Stechler, G., and Halton, A. (1987). The emergence of assertion and aggression during infancy: a psychoanalytic systems approach. *Journal of the American Psychoanalytic Association* 35:821–838.

Stein, M. R. (1979). Book review of *The Restoration of the Self*. *Journal of the American Psychoanalytic Association* 27:665–680.

Steinberg, B. S. (1993). The need to know and the inability to tolerate not knowing. *Canadian Journal of Psychoanalysis* 1:85–103.

Sterba, E. (1940). Homesickness and the mother's breast. *Psychiatric Quarterly* 14:701–707.

Stern, D. N. (1976). A microanalysis of mother–infant interaction: behavior regulating social contact between a mother and her 3 ½ month old twins. In *Infant Psychiatry*, ed E. Rexford, L. Sanders, and T. Shapiro. New Haven, CT: Yale University Press.

Stoller, R. J. (1975). *Perversion: The Erotic Form of Hatred.* New York: Pantheon.

——— (1979). *Sexual Excitement.* New York: Pantheon.

Stone, L. (1954). The widening scope of indications for psychoanalysis. *Journal of the American Psychoanalytic Association* 2:567–594.

——— (1961). *The Psychoanalytic Situation.* New York: International Universities Press.

——— (1971). Reflections on the psychoanalytic concept of aggression. *Psychoanalytic Quarterly* 40:195–244.

——— (1981). Notes on the noninterpretive elements in the psychoanalytic situation and process. *Journal of the American Psychoanalytic Association* 29:89–118.

Stone, M. H. (1980). *The Borderline Syndromes.* New York: McGraw-Hill.

——— (1989). Murder. *Psychiatric Clinics of North America* 12(3):643–652.

Storr, A. (1968). *Human Aggression.* New York: Atheneum.

Strachey, J. (1934). The nature of the therapeutic action of psychoanalysis. *International Journal of Psycho-Analysis* 15:127–159.

Strassman, H., Mann, J., Madow, L., and Wood, E. (1976). The impact of psychiatric residency training on choice of analytic training. *Journal of the American Psychoanalytic Association* 24:347–356.

Strauss, G. D., Yager, J., and Strauss, G. E. (1984). The cutting edge in psychiatry. *American Journal of Psychiatry* 114:38–43.

Strenger, C. (1989). The classic and romantic visions in psychoanalysis. *International Journal of Psycho-Analysis* 70:595–610.

Summers, F. (1994). *Object Relations Theories and Psychopathology: A Comprehensive Text.* Hillsdale, NJ: Analytic Press.

Suttie, I. (1924). Metapsychology and biology: some criticisms of Freud's "Beyond the Pleasure Principle." *Journal of Neurology and Psychopathology* 5:61–70.

——— (1935). *The Origins of Love and Hate.* London: Kegan, Paul, Trench, Trubner.

Svrakic, D. M. (1985). Emotional features of narcissistic personality disorder. *American Journal of Psychiatry* 142:720–724.

Tahka, V. (1993). *Mind and Its Treatment: A Psychoanalytic Approach.* Madison, CT: International Universities Press.

Teja, J. S., and Akhtar, S. (1981). The psycho-social problems of FMGs with special references to those in psychiatry. In *Foreign Medical Graduates in Psychiatry: Issues and Problems,* ed. R. S. Chen, pp. 321–338. New York: Human Sciences.

Thomas, A., Chess, S., and Birch, H. G. (1963). *Behavioral Individuality in Early Childhood.* New York: International Universities Press.

——— (1968). *Temperament and Behavior Disorders in Children.* New York: International Universities Press.

Thoreau, H. D. (1854). *Walden,* ed. S. Fender, p. 92. New York: Oxford University Press, 1997.

Tinbergen, N. (1951). An attempt at synthesis. In *The Study of Instinct,* pp. 101–127. New York: Oxford University Press.

Tolpin, M. (1980). Discussion of *Psychoanalytic Developmental Theories of the Self: An Integration* by M. Shane and E. Shane. In *Advances in Self Psychology,* ed. A. Goldberg, pp. 47–68. New York: International Universities Press.

Varma, V. K., Akhtar, S., and Kulhara, P. N. (1973). Measurement of authoritarian traits in India. *Indian Journal of Psychiatry* 15:156–175.

Volkan, V. D. (1976). *Primitive Internalized Object Relations.* New York: International Universities Press.

——— (1980). Narcissistic personality organization and "reparative" leadership. *International Journal of Group Psychotherapy* 30:131–152.

——— (1981). *Linking Objects and Linking Phenomena.* New York: International Universities Press.

——— (1986). The narcissism of minor differences in the psychological gap between opposing nations. *Psychoanalytic Inquiry* 6:175–191.

——— (1987a). *Six Steps in the Treatment of Borderline Personality Organization.* Northvale, NJ: Jason Aronson.

——— (1987b). Psychological concepts useful in the building of political foundations between nations: track II diplomacy. *Journal of the American Psychoanalytic Association* 35:903–936.

——— (1988). *The Need to Have Enemies and Allies.* Northvale, NJ: Jason Aronson.

Volkan, V. D. and Akhtar, S. (1979). The symptoms of schizophrenia: contributions of the structural theory and object relations theory. In *Integrating Ego Psychology and Object Relations Theory,* ed. L. Saretsky, G. D. Goldman, and D. S. Milman, pp. 270–285. Dubuque, IA: Kendall/Hunt.

Volkan, V. D., and Corney, R. T. (1968). Some considerations of satellite states and satellite dreams. *British Journal of Medical Psychology* 41:283–290.

Voltaire. (1759). *Candide,* trans. R. Pearson, p. 54. New York: Oxford University Press.

Waelder, R. (1933). The psychoanalytic theory of play. *Psychiatric Quarterly* 2:208–225.

—— (1936). The principle of multiple function: observations on multiple determination. *Psychoanalytic Quarterly* 5:45–62.

—— (1956). Critical discussion of the concept of an instinct of destruction. *Bulletin of the Philadelphia Association for Psychoanalysis* 6:97–109.

Wallerstein, R. S. (1983). Self psychology and "classical" psychoanalytic psychology: the nature of their relationship. In *The Future of Psychoanalysis,* ed., A. Goldberg, pp. 19–63. New York: International Universities Press.

—— (1986). Book review of *Severe Personality Disorders: Psychotherapeutic Strategies. Journal of the American Psychoanalytic Association* 34:711–722.

—— (1990). Psychoanalysis: the common ground. *International Journal of Psycho-Analysis* 71:3–20.

—— (1993). On transference love: revisiting Freud. In *On Freud's "Observations on Transference-Love,"* ed. E. S. Person, A. Hagelin, and P. Fonagy, pp. 57–74. New Haven, CT: Yale University Press.

Warren, M. (1961). The significance of visual images during the analytic session. *Journal of the American Psychoanalytic Association* 9:504–518.

Webster's New Universal Unabridged Dictionary. (1983). Caveat. 2nd Edition. New York: Simon & Schuster.

Webster's Ninth New Collegiate Dictionary. (1987). Aggression. Springfield, MA: Merriam-Webster.

Weil, A. (1970). The basic core. *Psychoanalytic Study of the Child* 25:442–460. New York: International Universities Press.

—— (1976). The first year: metapsychological inferences of infant observation. In *The Process of Child Development,* ed. P. Neubauer, pp. 246–268. New York: Jason Aronson.

Weiss, E. (1935). Todestrieb und masochismus. *Imago* 21:393–411.

—— (1964). *Agoraphobia in the Light of Ego Psychology.* New York: Grune & Stratton.

Werman, D. S. (1977). Normal and pathological nostalgia. *Journal of the American Psychoanalytic Association* 25:387–398.

—— (1979). Chance, ambiguity, and psychological mindedness. *Psychoanalytic Quarterly* 48:107–115.

Wheelis, A. (1966). *The Illusionless Man.* New York: Harper Colophon.
———— (1971). The league of death. In *The Illusionless Man,* pp. 57–95. New York: Harper Colophon.
———— (1994). *The Way Things Are.* New York: Baskerville.
Willick, M. S. (1983). On the concept of primitive defenses. *Journal of the American Psychoanalytic Association* 31 (suppl.):175–200.
Wilson, E. O. (1975). *Sociobiology: The New Synthesis.* Cambridge, MA: Harvard University Press.
Winer, J. A. (1994). Panel report: hate in the analytic setting. *Journal of the American Psychoanalytic Association* 42:219–232.
Winnicott, D. W. (1947). Hate in the Countertransference. In *Collected Papers: Through Paediatrics to Psychoanalysis,* pp. 194–203. London: Hogarth, 1958.
———— (1950). Aggression in relation to emotional development. In *Collected Papers: Through Paediatrics to Psycho-Analysis,* pp. 204–218. New York: Basic Books, 1958.
———— (1953). Transitional objects and transitional phenomena. *International Journal of Psycho-Analysis* 34:89–97.
———— (1956). The antisocial tendency. In *Collected Papers: Through Paediatrics to Psycho-Analysis,* pp. 306–316. New York: Basic Books, 1958.
———— (1959). Classification: Is there a psychoanalytic contribution to psychiatric classification? In *The Maturational Processes and the Facilitating Environment,* pp. 124–139. New York: International Universities Press, 1965.
———— (1960a). Ego distortion in terms of true and false self. In *The Maturational Processes and the Facilitating Environment,* pp. 140–152. New York: International Universities Press, 1965.
———— (1960b). String: a technique of communication. In *The Maturational Processes and the Facilitating Environment,* pp. 153–157. New York: International Universities Press, 1965.
———— (1960c). The theory of the parent–infant relationship. *International Journal of Psycho-Analysis* 41:585–595.
———— (1960d). Comments on Joseph Sandler's *On the Concept of the Superego.* In *Psychoanalytic Explorations: D. W. Winnicott,* ed. C. Winnicott, R. Shepherd, and M. Davis, pp. 465–473. Cambridge, MA: Harvard University Press, 1989.
———— (1962). Ego integration in child development. In *The Maturational Processes and the Facilitating Environment,* pp. 56–64. New York: International Universities Press, 1965.

————— (1963). The development of the capacity for concern. *Bulletin of the Menninger Clinic* 27:167–176.

————— (1965). *The Maturational Processes and the Facilitating Environment.* New York: International Universities Press.

————— (1967). The mirror-role of the mother and family in child development. In *Playing and Reality*, pp. 130–138. Middlesex, England: Penguin, 1971.

————— (1969a). The use of an object in the context of *Moses and Monotheism.* In *Psycho-Analytic Explorations: D. W. Winnicott*, ed. C. Winnicott, R. Shepherd, and M. Davis, pp. 240–246. Cambridge, MA: Harvard University Press, 1989.

————— (1969b). The mother–infant experience of mutuality. In *Psycho-Analytic Explorations: D. W. Winnicott*, ed. C. Winnicott, R. Shepherd, and M. Davis, pp. 251–260. Cambridge, MA: Harvard University Press, 1989.

————— (1971). *Playing and Reality.* New York: Basic Books.

Wolf, E. (1988). *Treating the Self: Elements of Clinical Self-Psychology.* New York: Guilford.

————— (1994). Selfobject experiences: development, psychopathology, treatment. In *Mahler and Kohut: Perspectives on Development, Psychopathology, and Technique*, ed. S. Kramer and S. Akhtar, pp. 65–96. Northvale, NJ: Jason Aronson.

Wolman, T. (1991). Mahler and Winnicott: some parallels in their lives and works. In *Beyond the Symbiotic Orbit: Advances in Separation-Individuation Theory—Essays in Honor of Selma Kramer, M.D.*, ed. S. Akhtar and H. Parens, pp. 35–60. Hillsdale, NJ: Analytic Press.

Yeomans, F. E., Selzer, M. A., and Clarkin, J. F. (1992). *Treating the Borderline Patient: A Contract Based Approach.* New York: Basic Books.

Zerubavel, E. (1991). *The Fine Line: Making Distinctions in Everyday Life.* New York: The Free Press.

Zetzel, E. (1965). The theory of therapy in relation to a developmental model of the psychic apparatus. *International Journal of Psycho-Analysis* 46:39–52.

Zonis, M. (1980). Some possible contributions of the psychology of the self to the study of the Arab Middle East. In *Advances in Self Psychology*, ed. A. Goldberg, pp. 349–446. New York: International Universities Press.

CREDITS

CHAPTER 1

CHAPTER 2

CHAPTER 3

CHAPTER 5

CHAPTER 6

CHAPTER 7

CHAPTER 8

INDEX

Abend, S. M., 207, 208
Abraham, K., 45, 85, 210, 212, 246
Abrams, S., 24, 120, 198
Adler, G., 14, 207, 247
Adolescence, object constancy, 11–12
Aggression, 31–61
  contemporary reformulations, 51–56
  definitions of, 32–35
  Freud's view of, 35–41
  hate, 98
  Klein and Hartmann, 41–47
  object relations theory and self psychology, 47–51
  overview, 31–32
  synthesis and reflections, 56–61
Akhtar, S., 9, 11, 13, 14, 16, 17, 18, 23, 50, 51, 59, 60, 79, 83, 84, 85, 87, 88, 89, 91, 93, 101, 102, 119, 120, 122, 124, 132, 136, 139, 150, 160, 184, 190, 192, 193, 195, 209, 213, 217, 218, 223, 228, 230, 233, 234, 247, 248, 249, 259, 260, 267

Alexander, F., 172
Altman, L. L., 72, 75, 76, 92
Altschuler, K. Z., 133, 137
Amati-Mehler, J., xv, 213, 219, 228, 230
Ambitendency, object constancy, 8
Anatomy, ego and, 237
Angel, A., xv, 212
Argentieri, S., 213, 219, 228, 230
Aristotle, 125
Arlow, J. A., 46, 207
Arnold, M. B., 55
Arrogance, hate, 101–104
Asch, S., 24, 266, 267
Atkin, S., 142

Bacal, H. A., 48, 50, 139, 140, 141
Bach, S., 155, 238
Baker, H. S., 136
Baker, M. N., 136
Balint, M., xv, 17, 48, 49, 71, 72, 98, 120, 140, 141, 142, 143, 168, 178, 179, 190, 195, 207, 208, 211, 229, 241, 242, 243, 257, 258, 267

Bartlett, J., 125
Begley, L., 91
Benedek, T., 72, 75, 77, 211
Bergman, A., 79, 172, 243, 259
Bergman, P., 142
Bergmann, M., xiii, 72, 73
Berliner, B., 102
Biology, ego and, 237
Bion, W., xiii, 12, 23, 42, 103, 210
Blashfield, R. K., 136
Blos, P., 11, 12, 180, 259
Blum, H. P., xiii, 13, 14, 15, 16, 18,
    22, 25, 26, 89, 92, 101, 107, 110,
    123, 125, 218, 232, 248
Bollas, C., 82, 83, 101
Boris, H. N., 211, 233
Bouvet, M., xv, 9, 23, 122, 193, 239,
    240, 265
Boyer, L. B., 263
Braunschweig, D., 75
Brenman, E., 103, 108
Brenner, C., 47, 58, 105, 106, 142,
    148, 167, 185, 207
Britton, R., 114
Buie, D. H., 111, 114, 115
Burgner, M., 173, 175, 177
Burland, J. A., 22, 24, 25, 209, 249
Burnham, D. L., 13, 80, 84, 172, 247
Bychowski, G., 72
Byrne, J. P., 14

Calef, V., 132, 142, 146, 147
Campbell, R. J., 238
Carlyle, T., 124
Casement, P., 80, 180, 188, 190, 192,
    200, 208, 214, 226
Chasseguet-Smirgel, J., xiii, 59, 72,
    75, 77, 216
Chirico, G. de, 223
Chmiel, A. J., 258
Coen, S. J., 99
Coltart, N., 121
Conflict, Kohut versus Kernberg,
    148–151

Cooper, A. M., xv, 132, 162, 216
Corney, R. T., 254
Countertransference, hate in, 114–116
Curtis, H. C., 186

Death instinct
    aggression, 38–39, 41, 49
    Hartmann, 43
    Klein, 42
DeClerambault, C. G., 93
Deutsch, F., 237
Deutsch, H., 13, 93, 100, 136, 246,
    247, 248
Dewall, R., 259
Distance. See Optimal distance
Dora case (Freud), 36
Dorpat, T., 149
Drive theory, aggression, 37–39, 40,
    46–47

Edgcumbe, R., 173, 175, 177
Ego
    aggression, 38
    biology and, 237
Ehrlich, H., 180
Eickhoff, F. W., 89, 218
Eidelberg, L., 33, 34
Eissler, K. R., 56, 58, 59, 105
Eitingon, M., 42
Emch, M., 172
Emde, R., 55, 142
Emotional flooding, object
    constancy, disturbances in, 14–
    15
English, A. C., 33, 34
English, H. B., 33, 34
Envy, hate, 101–104
Erikson, E. H., 14, 190, 211, 257
Erotic transference, malignant,
    object constancy, disturbances
    in, 17–18
Escalona, S. K., 142
Escoll, P., 12, 22, 23, 84, 122, 193,
    195, 198, 228, 249

Fain, M., 75
Fairbairn, W. R. D., 14, 48, 49, 50, 51, 56, 58, 102, 105, 106, 140, 143, 178, 179, 248
Fantasy. *See* "Someday" and "If only" fantasies; Tether fantasy
Federn, P., 42, 58
Fenichel, O., 88, 101, 172, 219, 220, 237, 238
Ferenczi, S., 6, 42, 58, 105, 168
Fine, B., xii, 33, 34, 35, 91, 239
Fink, P., 135
Fischer, N., 255
Fleming, J., 22, 198
Fliess, R., 36
Fodor, N., 220
Frank, A., 23, 24, 209, 249
Freedman, A., 135, 229
French, T. M., 212
Freud, A., 5, 46, 48, 52, 75, 105, 123, 137, 149, 172, 175, 176, 265
Freud, S., 22, 32, 35–41, 42, 43, 45, 49, 55, 58, 67–71, 77, 82, 86, 87, 104, 105, 106, 109, 110, 117, 121, 124, 136, 137, 139, 143, 148, 153, 168–171, 172, 182, 188, 199, 200, 201, 209, 212, 216, 219, 223, 227, 237, 238, 246, 248, 250, 255, 257, 259, 266
Friedman, L., 225, 229
Frustration, aggression, 50
Furer, M., 6, 7, 52, 55, 150
Furman, E., 175, 177

Gabbard, G. O., 102, 191
Galdston, R., 100, 120
Gaoni, B., 84
GAP report, 132
Gay, P., 36, 42, 124, 170
Geahchan, D., 221
Gediman, H. K., 14, 16, 215, 248
Gedo, J. E., 149, 230
Gibran, K., 256

Gillespie, W. H., 46, 72
Gitelson, M., 137, 225
Glenn, J., 11, 257
Glover, E., 212, 232
Goldberg, A., 149, 230
Greenacre, P., 22
Greenberg, J. R., 157
Greenson, R. R., 225
Greenspan, S. I., 150
Grinberg, L. R., 259, 260
Grinberg, R., 260
Grinspoon, L., 135
Grinstein, A., 258
Grotstein, J. S., 42
Gruenert, U., 24, 267
Grunberger, B., 155
Gunderson, J. G., 14, 196, 247
Gunther, M., 53
Guntrip, H., 48, 50, 58, 71, 80, 84, 105, 140, 141, 180, 248, 264
Gurewich, J. F., xiv

Halton, A., 60
Hamburg, D. A., 45
Hamilton, J. W., 223
Harnik, E. J., 172
Hart, J., 87
Hartmann, H., xii, 5, 32, 41–47, 51, 52, 55, 56, 58, 105, 139, 173, 174, 186, 191, 220
Hate, 97–125. *See also* Love-hate
  in countertransference, 114–116
  definition and overview, 97–98
  ego, 38
  manifestations of, 98–101
  origins of, 104–108
  rage, envy, and arrogance, 101–104
  sociocultural vicissitudes, 108–110
  technical implications, 116–122
  in transference, 110–114
Hayman, A., 43
Heimann, P., 42, 46
Hendrick, I., 46

Henman, J. L., 106
Hensie, L. E., 238
Hill, L. B., 102
Holzman, P., 142
Horowitz, M., 124
Howell, N., 100

"If only" fantasy. *See also* "Someday"
    and "If only" fantasies
    described, 219–223
    object constancy, disturbances in,
        18–21
Inability to mourn, object constancy,
    disturbances in, 18–21
Inconstant object, paranoia and,
    object constancy disturbances,
    15–16
Individuation, object constancy, 8
Inordinate optimism, object
    constancy, disturbances in, 16–
    17
Invisible fences. *See* Optimal distance
Isakower, O., 209
Izard, C., 55

Jacobs, T., 198
Jacobson, E., 45, 51, 55, 59, 101, 142,
    143, 172
Jones, E., 38, 42, 98, 102, 137
Joseph, B., 89, 116, 218
Joseph, E. D., 46

Kafka, J. S., 124
Kaplan, L., 14, 59, 82, 84
Kernberg, O., xii, xiii, xiv, 12, 14, 17,
    23, 51, 55, 56, 59, 61, 67, 72, 73,
    74, 75, 78, 79, 80, 81, 82, 84, 87,
    88, 89, 91, 94, 98, 99, 100, 101,
    105, 106, 107, 108, 113, 115,
    117, 118, 119, 120, 121, 122,
    123, 124, 190, 207, 208, 216,
    225, 229, 247. *See also* Kohut
    versus Kernberg

Khan, M. M. R., 83, 84, 119, 180, 208,
    214
Kiell, N., 122
Killingmo, B., 168, 186, 190, 228, 230
Klauber, J., 262
Kleeman, J. A., 7, 257
Klein, G., 173, 174, 175
Klein, H., 137
Klein, M., xii, xiii, 25, 32, 41–47, 48,
    58, 59, 105, 106, 112, 116, 117,
    142, 143, 168, 221
Kleiner, J., 220, 223, 224
Knapp, P. H., 55
Koenigsberg, H. W., 135
Kohon, G., 121
Kohut, H., xiv, 48, 50, 51, 53, 58,
    105, 106, 117, 120, 167, 180,
    181, 190, 199, 207, 208, 230, 246
Kohut versus Kernberg, 131–164
    general psychiatry, 133–139
    mainstream psychoanalysis, 144–
        154
        conflict, 148–151
        generally, 144–148
        Oedipus complex, 152–154
    narcissistic personality, 154–162
        pathogenesis and
            metapsychology, 157–159
        phenomenology, 154–157
        treatment technique, 159–162
    overview, 131–133
    regard for others' contributions,
        139–144
Krafft-Ebing, R. von, 37
Kramer, S., 9, 11, 105, 120, 198
Kris, E., 51, 58, 148, 167, 226
Krystal, H., 223
Kundera, M., 102
Kurtz, S. A., 197

Lafarge, L., 113
Lantos, B., 60
Laplanche, J., 36, 238–239

Latency, object constancy, 11
Lax, R., 22
Lerner, B., 172
Lester, E. P., 191
Levarie, S., 132, 144
Levin, F. M., 133
Levy, S. T., 117
Lewin, B. D., 59
Lewin, R. A., 80, 119, 208, 246
Lichtenberg, J. D., 60, 61, 175, 178, 185
Lichtenstein, H., 59
Little, M., 187
Loewald, H. W., 22, 194, 198, 215, 231, 232
Loewenstein, R., 58, 265
Lorenz, K., 55
Love, 67–94
    contemporary view of, 71–78
    Freud's view of, 67–71
    inability to fall in love, 79–81
    inability to fall out of love, 88–90
    inability to feel loved, 90–92
    inability to remain in love, 81–85
    wrong choice, 85–88
Love-hate, aggression, 48–49, 55–56
Lussier, A., 33, 47
Lustman, S. L., 142

Madonna–whore images, oedipal phase conflicts and, 10
Mahler, M., xii, xv, 5, 6, 8, 9, 10, 13, 14, 16, 21, 23, 26, 27, 52, 53, 55, 59, 73, 82, 84, 92, 105, 140, 142, 150, 172, 175, 176, 195, 215, 216, 221, 226, 227, 239, 240, 243, 244, 249, 254, 257
Malignant erotic transference, object constancy, disturbances in, 17–18
Maltsberger, J. T., 111, 114, 115
Marcovitz, E., 33, 45
Masson, J. M., 36
Mastery, aggression, 37, 40

McDevitt, J. B., 6, 8, 52, 53
McElroy, R. A., 136
McLaughlin, J. T., 24
Meissner, W. W., 137
Melges, F. T., 14, 247
Menninger, K., 42, 58, 105, 212
Mitchell, S. A., 157, 232, 234
Mittelman, B., 246
Modell, A., 24, 80, 119, 174, 192, 200, 227, 266, 267
Moore, B., xii, 33, 34, 35, 72, 91, 239
Mourning, disability in, object constancy, disturbances in, 18–21
Mullen, P. E., 93

Narcissistic personality, Kohut versus Kernberg, 154–162
Nasio, J.-D., 221–222
Needs versus wishes, 167–201
    contributions, 171–182
        British independent school, 178–180
        generally, 171–173
        infant and child development studies, 175–178
        metapsychology, 173–175
        self psychology, 180–181
    Freud's views, 168–171
    overview, 167–168
    synthesis, caveats, and beyond, 182–187
    technical implications, 187–199
    theoretical postscript, 199–201
Nemiah, J. C., 155
Neubauer, P., 110
Newman, K. M., 48, 50
Nickman, S. L., 172
Nirvana principle, 39
Nixon, R. M., 125
Nostalgia, object constancy, disturbances in, 18–21
Nunberg, H., 42, 172, 173, 174, 193

Object constancy, 5–27
  concept of, 5–6
  disturbances in, 13–21
    inability to mourn, nostalgia,
      and "if only" fantasy, 18–21
    inordinate optimism and
      someday fantasy, 16–17
    malignant erotic transference,
      17–18
    optimal distance, 13–14
    paranoia and inconstant object,
      15–16
    splitting, emotional flooding,
      and violence, 14–15
  initial achievement of, 6–9
  reverberations of, 9–12
  technical implications, 21–26
Object relations theory, aggression,
  47–51
Ocnophilia, optimal distance, 241–245
Oedipus complex
  Klein, 43
  Kohut versus Kernberg, 152–154
  love, 76
  separation-individuation and, 10
Olden, C., 109
Optimal distance, 237–269
  definitions, 238–241
  developmental perspective, 241–
    245
  object constancy, disturbances in,
    13–14
  overview, 237–238
  psychopathology of, 245–248
  sociocultural vicissitudes, 256–261
  technical implications, 261–267
  tether fantasy, 248–256
Optimism, inordinate, object
  constancy, disturbances in, 16–17
Orbits. See Optimal distance
O'Shaughnessy, E., 113
Ostow, M., 72
Ovesey, L., 72

Pain, love and, 71
Pao, P.-N., xiii, 102, 120
Paranoia, object constancy,
  disturbances in, 15–16
Parens, H., xii, 10, 38, 40, 51, 52, 53,
  54, 58, 60, 61, 105, 106, 107,
  175, 177
Paris, J., 106
Perry, J. C., 106
Person, E., 72, 75, 77
Phillips, R. H., 257
Philobatism, optimal distance, 241–245
Phobias, optimal distance, 246–247
Piaget, J., 5
Pine, F., 107, 113
Poland, W. S., 10, 122, 193, 228, 261,
  265
Pollock, G., 259
Pontalis, J.-B., 36, 238–239
Potamianou, A., xv, 213
Potter, H., 137
Povl, W. T., 172
Projection, optimal distance, 240–241
Proust, M., 223
Psychoanalysis, indications for, 131–
  132
Pulver, S., 197, 234

Rage, hate, 101–104
Rangell, L., 35
Rapaport, D., 173, 174, 195
Rat Man case (Freud), 188
Reich, W., 155, 172
Reiser, M., 133
Renik, O., 217
Rich, H., 125
Richards, A., 182, 183
Riviere, J., 123
Robbins, F. P., 22
Robbins, M., 22, 50, 140, 198
Rochlin, G., 53
Rockwell, N., 223
Rollman-Branch, H., 199

Rosenfeld, H., 42, 46, 58, 61, 91, 105
Rossner, J., 238
Roth, M., 246
Rothstein, A., 139, 145, 158, 163
Rubovitz-Seitz, P., 209
Rudolph, L. I., 124
Rudolph, S. H., 124
Rushdie, S., 115
Rycroft, C., 33, 34, 239

Sadomasochism
    aggression, 37, 38, 39, 45, 49, 55
    hate, 99
Samuel, S., 14, 190
Sandford, B., 172
Sandler, J., 33, 47, 240
Savitt, R. A., 172
Schafer, R., 71
Schlessinger, N., 22
Schmale, A. H., 88, 221
Schopenhauer, A., 246, 247
Schulz, C., 80, 119, 208, 246
Schur, M., 52, 173, 174
Schwaber, E., 190
Schwartz, H. J., 193
Searles, H. F., 102, 111, 116, 207,
    212, 213, 232
Seeman, D., 93
Segal, H., 42
Segal, J. H., 93
Segal, N. P., 142
Self psychology
    aggression, 47–51
    needs versus wishes, 180–181
Selzer, M. A., 135
Separation-individuation
    object constancy, 8–9
    oedipal phase conflicts and, 10
    optimal distance, 242–243
Settlage, C. F., 6, 8, 21, 22, 24, 25,
    105, 192, 196, 198, 261
Sexuality, aggression, 36–37. *See also*
    Love

Shakespeare, W., 237
Shapiro, D., 101
Shengold, L., 60, 107, 191
Shevrin, H., 172
Socarides, C. W., 72, 110
Sociocultural vicissitudes
    hate, 108–110
    optimal distance, 256–261
    "someday" and "if only" fantasies,
        223–224
Sohn, L., 229
Solnit, A. J., 52
"Someday" and "If only" fantasies,
        207–234
    caveats, 209–210
    overview, 207–209
    sociocultural vicissitudes, 223–224
    "someday" fantasy, 16–17, 210–218
    technical implications, 224–234
Sperling, M., 172
Spitz, R., 5, 52, 142, 175, 176, 209, 242
Splitting, object constancy,
        disturbances in, 14–15
Stalin, J., 102
Stechler, G., 60, 106
Stein, M. R., 139
Steinberg, B. S., 172, 173
Sterba, E., 220, 259
Stern, D. N., 142
Stoller, R. J., 72, 99
Stone, L., 32, 59, 131, 132, 162, 198,
        207
Stone, M. H., 61, 106
Storr, A., 53
Strachey, J., 265
Strassman, H., 137
Strauss, G. D., 133
Strenger, C., xiii, 117, 119, 168
Summers, F., 139
Suttie, I., 48, 49, 58, 90, 104, 105,
        178, 179
Svrakic, D. M., 155
Swartz, M. S., 14, 247

Tahka, V., 198
Teja, J. S., 260
Tether fantasy, optimal distance, 248–256. *See also* Optimal distance
Thomas, A., 142
Thomson, J. A., 132
Thoreau, H. D., 209
Tinbergen, N., 55
Transference
hate in, 110–114
malignant erotic, object constancy, disturbances in, 17–18
Tribich, D., 142, 143

Valenstein, A. F., 46
Violence, object constancy, disturbances in, 14–15
Volkan, V. D., 19, 61, 109, 124, 132, 172, 208, 228, 254, 263

Waelder, R., 45, 58, 105, 111, 161, 186, 233, 257
Wallerstein, R. S., 147, 150, 151, 160, 197, 209, 218
Warren, M., 251

Weil, A., 7, 52
Weinshel, E., 132, 142, 146, 147
Weiss, E., 42, 246
Werman, D. S., 194, 220, 221, 223, 229
Wheeler, D. R., 212
Wheelis, A., 56, 59, 90, 223, 238
Willick, M. S., 207
Wilson, E. O., 55
Winer, J. A., 102, 124
Winnicott, D. W., 9, 23, 48, 49, 50, 51, 58, 71, 105, 106, 117, 119, 120, 121, 122, 124, 125, 140, 141, 171, 178, 179, 200, 207, 208, 213, 214, 216, 226, 227, 233, 255, 257, 260, 263, 264
Wishes. *See* Needs versus wishes
Wolf, E., 134, 148, 149, 155, 156, 167, 181, 207, 208

Yeomans, F. E., 118, 208

Zerubavel, E., 256
Zetzel, E., 22
Zonis, M., 132